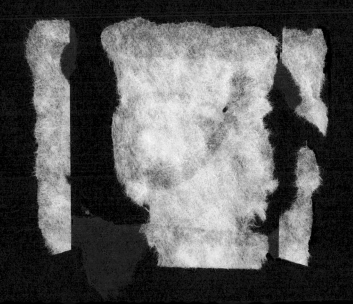

Nature and Values

Published in Columbia, South Carolina, during the one hundred and seventy-fifth anniversary of the establishment of the University of South Carolina and the two hundredth anniversary of the establishment of the United States of America.

PUBLICATION OF THIS BOOK WAS MADE POSSIBLE BY A GRANT
FROM THE PUBLICATIONS FUND OF THE PHILOSOPHY DEPARTMENT
OF THE UNIVERSITY OF SOUTH CAROLINA

Nature and Values

PRAGMATIC ESSAYS IN METAPHYSICS

Theodore T. Lafferty

CARL A. RUDISILL LIBRARY
LENOIR RHYNE COLLEGE

University of South Carolina Press
Columbia, South Carolina

Copyright © University of South Carolina 1976

FIRST EDITION

Published in Columbia, S.C., by the
University of South Carolina Press, 1976

Manufactured in the United States of America

/ / O

L / 3 N

9 9 4 4 0

2 an . / 9 7 7

Library of Congress Cataloging in Publication Data
Lafferty, Theodore Thomas, 1901–1970.
    Nature and values.
    Bibliography: p.
    1. Metaphysics—Addresses, essays, lectures.
2. Pragmatism—Addresses, essays, lectures.   3.   Worth
—Addresses, essays, lectures.   I.   Title.
BD41.L27   1976   110   78–120586
ISBN 0–87249–193–5

CONTENTS

EDITOR'S NOTE

Dr. Theodore T. Lafferty was Professor of Philosophy at the University of South Carolina from 1946 until his retirement in 1969. He was born in the Cherokee Nation, Indian Territory (later to become the State of Oklahoma), on June 3, 1901. He dropped out of school to join the Army at fifteen, giving his age as seventeen. He served in the Philippines, Siberia, Japan, and China. After demobilization, he returned to school and received his high school diploma, A.B., M.A., and Ph.D. (University of Chicago) in the space of six and a half years. Before coming to the University of South Carolina, he had taught at A and M College in Jonesboro, Arkansas, the University of Chicago, Lehigh University, and Hood College. After retirement he completed a year as Visiting Professor at Columbia College (S.C.) before his death on June 10, 1970. He was the author of a number of articles and of *Elements of Logic* (1963).

At the time of his death, the manuscript of the present volume was complete, and the University of South Carolina Press had accepted it for publication. He had begun to consider a set of queries from the Press's editor, but a number of small details remained, and I undertook to complete the manuscript for the printer. Some references have been added, and some sentences have been slightly changed for smoothness of reading. My aim has been, however, to make the minimum alteration in the manuscript. The present work does faithfully represent Dr. Lafferty's views.

The index, based in part on Dr. Lafferty's draft, has been prepared by Miss Louise A. Kohl.

JAMES WILLARD OLIVER

PREFACE

It has recently been noted that there is a ground swell of reaction against the more narrow, restricted, and highly skeptical philosophical views of the logical positivists and the analysts. This book follows that new and growing movement.

It should be added hastily, though, that my intent is not to disparage the contributions of those other views, for all philosophies have had invaluable contributions to make toward the development of thought, and none has said the last word, nor could such a thing be possible so long as thought is not dead.

If I have been critical of logical positivism and analysis, as well as of other movements, it is often merely for the sake of contrast in order to sharpen ideas. Beyond that, I would nudge the extreme skeptics over a bit in order to find a foothold for possibilities that I think they overlook. I would like to dissolve the myth that all metaphysical, ethical, and value judgments of whatever kind must be relegated to the realm of crude, subjective, and emotional nonsense, built on bad grammar, in contrast to the supposedly neat, precise, rigorous, and rational certainties of linguistic analysis. If I find that the latter is sometimes confused, evasive, and inadequate, that, I fear, is a rather common human failing which the present work does not escape.

One mark which the positivists and analysts have left is that the more speculative works appear to be more self-conscious, cautious, and critical than were the freewheeling speculations of the late nineteenth or early twentieth centuries. The pragmatists, of course, had already struck that note.

The felicity of human life is that man may love things that prove themselves worthy of being loved. The basic idea is the naturalistic view that man may find and, by art, may create values, ends, or purposes in this world, including the social world. Such values are not always merely vaporous, subjective figments of mental aberrations, because many of them are actual achievements in the world created by art—including the art of social conduct—and not by magic; and art involves trial and error and work. Ideas, including those that are cataloged as religious or philosophical, are, willy-nilly, proposals that are to be evaluated or tested as they may facilitate this creation of values, no matter how dogmatically they may be asserted in the first instance or for however long periods of time. Thus, men eventually get around to the question of intelligence which Socrates asked of old, "What will it do to you?" The criterion to be applied is that such ideas must contribute to a better life for men here and now, and all else which is persisted in is superstition. And "better" must be stated, not in terms of dogmatic prescription, but in terms of the hope that as men live with the consequences of their acts they may actually find some of these consequences to be better, among the possibilities that for the time are open to them; and then the results may teach them the need to revise their ideas of what is better. This, I propose, is the kind of world we live in, but, if so, its implications should be elaborated.

The expression, "Pragmatic Essays," in the title of this book, may call for the remark that I do not, of course, presume to speak for others to whom the word "pragmatist" may be applied. I can speak only for myself in developing some possibilities that I see within the general framework of pragmatism.

For some materials, I have drawn on articles previously published, mainly in the *Journal of Philosophy*. Chapters II, V, and VI bear the same or nearly the same titles as do three formerly published articles,[1] but they are not at all republications of those articles, although they deal with the same subjects and contain some of the same materials.

I wish to express my gratitude to the *Journal of Philosophy* for permission to use much of the material in the three articles mentioned above and to Lehigh University for permission to reprint the note by John Dewey. I also wish to thank *Harper's Magazine* for permission to quote from Walker Gibson's poem "Gotham."

THEODORE T. LAFFERTY
University of South Carolina

Nature and Values

I

Epistemological Preliminaries

I

In these studies I wish to present a view of the natural world that finds a place for values in that world. This involves a metaphysics, a "first philosophy" or a theory of reality which includes a theory of values capable of belonging to a naturalistic world. Some have suggested that metaphysical or speculative views have not been much in favor recently. Professor Morton White has called our age the "Age of Analysis," and that remark could be misread to mean "the age of the analyst." Such an idea overlooks a number of other movements.

It is not correct, of course, to refer to analysts as if they represent any common doctrine beyond method, if even that, for they disagree pretty much on everything else. It is still less possible to attribute any cosmic view to them; therefore, in the succeeding chapters, I shall look to older, more systematic philosophies for the purpose of orienting my views and for drawing contrasts.

In the interest of brevity and, perhaps, of clarity, I shall use the words 'analyst' and 'analysis' in the way in which J. O. Urmson does. He is concerned in the body of his treatment with what led up to a modified form of analysis as represented in the final chapter of *Philosophical Analysis*, "The Beginnings of Contemporary Philosophy." For my purpose, this will serve well enough, since I am not pretending to give a systematic evaluation of philosophies; rather, I am concerned to mention certain ideas that may have a bearing on what I shall have to say. It is necessary to enter this caveat because, like Urmson, I shall, for my purpose, treat analysts and logical positivists together, since the logical positivists were analysts; and yet the contemporary leading analysts are, in major respects, very different from the logical positivists.

Nevertheless, a minor dilemma appears at the moment. On the one hand, the power and influence of the attack on metaphysics by the analysts and logical positivists would seem to require any attempt at proposing a metaphysical theory to take these views into account. Yet, on the other hand, there are indications that the views in question show signs of fading or, at least, of withdrawing from some of the more startling of the earlier positions—a fact which may give one the uncomfortable feeling that any considerable attempt to deal with them would be engaging in the passé. Yet these doctrines, although largely abandoned by the principals, are still retained and taken for granted by many in discussions of metaphysics and ethics. Perhaps one should not beat a dead horse, but its ghost still haunts philosophic discussions. In any case, I have no desire to document with an extensive catalog the stubborn manner in which these ideas live on, but a few abbreviated examples may suffice for illustration.

Certainly, Urmson has given us a remarkable account of the rapid molting in the general movement.[1] Furthermore, G. J. Warnock asserts "in very plain terms that I am not, nor is any philosopher of my acquaintance, a Logical Positivist,"[2] even though A. J. Ayer was at the moment associated with him. Of course, with respect to one branch of the movement, Ayer himself observes, "It is not clear to me, however, that the logical study of semantics has yet produced anything of philosophical importance, with the notable exception of Tarski's semantic restatement of what was rather vaguely implied in the correspondence theory of truth."[3] Others, it might be said, have found Tarski's achievement in this particular respect to be less notable and comprehensive in significance than Ayer's remark would suggest.

Bertrand Russell's more recent remarks exhibit a far more

critical attitude toward analysis than was evident in his *History of Western Philosophy*, chapter 31. Referring to "linguistic analysis," Russell observes:

A new kind of scholasticism has sprung up, and like its medieval forerunner, is running itself into a somewhat narrow groove. What most of the various strands of linguistic analysis share is a belief that ordinary language is adequate, and puzzles arise from philosophic solecism. This view ignores the fact that ordinary language is shot through with the fading hues of past philosophic theories.

... As a philosophic doctrine it has, however, some weaknesses. I should have thought, indeed, that philosophers had been doing this sort of thing on the quiet all along. That this is not willingly acknowledged nowadays is due to a certain intellectual parochialism which has been somewhat the fashion recently. A more serious matter is the enthronement of ordinary language as an arbiter in all disputes. It does not seem at all clear to me that ordinary language could not itself be seriously confused. At the very least it must be a risky business to treat it like the form of the Good without asking what language is, how it arises, functions and grows. The tacit assumption is that language as ordinarily used is possessed of some superior genius or hidden intelligence. A further assumption, linked indirectly with this, allows that one may ignore all unlinguistic knowledge, a dispensation liberally indulged by its adherents.[4]

The major point of this chapter is to indicate, and to do little more than that, some limitations and inadequacies of the epistemological views common to much of logical positivism and analysis. These doctrines are altogether too simple in conception to be adequate for much fruitful human thought, especially in science and philosophy, the latter including metaphysics and ethics.

What I have to say respecting the analysts does not express my appreciation for the number of careful studies which they have produced. My own critical remarks on these views are not intended as a general disparagement, nor as a balanced evaluation, but as a kind of apology for my temerity in offering a metaphysics and a value theory in the face of these vigorous objections. Although the analyst and the logical positivist may object to the speculative, nonetheless, any new ideas, including their own, however hopeful and optimistic, are themselves no less speculative, precisely for the reason that their fruitfulness cannot be foreknown. They are proposals to be evaluated for good or ill, probably for both.

The historic advancement of philosophy has come about through the discovery of new and different ways of looking at things. All great movements of human inquiry have made invaluable contributions to human thought, and this is no less true of the analyst and the logical positivist. The expression, a new broom sweeps clean, is often made in a tone of disparagement, suggesting superficiality and the transiency of a passing fad. But the expression per se is not a conclusive argument against having new brooms. New ideas, new points of view, permit a fresh look and stimulate thought. Moreover, the general movements presented by the logical positivists and the analysts have led to an emphasis upon logical rigor, which is surely helpful. And, more than that, their highly critical and skeptical evaluations of some traditional topics or problems, even while they uncritically accept others, are of the greatest value in helping us look at old problems in new ways, however likely it is that the destruction of these problems is not as complete or final as the logical positivists and analysts so quickly assume. The task of arousing philosophers from dogmatic slumbers is perennial. The skeptic is to be welcomed, for he is the great touchstone of truth, as Socrates taught us in the *Phaedo*, and it must be forever remembered that the burden of proof is on the affirmative side.

Perhaps, however, as John Dewey has noted, every good thing has its limitations, as a condition for its goodness. Certainly, the method of the logical positivist and of the linguistic analyst seems all too often to be the method of systematic oversimplification, with the consequence that questions are sometimes evaded rather than faced.

II

In this connection, I mention three views toward which I shall direct criticism, as they seem to run counter to views that I wish to develop. Succinctly stated, they are: (1) the view that all cognitive propositions are either tautologies or else are empirical; (2) the attack on metaphysics; and (3) the restrictions of the method of "linguistic analysis." These views are interrelated, and so, for convenience of exposition, I shall not entirely separate discussion of the three.

Respecting the first view, that all cognitive propositions are either tautologies or else are empirical, I am not concerned in this connection with the idea that some cognitive propositions are tautologies, but rather with the implications that all other cognitive propositions are empirical. The nub of the objection to the latter is to the way in which it characteristically *has* been interpreted. It may be added that the method of linguistic analysis does not necessitate acceptance of this limited epistemology, but it is actually accepted by a number of linguistic analysts. Thus their method is no guide.

The characteristic interpretation of the "empirical," except as the pragmatist has reconstructed the notion, is a relic of seventeenth- and eighteenth-century empiricism, which stated, essentially, that a proposition is empirical in the sense that it can be directly analyzed into empirical elements. Early in his career, Russell carried this view over into a metaphysical position which reappears in the linguistic form of "reductive analysis" by which all sentences containing "object words" can be replaced equivalently by sets of sentences which refer only to "sense-data." This reductionist principle has presumably been abandoned, at least officially, but a concomitant view has treated all empirical propositions as descriptions.

The reduction principle was used ambiguously to cover at least three very different types of analysis—the reduction of things to sense-data, of nations to persons, and of propositions of one type to propositions of another type. Some later analysts have rejected all three, but, in rejecting the third, they have gone to the opposite extreme, adopting the view that every different type of proposition has its own peculiar logic. Worse, this "idiosyncrasy platitude" leads to the chaotic idea that "every single sentence will have its own logical criteria."[5] One objectionable implication of this view, to which I shall return, is that it makes ethical statements *sui generis*, because it makes all sentences *sui generis.*

Russell has said that "every proposition which we can understand must be composed wholly of constituents with which we are acquainted."[6] In isolation, this statement could be interpreted ambiguously as a truism, namely that we must understand the constituents of a proposition if we are to understand the proposition. However, like Ayer, I interpret Russell's statement in terms of his concept of "knowledge by acquaintance," which leads us back to the eighteenth-century doctrine. Yet there is a problem which must be solved, and there is some indication that Russell may have recognized it; for elsewhere, with more perception, he remarks, "In using causal laws to support inferences from the observed to the unobserved, physics ceases to be *purely descriptive.* . . ."[7] But if the use of causal laws is not descriptive, whether purely or impurely, how can they be empirical in the traditional and narrow sense of that term? The common notion of the logical positivist, that empirical concepts or propositions are merely correlations of phenomena, is a further case in point.

The difficulty, on which I shall elaborate, stems not only from the idea that all cognitive propositions are either tautological or empirical, but also from the connected view that equates empirical propositions with descriptions. On the contrary, I wish to use the word 'empirical' in a broader sense in the interest of verification, accepting the view that equates the empirical with the verifiable. Urmson, presumably a member of the group discussed in his chapter on contemporary philosophy, can still remark that "metaphysics and moral statements must be thrown overboard by the empiricist."[8] This conclusion, I suggest, arises from the identification of the empirical with description. I do not doubt the accuracy of his comment as a historical statement, but it must be recognized that some hypotheses that are not descriptions are indirectly verifiable and are thus empirical in that sense. Moreover, further consideration has forced recognition of this point, as has been seen in the case of Russell. A counterproposal might be that the traditional view of empiricism needs to be thrown overboard, along with some views of metaphysics and moral philosophy. Nevertheless, the necessity of recognizing and dealing with realities, as well as the need for some guidance of conduct, would seem to be elementary in experience.

The pragmatist philosopher's method of formulating hypotheses required that all hypotheses be verifiable but recognized that very often hypotheses are not descriptions. In the revision of his view contained in the introduction to his book *Language, Truth and Logic,* Ayer comments:

I propose to say that a statement is indirectly verifiable if it satisfies the following conditions: first, that in conjunction with certain other premises it entails one or more directly verifiable statements which are not deducible from these other premises alone; and secondly, that these other premises do not include any statement that is not either analytic, or directly verifiable, or capable of being independently established or indirectly verifiable.[9]

Certainly, as Ayer remarks, this is a "more liberal" version of the "empiricist principle" which had implied "that it was illegitimate to introduce any term that did not itself designate something observable."[10] Indeed, Ayer specifically intends "to allow for the case of scientific theories which are expressed in terms that do not themselves designate anything observable."[11] Yet even this liberalization is scarcely sufficient, because it is not correct to suppose that all scientific theories are so much matters of formal logic and mathematics as even the liberal version of Ayer seems to assume. The explanatory function of theories is not always one of necessary implications,[12] although in some cases it is, and perhaps those are the ideal cases. The explanatory value of the evolutionary theory is not merely and strictly deductive. Theory is suggestive and heuristic as well as strictly implicative and may tie together many areas without necessarily implying any of them or being implied by them. The use of models, as of atoms or of molecules, is another illustration; and models are used in quite different ways.

Yet this new view of Ayer's was immediately qualified by the restriction that a "dictionary" be provided, by which statements which contain such terms "can be transformed into statements that are verifiable."[13] This qualification, "transformed," is most vague, except as it may seem to reintroduce the doctrine of reduction, and, because it is vague, it is subject to such different interpretations as may suit the prejudice of the moment. What does 'transformed' mean? And if the verifiable includes the indirectly verifiable, we have nothing but a reiteration of what has been previously said.

Let us consider Bohr's equation of atomic structure, in a simplified form

$$\nu = Z^2 R \left(\frac{1}{n^2} - \frac{1}{n'^2} \right)$$

In what sense is it a description or may it be "transformed" into a description? Now it may be said that descriptive interpretation of the law has indeed been given—in fact, too many and too varied interpretations. Bohr himself interpreted it in terms of a solar system atom in which the law expressed the radii or distances of the orbits of electrons from the nucleus. DeBroglie gave it a wave interpretation, for it has the typical form of a wave formula. Schroedinger suggested that it represented distribution of negative electric density, whatever that may mean phenomenologically. Actually, these interpretations are not so much descriptions as they are the construction of models with whatever value they may have. Much less do they constitute "reduction" of the theory to observation statements. These models are not verifiable in any sense that the formula is not, for any verification is related to implications of the formula. Moreover, still others, more recently, treat the formula as merely a mathematical instrument for computing probabilities. It does not seem clear that this law is a description in any obvious sense, or is to be "transformed" into descriptions by any "dictionary."

S. E. Toulmin and K. Baier remark, "In recent analytical philosophy it has often been taken for granted that the terms 'describe', 'description' and 'descriptive' are so simple as hardly to need examination."[14] I do not suggest that the analyst broadens the notion of description illegitimately, for, especially when dealing critically with metaphysics or with ethics, he does not ordinarily do so. That is precisely where the difficulty appears, for the idea that all propositions—if they are to be cognitive and yet not be tautologies—must be descriptions, would require that the notion of description be enlarged out of all ordinary usage of the term and certainly much beyond the proclaimed meaning of 'protocol sentences'; or else it fails utterly to give any account of the great mass of highly sophisticated scientific theory, especially when it must be recognized that such theory does not consist of purely formal tautologies but rather is focused ultimately on scientific research.

The paradigm examples and stock illustrations of knowledge given by the analyst are of the type 'this is red', 'I was in this room yesterday', or 'there is a cat on the mat'. These illustrations, of course, occur in sophisticated discussions of technical questions. They perhaps do not go out of the bounds of description, although they surely use "object words"; but as far as a more general epistemological doctrine is concerned, it must also be noted that they are not illustrations which remotely suggest scientific theory or any cognitive function beyond the naive level of a child. Respecting ethical trivialities, the addition of evinced emotions, cheers and jeers, does not raise the level significantly.

Warnock suggests that difficulties arise when we "take as a standard case of knowledge my knowledge that there is a cat on the mat now before me,"[15] but he does not elaborate the alternative, except to recommend an examination of language. Now, certainly, a subject matter is never the basis for an invidious reflection on an inquiry. My objection is not to the study of such instances, but to the exclusive concern with them as examples of cognition, so that cognition comes to be stated in such limited ways. In any case, they are inadequate models for any general theory of cognition, and a theory based on them must be a gross oversimplification if the word 'description' is taken in the commonsense or ordinary meaning of the term—as a direct report of experience—and, what is worse, if experience is identified with the results of an abstract analysis of experience into its simplest elements of immediacy.

The idea that Newton's law of gravitation is merely a direct report of experience has little to recommend it. Moreover, we have the testimony of Newton that he invented the idea, and descriptions are not inventions except in fiction. Dewey long ago criticized seventeenth- and eighteenth-century empiricism on that point. These epistemological views must be held in question until they have faced the fact that the Newtonian system did not, on the one hand, break down because it was found to be self-contradictory. Neither, on the other hand, was the system found to be false as a direct empirical description, for it is no more a direct empirical description than is that of Einstein; but, together with particular minor premises, it does imply direct descriptions which are false.

As the logical implications of these narrow and oversimplified epistemological views have become more clearly realized, the conclusion has been reached, not merely that the products of the tortured grammar of philosophers cannot be classified as respectable propositions, but, still more sweeping and startling, that we cannot even say that what have been called "general propositions" are propositions;[16] for, after all, there are no general things to be described by general propositions. The "linguistic" excuse later given for this curious view is that it was just a matter of "words," a recognition that universal propositions are, after all, different from singular propositions—not a very recent discovery.

That the logical positivist is quite capable of extending the bad word 'metaphysical' to sentences or propositions in unusual and esoteric ways is illustrated by Ayer's very definition of the word. "We may accordingly define a metaphysical sentence as a sentence which purports to express a genuine proposition, but does, in fact, express neither a tautology nor an empirical hypothesis."[17] May I repeat that this is an unusual definition because of the connected idea that, for a proposition to be an empirical proposition, it must be reducible to "protocol sentences"? More positively, according to Ayer, "metaphysicians" lapse into such propositions "through being deceived by grammar, or through committing errors in reasoning."[18] Similarly, Wittgenstein says, "Our investigation is a *grammatical* one."[19]

A direct consequence is that the analyst and the logical positivist run into difficulty in classifying their own assertions according to their all-too-limited scheme. Is the verifiability principle of the logical positivist itself a tautology or an empirical description or else mere nonsense?[20] Ayer says that "the verification principle . . . was put forward as a definition, not as an empirical statement of fact. But it is not an arbitrary definition. It purports to lay down the conditions which actually govern our acceptance, or indeed our understanding, of commonsense and scientific statements, the statements which we take as describing the world 'in which we live and move and have our being'."[21] Thus, at first, Ayer claims that this is but a definition. Yet if he also claims that the principle is a statement of "the conditions which actually govern," then it would seem to be a claim to being "an empirical statement of fact," or an attempt to acquire the prestige of such statements. And yet again, if "it purports to lay down the conditions," then there is no noticeable difference between such a "definition" and a normative statement. The argument seems to want it all three ways at once: a definition, a factual statement, and a normative statement.

Under pressure of philosophical suicide, Ayer seems to have had some second thoughts. "I now think that it is incorrect to say that there are no philosophical propositions. For, whether they are true or false, the propositions that are expressed in such a book as this do fall into a special category; and since they are the sort of propositions that are asserted or denied by philosophers, I do not see why they should not be called philosophical. To say of them that they are, in some sense, about the usage of words, is, I believe, correct but also inadequate."[22]

One problem which this suggests is that, if some propositions are to be called philosophical because they are asserted or denied by philosophers, how does one know in the first place who are philosophers? A second question would be whether or not all propositions that are asserted or denied by philosophers are to be called philosophical. Or else, does Ayer simply offer "such a book as this" as a paradigm of philosophy? Unfortunately, his remarks would serve to end an account rather than to begin one, so that what would be necessary for the reconstruction of the admittedly "inadequate" cognitive theory is merely left to our imagination.

The characteristic view of the logical positivist and of the analyst, not to mention the realist who went before them, has been that all cognitive propositions are either tautologies or else descriptions. I suggest that if the idea of description is not broadened illegitimately, then this is an overly simplified epistemological doctrine that is quite inadequate as an account of the cognitive function in general. This naive simplicity may give it popularity, but it will not provide it with any other desirable virtue. Any acceptable epistemology or theory of knowledge must, at the least, acknowledge and account for the elaborate and varied kinds of theoretical propositions, such as those of the theoretical sciences.

Some such theoretical propositions or hypotheses are little more than simplifications, involving solely what Aristotle called "middle terms." Lorenz and Fitzgerald found that Maxwell's field equations can be simplified by the expression

$$\frac{1}{\sqrt{1-\frac{v2}{c2}}}$$

Another kind of theoretical proposition is represented by Einstein's statement that the speed of light is constant for all frames of reference, which is not a description of anything observable. As a third example, mention may be made of the recent concept of "quarks" in physics; this may turn out to be a significant advance or it may be dropped, depending on the outcome of its use, but it is not a description.

In speaking of metaphysics, it may be in the interest of precision to note a distinction that is sometimes made between the positions of the logical positivist and of the linguistic analyst. The attitude of the logical positivist has been to attack metaphysics, whereas that of the linguistic analyst has often been to ignore it as meaningless and to transform supposedly metaphysical questions into linguistic questions.

The term 'metaphysics' as I shall use it is defined in a way neutral to any particular view of metaphysics. I mean by 'metaphysics' any theory of reality. It would follow that anyone who uses the word 'real' or any substitute meaningfully would have some glimmer of metaphysics. There is, of course, the more limited definition which identifies the concept with a particular theory of reality or metaphysical view. Kant apparently derived his definition from the etymology of the word itself, when he remarked, "As concerns the sources of metaphysical knowledge, its very concept implies that they cannot be empirical."[23] The logical positivist and the analyst, as well as others, appear, in turn, to derive their concept of metaphysics from Kant.

There is the ancient story that in actual origin the word 'metaphysics' merely indicated an unnamed work by Aristotle that was in the Alexandrian library beside the *Physics*. Whether this story is true or false, it at least suggests that a first philosophy concerned with being or reality need not necessarily be bound by the etymology of a word that was long afterwards attached to such inquiry.

My position is one which, while agreeing with criticism of transempirical metaphysics, nevertheless finds gaps in the arguments which would lead one to draw too sweeping negative conclusions. However valid may be the attack upon transempirical metaphysics, it does not destroy all theories of reality or metaphysics. For instance, having identified 'metaphysics' as a bad word, the logical positivist and analyst, abandoning analysis, extend the term to cover all hypothetical entities including "object words," where the latter term is used to indicate the continuity of things rather than mere phenomena. And, again, while much of what is termed morality may indeed be little more than the evincing of emotions, just as the logical positivist and analyst say, we may, nevertheless, ask the question: Is it not possible to be intelligent or at least more intelligent about human conduct and human aims or values? The very job of philosophy, in these respects, as I see it, is to propose and evaluate presuppositions on which we can make better judgments. In other words, philosophy is basic theory.

The denial of metaphysics has been more often a matter of creed than of practice. Urmson, speaking of logical atomism, says, "It rejects speculative metaphysics, the metaphysics of inferred entities."[24] But, of course, the whole doctrine is speculative and, furthermore, it is concerned with "inferred entities." Thus, the "atomic fact" which answers to the propositional function, fx, and which has never been seen on land or sea, is asserted to consist of a "constituent," a particular, and a "component," a universal element. According to the earlier Wittgenstein of the *Tractatus*, the language "pictures" reality, but that is because the "fact" or "reality" already was created in the image of logic or language, in the time-honored tradition.

It has been noted and documented often enough that the logical positivists and analysts have been by no means innocent of metaphysics. Hence, their avowed eschewal of the idea has the further difficulty of leading to an evasion or, at least, to a failure to recognize the need for critical support of the metaphysics which they do introduce as though it were merely a matter of course, often under the guise that it is just a given linguistic expression. As one example of metaphysics, as pure and undefiled as that of Herbert Spencer, and in an equal, if opposite, direction, I might quote a statement by Moritz Schlick:

As a matter of principle, it should be realized and noted that in scientific cosmology, the present more complex and ordered state of the world, can never be derived from simpler and more chaotic conditions. The degree of differentiation, order and multiplicity remains the same throughout all transformations. As a result of this observation, the philosophical significance of theories of the evolution of the world is reduced to a minimum.[25]

One will immediately be struck by the metaphysical doctrine, the contrary of the view of Spencer, that there can only be a certain amount of order in the universe. But attention may be called to something else: anyone after David Hume should be sensitive to a significant ambiguity in the word 'derived' as used by Schlick in this quotation. Derived in what sense? Does the word mean a logical derivation from a set of propositions, or does 'derive' refer to something which may arise out of prior conditions in some actual process? There *is* a difference. Descartes may have identified the two in the doctrine that there can be nothing more in the effect than there is in the cause, confusing reality with logical systems, but he and his metaphysics came before Hume.

The example quoted from Schlick may not be as broadly representative of the metaphysics characteristic of the analyst and logical positivist as are the commonly used "sense-data" and "phenomenological" concepts that one finds taken for granted; although, more recently, there have been criticisms of these notions by some analysts, the criticisms consist largely of negative dialectic and do not propose alternatives.

The standard method of the linguistic analyst is to pose metaphysical problems but to deal with them in a sub rosa fashion by the curious claim that they are merely questions about linguistic expressions. Like Hamlet, it seems that one only reads words; but word readers need remedial reading. Thus, the problem of universals is raised but is then translated into the verbalistic question of whether to reclassify abstract words as proper names. In the *Philosophical Investigations*,[26] Wittgenstein attempts to deal critically with what would ordinarily be stated as the question of a metaphysical subjective realm. But he does not meet the issue head on.

Rather, he deals with it in an oblique fashion by raising the issue of whether there can be a private language. The result is a discussion so vague that serious scholars may be left at a loss to know what Wittgenstein is saying.[27] Though the issue is metaphysical, obviously no clarity is added by dealing with it in obscure ways.

Since the views which I propose to set forth have nothing to do with the transempirical, against which the logical positivist inveighs under the title of metaphysics, the implication would seem to be one of peaceful irrelevance. It would be, except for a logical howler that was rife among the logical positivists. Having defined 'metaphysics' in the limited term of being concerned merely with the transempirical, and having eliminated that, they forthwith concluded that nothing is left to philosophy but "logic." (I am not concerned with ethics at this point.) What, we ask, happened to theories of reality, including perhaps their own, which may not be transempirical? To this question, the logical positivist had his simple little out. Such theories, he said, are science.

Although the way is open for the logical positivist to classify ideas in any way he likes, still, if this is an arbitrary matter, then those who are not logical positivists are equally free and are not bound to follow him, especially when he uses commonly accepted words in ways so far removed from their accepted meanings that they are grossly misleading. In any case, this would *not* be an example of the "common language usage" technique. The one function of philosophy recognized by analysts and logical positivists is that philosophy should clarify concepts, not confuse them.

That the methods of philosophy should be somewhat similar to the general methods of science has long been a thesis of pragmatism, but there is a major distinction. The word 'science', in its more specific sense, has come to signify the plural 'sciences'. That is, the sciences characteristically have limited or delimited subject matters, whereas any theory of reality, like any inquiry, provides answers to a limited or specific set of questions, but, in the nature of the case, it does not have a limited subject matter, at least not in the same sense as the sciences.

Then too, the term 'sciences' has come to signify, almost inevitably, theories that are well verified or at least that aim more or less directly at precise experimental verification. To apply the word 'science' to philosophical views which, at first, are merely hopeful proposals—and that is the most that I could claim for my views—would seem to border on the boastful. I suggest that these views of the logical positivist have the unphilosophical feature of serving to confuse ideas, rather than to distinguish and clarify them. Analysis, presumably, is the boast of the analyst.

It is appropriate, in this connection, to note the views of the pragmatists on metaphysics, more especially those of Dewey. These remarks are necessary because of the rather frequent statements suggesting that he discarded metaphysics. Dewey had his own particular metaphysical views, just as other philosophers have had throughout history in their variety of ways. In any case, he was concerned with "existence," and that concern would bring his views under the neutral definition adopted here of 'metaphysics', namely, any 'theory of reality'.

Dewey made a number of critical remarks about metaphysics, sometimes without obviously qualifying them, except as might be appropriate to the particular views against which they were directed. Thus, the remarks may seem general with respect to all metaphysics, and some readers have been led to conclusions similar to those indicated above. Dewey, for instance, speaks of "vain metaphysics" and "sterile metaphysics"[28] without any special qualifications; furthermore, the remarks occur in what is perhaps his most widely read book. Yet, he often did make a very significant qualification: "It is not meant, of course, to deny all metaphysical implications in a certain sense of 'metaphysical'."[29] Dewey, in fact, had an early and continuing interest in metaphysics. In 1915, he published his views on "The Subject Matter of Metaphysical Inquiry."[30] However, one of his most daring excursions into metaphysics, "Time and Individuality,"[31] does not use the word, I think, except in a pejorative sense.

Dewey viewed metaphysics as "being a detection and description of the generic traits of existence."[32] Thus, it was for him a "naturalistic metaphysics."[33] Others, of course, might continue to apply the term to older metaphysical views and, with whatever legitimacy one might have in insisting upon a particular definition, might object to Dewey's use of the word. What discouraged Dewey was not any such clear and definite difference as that, but the muddled assumption that, in using the term, he was carrying over the older ideas and accepting those ideas himself. To assume this could only be, on their part, a lack of scholarship on the order of a radical misstatement of the views of Aristotle or of Kant, diametrically opposite to what they said. So, eventually, Dewey said:

I now realize that it was exceedingly naive for me to suppose that it was possible to rescue the word 'metaphysics' from its deeply engrained traditional use. I derive what consolation may be possible from promising myself never to use the word again in connection with any aspect of my own position. Nevertheless, the text of my book [*Experience and Nature*] makes it clear that I was proposing a use of the word so different from the traditional one as to be incompatible with it.

The relevant point is that this does not represent a change of viewpoint respecting meaning or subject matter, nor a denial of the legitimacy of his former use of the term 'metaphysics'. Thus, he added, "The foregoing is not an apology for my use of the word metaphysical. It is evoked by the misreading of my use of the word."[34] In any case, Dewey's view was that "Pragmatism thus has a metaphysical implication."[35]

There is a rather vague sense, I think, in which philosophies do have something in common with verification, for they, too, may be applied. Plato said that philosophy is concerned with ways of life. One might hazard the idea that, in modern times, it has taken about a hundred years for major philosophies to permeate the social atmosphere, to become the common ideas in terms of which men define their problems and seek solutions. In the social and political worlds, an applied philosophy may be called an ideology; and ideologies have consequences in terms of which they eventually come to be evaluated. But, in any case, all this is rather distantly related to the more precise experimental verification which we expect of the several sciences.

III

The general philosophical view of the logical positivist and the analyst has been that all philosophical problems are pseudo-problems, brought about through the misuse of language; therefore their endeavor is "therapeutic," to save men from the delusions of philosophy; and this, of course, applies also to ethics. They prefer to think that the difficulty stems from ethics rather than from their own epistemology.

Now I think it may be stipulated that it is not the business of philosophical ethics to prescribe little rules or commandments for daily guidance. Ethics does not make particular moral decisions. But, if not, then what does it do? I suggest that, as a philosophical endeavor, the problem of philosophical ethics is to propose considerations upon which more intelligent moral decisions may be made; and this is neither a pseudoproblem nor is it merely a verbal one. However, Ayer concludes, "We find that ethical philosophy consists simply in saying that ethical concepts are pseudo-concepts and therefore unanalyzable."[36] It seems clear that Ayer's brand of philosophy cannot provide a solution that meets the conditions of our problem; therefore we shall have to get a different philosophy, if one exists that can offer such a solution.

Assuming that all cognitive functions are either tautologies or descriptions, what can be said of ethical or value judgments or supposed judgments? Ayer, resorting to "radical subjectivism" says that they "merely evince moral disapproval,"[37] presumably by way of cheering or jeering. Now, even if the moral attitude is one of approval and disapproval, or approbation and disapprobation, and this attitude is exhibited directly by cheering and jeering, it may yet be that, in the intelligent act, the attitude is temporarily inhibited and its energy channeled into acts of inquiry.

The difficulty with Ayer is that he seems to think that he has settled the issue when he has only raised it. The question of rational morality is whether approval or disapproval can be guided rationally in some cases, that is, whether there are or can be rational grounds for approval or disapproval. If so, then moral approval and disapproval are in such cases more than mere cheering and jeering. Approval and disapproval are natural emotional reactions which may have causes of various kinds—nonrational, irrational, or rational. The question at issue, if Ayer wishes to make it an issue, is whether approval and disapproval *can* be based on rational grounds, not whether they necessarily are.

Ayer says that the feelings are matters of "conditioning."[38] This is a question for psychologists to decide, and I have no desire to dispute it. But, if so, then it would seem that people can be conditioned to desire to be intelligent, and this may be a prerequisite to dealing with any problem rationally, whether in physics or in ethics. I mean a precondition of rational treatment of problems is that we seek rational solutions by rational methods. The fact that the insane or the hysterical or the infantile or the irresponsible or the prejudiced or those with ulterior motives or anyone else may not wish to do so is irrelevant. The only relevant philosophical questions are, whether it is possible to make rational moral judgments, and what the general conditions for that possibility are. Later, I shall argue that the objective of making approval and disapproval rational is that they may better serve the larger ends of human life. This is an evolutionary development of the means-end relation of the biological act. That is, rational approval and disapproval of conduct is concerned with means, as means affect ends of value.

If Ayer says that it is not possible to base moral judgments on rational grounds, then he must provide evidence. His argument for this point leaves something to be desired. According to him, ethical concepts "are mere pseudo-concepts." The major proof he offers of this view is this: "The presence of an ethical symbol in a proposition adds nothing to its factual content. Thus, if I say to someone, 'You acted wrongly in stealing that money,' I am not stating anything more than if I had simply said, 'You stole that money.' . . . In adding that this action is wrong . . . I am simply evincing my moral disapproval of it."[39] In Ayer's non sequitur above, I wish to agree with the premise: "If I say to someone, 'You acted wrongly in stealing that money,' I am not stating anything more than if I had simply said, 'You stole that money'." This is perfectly true and quite irrelevant to the conclusion that ethical concepts "are mere pseudo-concepts." The reason why the premise is true is that it is a tautology. 'Stealing' means the wrongful taking of property. The statement, 'stealing is wrong', is therefore an analytic truth. Certainly, the predicate adds nothing to the subject, but the tautologous use of a term does not make it a pseudoconcept.

It is quite a different matter, however, if we are considering whether certain corporation practices should be regarded as wrong, especially when the consideration is not limited to immediate likes or dislikes of the practices but involves a thorough investigation of their effects, as well as the effects of alternatives, upon furthering the conditions and major ends of people involved. I refer to practices of corporations because they are more recent in our history and raise genuine problems, whereas ordinary cases of murder and thievery may not seem to present any real moral issue; such an issue may have long since been settled. An example is the consideration of the manipulations of the old Standard Oil trust. The question to be adjudged is whether we should consider a certain practice to be stealing, or something of the sort. The judging does not consist of shouting that stealing is wrong, nor merely of cheering and jeering. The question is, what are the rational grounds on which we may approve or disapprove certain practices?

According to Ayer, "It appears, then, that ethics, as a branch of knowledge, is nothing more than a department of psychology or sociology. . . . For one finds that one of the chief causes of moral behavior is fear . . . of a god's displeasure, and fear of the enmity of society."[40] Doubtless, this remark clarifies Ayer's conception of ethics and thus illuminates his attitude toward it. Admittedly, there is such a type of "moral" behavior as he describes, and perhaps his treatment of it is justified. But I am concerned with a very different kind of ethics—namely, the question of getting something of worth out of life and the conditions which will more probably enable people to do so. Thus, its main virtue is not fear of gods or of society.

In passing, Ayer does mention something along this line, although, I suspect, on a different tangent. He says, "In short, we find that argument is possible on moral questions only if some system of values is presupposed."[41] I shall discuss the question of values in later chapters, but, for the moment, I shall agree hypothetically with Ayer's "radical subjectivism." If there is nothing of worth in life and cannot be, then what difference does it make what one does? At that point, however, my agreement ends. If important things are at stake, then one had better walk warily.

There are others who agree with Ayer that all cognitive judgments are either tautologies or descriptions but who give a somewhat different account of ethical and value judgments. They equate such judgments with "decisions," which have no evidential grounds and which are, therefore, arbitrary. They assume that the appeal to decisions merely serves to end the matter. Thus, R. M. Hare closes his discussion of this question by saying, "I have in the end to decide for myself what I ought to do."[42] This is undoubtedly true, but on what grounds does one decide? Hare offers only the most meager help.

Hare does say that "if asked to justify as completely as possible any decision, we have to bring in both effects—to give content to the decision—and principles, and the effects in general of observing those principles, and so on, until we have satisfied our inquirer."[43] And, again, I do not overlook the possible empiricism in Hare's demand that one "try to live by it." Both of these remarks may seem to provide room for naturalistic inquiry, but at least four things invalidate any such interpretation.

First, Hare emphatically repudiates naturalism in this connection. Second, in the first of the two remarks just quoted, the decision has already been made and the only point is to "justify" it. Thus, neither the decision nor the attempt at justification is a genuine inquiry.

Third, Hare does not follow up these apparently empirical suggestions with any further elaboration. The word 'effects' in the context, "effects in general of observing those principles," may suggest consequences of the behavior which consists of "observing those principles," but the logical significance of such behavior or conduct, so briefly recognized, is never elaborated, as, for instance, the pragmatist elaborates it in his experimental theory. Nor is the concept of effects or consequences elaborated in any other way. What kinds of effects or consequences are relevant in making value judgments? Not only is Hare merely justifying decisions already made, but he also soon ignores effects or consequences by turning to decisions of principle when he says, "For in the end everything rests upon such a decision of principle."[44] Thus, "it will be noticed how, in talking of decisions of principle, I have inevitably started talking value-language," and, again, "to make a value judgment is to make a decision of principle."[45] The two would seem to be equivalent. But when I am talking of value judgments I may be speaking of judgments of particular things. Is this a good painting or is it trash? Principles are used in judgments of any kind, I presume, but values, as I am concerned with them, are, concretely, particular and individual things.

Fourth, at another point Hare says, curiously, that there is an "analogy" with the position of the scientist, and that the difference "between decisions and observations is only apparent."[46] One might rather have thought that decisions, in the ordinary sense, would in part rest on observations, including observations of preferences, discovered likings and dislikings, when relevant. But it would hardly seem profitable to our purpose to speculate on Hare's curious analogy, for whatever analogy there is does not go far. Hare's central theme, in respect to value judgments, whether they are concerned with morals or with ends, is that such "judgments" are "not informative in the least."[47] Contrary to any empiricism which "observations" might suggest, Hare believes that we should "learn to use 'ought' sentences in the realization that they can only be verified by reference to a standard or set of principles which we have by our own decision accepted and made our own."[48]

Again, the appeal is merely to a decision, and one already made at that. In the context, one gathers that the "standard or set of principles" referred to for verification consists itself of moral principles; and he says, in that respect, that people must "decide between their rival principles."[49] Rather, I would suggest that these principles might be verified, if at all, by reference to non-ethical principles of verification, plus some nonethical facts. The philosophical question is *how* we may validly decide, whereas Hare only praises the glory of making decisions. "Morality regains its vigour when ordinary people have learnt afresh to decide for themselves what principles to live by."[50] Thus it is reiterated over and over that we must decide—even ordinary people must decide—but on what grounds? And how shall we decide? Since I have previously discussed a similar view in an article in the *Journal of Philosophy*,[51] I shall not further extend my remarks on this point.

It has been rather characteristic of logical positivists and analysts to point out that similarity of grammatical structure does not imply sameness of meaning. They are not the first to notice that point. It is, however, quite strange that in their linguistic analysis they frequently assume that a word must always mean the same thing wherever it occurs. For instance, consider the expressions 'good for' and 'good'. Hare asserts that "the word 'good' has a constant meaning."[52]

Another attempt to settle the problem merely by means of consideration of language does so by listing a number of isolated sentences in which the word 'good' appears and seeking to find a common meaning, assuming without question that there is a common meaning.[53] Among these sentences are:

This is a good electric blanket.
This soup is good to eat.

One might have supposed that the word 'good' meant rather different things in the different contexts. In the first sentence, 'good' refers to instrumental or effective characteristics; the blanket is durable, it regulates heat well, etc. In the second sentence, the word 'good' may refer to affective characteristics—the soup is delicious.

Of course, it is not entirely clear that Hare does mean that "the word 'good' has a constant meaning," for elsewhere he says that there are "many ways in which we use the word 'good'," [54] different ways, that is to say, which give the word a different "meaning." [55] However that may be, Hare nevertheless proceeds to argue that attempts to distinguish "instrumental good" from "intrinsic good" [56] fail because "instrumental good" also involves "choosing." [57] This leaves us with decisions again.

I suggest that the confusing result of unbridled dependence on linguistic usage may be corrected in this instance by not using the expression 'instrumental good'. There is nothing that we can say by using the word 'good' in reference to an instrument as such that we cannot say more precisely by using other general words such as 'effective'. Yet the major point is not the use of this or that word, but to note a confusion that genuine analysis would clarify. The question whether a means or an instrument is effective toward achieving an end, or is more effective than other means or instruments, is a question of fact, and it is such a fact, not the end, which is in question.

If we do not use the word 'good' for means or instruments as such, we may reserve the word for something like what Hare calls "intrinsic good," and thus rid ourselves of that expression also. The expression 'intrinsic good' is so closely associated with 'good in itself' as to suggest a *Ding an sich*, or, as Hare says, "the object" in distinction from its functions. Perhaps the expression could be saved by explicit definition, but bad associations are notorious for bad influences; and it suggests altogether too much the absolute, nonfunctional good of older views. Such a good is as nonrational and as arbitrary as any positivist or analyst might claim.

Strictly, ethical judgments are not primarily value judgments but are validated by reference to ends or values. Value judgments are judgments about ends and are concerned with good and bad in the nonethical use of those terms. Ethical judgments are concerned with conduct—right and wrong conduct—and 'conduct' means what it says, it conducts or leads to something. Nevertheless, the views I am discussing mix the two, in a rather unanalytic fashion, and I shall not take space to separate them.

Margaret Macdonald adopts an epistemological view similar to that previously noted, namely that all propositions are either (1) tautological or (2) empirical.[58] While she does not elaborate on her meaning of 'empirical', still it is such that she must find another category for (3) assertions or expressions of value. She goes on to say that "ethical judgments . . . are value decisions," and in turn, "value utterances are more like records of decisions than propositions." Thus, so far, we are back to Hare's "decisions."

Miss Macdonald goes further, however, by at least posing the all-important question, "Upon what grounds or for what reasons are decisions reached?" But then she vitiates this, for she follows the lead of many in transforming the question of validity into one of supporting or defending decisions; the decisions, presumably, have already been made. More plaintively, Russell says that an ethical judgment merely expresses a wish plus "the wish that others should share my wish."[59]

There is a strange propensity to use "ought" sentences in the second person, possibly because such sentences are frequently nonsense and the intent is to generalize this characteristic. Hare says that "the words 'right' and 'ought' . . . are used primarily for giving advice or instruction,"[60] and, again, "it is the purpose of the word 'good' and other value-words to be used for teaching standards."[61] Ayer also shares this forensic theory of ethics. The object of concern is "our opponent," and, hence, eventually, "it is because argument fails us when we come to deal with pure questions of value, as distinct from questions of

fact, that we finally resort to mere abuse." [62] Later, Russell made
a discovery of something new—theoretically new to him, at any
rate. "What we 'ought' to do is, by definition, the act which
is right." [63] This at least opens up a different approach. It is just
possible that there are occasions when I am not attending to the
improvement of other people's morals by forcing mine on them,
or concerned with warding off their imposition on me, but may
be more concerned with my own morals, and with finding out the
right thing for me to do. I have not made the decision; I am trying
to reach a decision that has some respect for truth. And Hare
keeps shouting at me, "Make a decision. Make a decision."

Following her argumentative lead, Miss Macdonald finds it
relevant to call upon all the histrionic tricks of a lawyer "to
impress and convince" but "not prove"—an appeal not to the
brains of the jury but to its viscera. I would suggest that her
courtroom analogy is not well developed, because the attorney
for the defense does not render the verdict. Attorneys usually
leave that decision to the court, or else assume that their clients
are innocent until proved guilty. The trial is concerned with
something that she never mentions—whether the accused did or
did not commit the crime with which he is charged. The rules of
evidence are not as stupid as she implies, and her analogy fails
to support her point that "assertions of value cannot be subjected
to demonstrative or inductive methods."

Perhaps a careful rereading of Plato's *Gorgias*, on persuasion,
would be helpful. It may be that in any actual case, I would
prefer to have both Socrates and Gorgias on my side, Socrates
to help me find out what I ought to do and Gorgias to help me
get it done. According to the story, Gorgias was great enough
to admit that point. But at the present moment, I am only
concerned with what is right, or, more strictly, with conditions
for finding out what is right. So I shall send Gorgias and Miss
Macdonald's lawyer about their business.

In the second of her two analogies, Miss Macdonald considers an argument as to whether George Crabbe or John Keats is the better poet. This is a stock argument frequently used for the sake of showing that value and ethical judgments are always inconclusive or futile. The sequel is that, having found the argument inconclusive, she compares it invidiously with a scientific example so chosen that the empirical evidence is fairly conclusive, as if science always knows the answers. The slanting of her argument is too evident. Whether the choice between Crabbe and Keats is or is not conclusive does not prove that there cannot be fairly conclusive value judgments. As an extreme example, why does she not consider such a value judgment as a choice between some ordinary doggerel written by a fifth-grade child and the poetry of either Crabbe or Keats? I am quite confident that, at that level, Miss Macdonald could distinguish the difference in aesthetic merit. The case is so obvious that it may seem condescending to mention it; but I wish to make a logical point.

Similarly, pictures of considerable aesthetic difference are indeed used in intelligence tests, such as the Stanford-Binet test of judgmental ability. The significant point is that one who could not render an appropriate aesthetic judgment in such simple cases would probably not be able to make much of any judgment at all. This is "significant" in the sense that it recognizes that judgment is judgment whether it involves aesthetic merit or other matters. Hence, philosophical views, for which this is an anomaly, do not discredit value judgments; they indicate their own inadequacy. Dewey makes some pertinent remarks on this matter in discussing "qualitative thought."[64] I hazard the guess that the real reason why it is so easy to think of aesthetic and moral judgments as inconclusive is that a vast mass of aesthetic nonsense and moralistic superstitions do pass for judgments, whereas they are on a level with Hottentot astronomy.

Now there is such a thing as decision in the sense of personal preference. But that is simply a matter of fact as it occurs; it is neither valid nor invalid and per se is neither defensible nor does it need any defense, for defense is irrelevant. It is simply a fact to be noted. What use may be made of it is another matter, as is the case with any other fact in the world.

IV

It sometimes seems that, not only do the logical positivist and the analyst raise the question, although confusedly rather than forthrightly, *Can* one be rational, but they also raise the question *Why* should one be rational? However, a rational answer would seem to be excluded as circular or as begging the question in presupposition. For this reason, they resort to persuasion or arbitrary decision. But rationality is not an all-or-none affair; we develop in a spiral, as Dewey says. People who manage to live outside of mental institutions may be rational enough in their more immediate and common affairs, even though, beyond that, they may be as superstitious as Hottentots. And, as Thomas Huxley says, science itself is developed common sense.

It is easier, however, to evade what is more remote. Few philosophers other than William James have tried to discover the more primitive foundations of rationality. His attempt, though often made the sport of dialecticians, is to "trace why people follow truth and always ought to follow it." [65] At higher levels, more sophisticated, abstract answers may indeed serve better, but they will nonetheless rest on this *arche*, to which we may return when our ideas are shaken to their foundations by catastrophe or by profound intellectual questions. The cynicism of the logical positivist and the analyst is only possible for people who make their living by words or have independent incomes and who do not practice what they preach. Russell at one time said that his social views had nothing to do with his philosophy—so much the worse for both.

Various philosophies have more or less independently found it necessary to return to this *arche*. When Santayana comes to his basic assumptions, he remarks, "When, as I must, I have yielded to this presumption and proceeded to explore the world, I shall find in its constitution the most beautiful justification for my initial faith and the proof of its secret rationality. This corroboration . . . will be only pragmatic."[66] Of course, Santayana's specific assumption in this case is his idea of "substance." I am not concerned with that but only with the method to which he thus resorts. Of his own view Whitehead remarks, "This doctrine places philosophy on a pragmatic basis."[67]

Russell states his problem as a disjunction: either we must accept solipsism or else we must accept some principle on faith. I am not concerned with the truth of this major proposition, but with the further method. The minor premise is, we cannot accept solipsism. Why not? Russell, of course, does not use the term 'pragmatic', but he writes, "As against solipsism it is to be said, in the first place, that it is psychologically impossible to believe, and is rejected in fact even by those who mean to accept it. I once received a letter from an eminent logician, Mrs. Christine Ladd Franklin, saying that she was a solipsist, and was surprised that there were no others. Coming from a logician, this surprise surprised me."[68] In an earlier version of this story, which I heard years before this one was published, he was surprised that the solipsist wrote a letter. The essence of Russell's argument against solipsism is pragmatic, for one cannot act on the hypothesis. Nor is he beyond making "pragmatic" appeals elsewhere and repeatedly, and in the loosest form of pragmatism: "In other cases, it is to be believed if it works."[69] "A fiction which is useful is not likely to be a mere fiction."[70] "The forming of inferential habits which lead to true expectations is part of the adaptation to the environment upon which biological survival depends."[71]

If some of the foregoing authors may be criticized for not developing their remarks, the criticism is not equally applicable to Stuart Hampshire. He remarks that "the justification of one method rather than another, in philosophy as in any other enquiry, is a pragmatic one—that, when we use it, we find answers to the questions we want to answer."[72] Furthermore, he raises the

question, "Why should we not now finally accept that philosophy itself must always be experimental?"[73]

Far from suggesting that these admissions constitute the em-
bracing of pragmatism, I should say that, except for that of
Hampshire, they are for the most part the most grudging of
admissions. Yet that is all the greater testimony to their necessity. And furthermore, the fact that they lie, not on the outer
fringes and among incidentals, but at the very foundations, the
basic presuppositions, of the respective systems, would seem
not only to give them a place of prominence, but also to call for
more investigation of the method to which appeal is made.[74]

The key idea to the present studies is indicated by the word
'experimental'. Life is inevitably experimental, both in respect
to its values and to its means of achieving them. At its best, it
is experimental in the most intelligent and broadly considerate
sense of the word; at its lowest and most primitive level, it is
experimental in the less intelligent sense of blind impulse and
dumb trial and error. There are many degrees in between. The
basic hypothesis of these studies is that knowing in its most
fruitful sense, including knowledge of values, is experimental.
The problem is to elaborate the metaphysical and moral implications of this point of view, not only to see what they mean in
that respect but also to see whether a reasonably adequate view of
life can be stated or at least intimated in such terms. The basis
of the hypothesis is that the development of thought is the history of the development of experimentation—either intelligent
experimentation or less intelligent trial and error and improvisa-
tion. Most often it has not been conceived as experiment, but
as dogmatic and final truth; but any actual attempt, whether
it be an intellectual enterprise or a practical endeavor, commits
one to a line of development which entails consequences, good
or bad, that one cannot always foresee.

The problem of developing truth is too often treated as an
oversimplified version of "verification"; as if we have already
posited a given, clear-cut proposition, and the only question lies

in determining whether it corresponds in some direct, simple fashion to some equally given reality. Truth must be *worked* out; it is not an automatic secretion of a mind or of a ganglion. Therefore, genuine concern as to whether one's ideas are true or not requires one to put them to the test, to apply them, to put them into practice to determine whether indeed they do solve the problem. Research scientists have laboratories, not merely to test their ideas, to confirm or disconfirm, but in order to develop their ideas in terms of dealing with things. While the motives of the research scientist and of the factory owner may be quite different in important respects, there is no impossible gap between the laboratory and the factory; sometimes they are in the same building.

I am concerned with science, not to overemphasize it at the expense of values, but, on the contrary, to avoid the hypostatization of scientific concepts as some philosophical arguments appear to do; that is, they identify absolutely scientific concepts with reality, which leaves no room in reality for values, or, as Dewey long ago pointed out, it "has no place for poetry or possibilities."[75]

Science, until modern times, has been defined as an organized body of knowledge. Thus any systematized body of dogmas claiming to be "knowledge" could be called a "science." However, modern science, as G. H. Mead points out,[76] is research science. Research science is concerned with problems and with the reconstruction and development of ideas in the resolution of the problems. In this process, the systematic or logical organization of ideas and the calculation of implication is an effective means, but it is to be treated functionally, that is, as a means of inquiry not as a final end.

In research science, a problem as a problem is stated as the clarification of a difficulty; and difficulties arise, not merely out of cognitive conditions, but out of precognitive conditions as well; ultimately, difficulties arise out of the business of life. At lower levels, difficulties suddenly confront and force themselves upon one, however inconvenient the time. At more advanced levels, more thoughtful levels, men actively seek out problems—this characterizes research procedures. The transformation of a difficulty into a problem is the first major intellectual step. In any case, no problem in its own terms is merely subjective; the very statement of any problem, whether theoretical or practical, presupposes realities. This does not guarantee that any particular presupposition is true, much less absolute, for it in turn might be questioned, as it might be if the original statement of the problem does not lead to a solution. But that constitutes another problem. It follows that the statement of the problem is itself hypothetical.

Secondly, the statement of the problem stipulates demands which must be met to provide a solution. Thus this statement specifies the conditions for the verification of ideas respecting a solution. This point is, I think, frequently overlooked in generalized discussions of verification, truth, and validity of knowledge. Thus verification of ideas is often talked about as if the ideas were in a vacuum, except that, in some other, far-off realm there is a static set of entities called "facts"—such a tendency is often signified by calling indicative sentences, per se, "judgments" or "propositions."

The view I am suggesting establishes a relativism. Any problem arises within a context or a situation, not only by virtue of its presuppositions, but also by virtue of the conditions which give rise to the difficulty and which provide at least some of the conditions for its solution. If its fails to provide conditions for its solution, the solution does not lie within that context, and so the context must be broadened. In the most narrow sense of the context of a difficulty, this must always be the case.

Any given situation of thought involves a background of ideas and facts, but it also involves the invention of new ideas or the inventive reconstruction of previous ideas. As R. A. Millikan wrote in 1917, "To be living in a period which faces such a complete reconstruction of our notions . . . is an inspiring prospect."[77]

The new idea is never strictly and necessarily or formally inferred from facts, any more than is any idea. In some cases, we can plot our data, and we may calculate a formula of best fit by the method of least squares, but such a method would give us only a meager portion of modern science. We can merely correlate data, as the logical positivists sometimes seem to suggest, but, in such a case, selection of one set of data rather than another would remain a matter of chance. Such random performance would be on the level of a child playing with measuring instruments, "measuring" merely to be measuring.

Theories are more than mere random correlations of data or of phenomena. A major function of theory is to suggest fruitful lines of investigation; therefore, to that extent, good theory does this and is good theory only so long as it does. Millikan wrote at the time the Bohr theory was formulated, "For the present at least it is the truth, and no other theory of atomic structure need be considered until it has shown itself able to approach it in *fertility*. I know of no competitor which is as yet even in sight."[78] Within a year after the second edition of Millikan's book, these statements could no longer be made about the Bohr theory, but his remarks still exhibit a truth about theory itself.

What alternative to an experimental philosophy have we in major contemporary philosophical movements? I must say, on the grounds of more consideration than appears in the following discussion, that, so far as I can see, they have nothing to offer as ultimate grounds but cynicism or dogmatism. That is to say, the alternative to experimental inquiry is either the silence of the logical positivist or else faith.

The word 'faith' can have different meanings. It may mean devotion or commitment of allegiance to values, "the substance of things hoped for," as Paul defines it. It can mean adopting principles upon the warrant of more evidence than not, as tentative heuristic ideals. But what it has most often meant in history and in common use is believing propositions without any evidence.

Russell observes that "philosophy is an offshoot of theology."[79] I do not accept this unqualified remark, even though various philosophies have borrowed much from religion. Xenophanes and Parmenides did not copy the religions of their day, and the Socratic method was not copied from any theologian as far as I know, certainly not from Euthyphro. On the contrary, theology, as a logical systematization of religious ideas, arose as an application of older philosophical methods to religion. However that may be, Russell's remark does describe the nature of his problem as he states it, because he, like the theologians, wants something to "justify our beliefs."[80] This way of stating the problem indicates that we already have beliefs, and now we seek some antecedent principle or authority which will justify them. Thus he abandons empirical method, for empirical method cannot guarantee justification for antecedent beliefs. According to him, "empiricism, as a theory of knowledge, is self-refuting."[81] Of course, this remark is directed toward empiricism as Russell interprets it.

We have seen that in respect to value judgments, the forensic method of Hare and of Miss Macdonald justifies decisions already made. Russell, on the contrary, has the perception to realize that the tail goes with the hide: the same doctrine would apply to all judgments, if to any. Consequently, the whole of epistemology must rest on "faith," as Russell says. This is the old theological doctrine that one must already believe what is to be proved in order to prove; and it may as well be admitted that the word 'justify' does imply antecedent belief, faith, or decision, respecting the conclusion in question. But, whatever that may be, it is not genuine inquiry. The difficulty, just as Russell suggests, is that he—as well as others—has adopted the methods of theology, rather than looking to experimental or research science for methodological suggestions. Of course, any problem or question does take something for granted in the very statement of the problem, although there is no absolute presupposition, because what is presupposed in one problem may be in question in another. But genuine inquiry does not presuppose the truth of the conclusion.

In seeking an alternative to the experimental use of ideas in their prospective and "speculative" sense, I therefore refer not only to theological conceptions presuming to rest upon antecedent revelation and authority, but also to such derivative views as those of Russell, who searches for a guarantee of the validity of knowledge in some antecedent axiom, such as the inductive principle, only to find that he cannot establish the inductive principle by a similar method without presupposing the inductive principle. Thus, he too must have "faith." As he says, "I do not see any way out of a dogmatic assertion that we know the inductive principle, or some equivalent." [82] Elsewhere, we find a similar appeal to this form of "epistemology": "Either we must accept skeptical solipsism in its most rigorous form, or we must admit that we know independently of experience, some principle or principles by means of which it is possible to infer events from other events at least with probability." [83] These propositions are "propositions having some intrinsic credibility." [84] And yet, according to Russell, they are not the tautologies of formal logic.[85] It is unfortunate that Russell does not go further in investigating this new avenue of epistemology, or that he does not at least explain what he means by something of such basic significance.

In the foregoing we have been concerned with general ideas. Somewhat pertinent to this, Russell says, "one important difference" between himself and Dewey is that "Dewey is mainly concerned with theories and hypotheses, whereas I am mainly concerned with assertions about particular matters of fact." [86] However, the principles we have mentioned, founded on faith, are not at all the end of Russell's belief in the unverifiable, for there is another whole class of propositions without verification. So, when we turn to the other end of the scale, to particulars, we find pretty much the same view. Thus Russell mentions "the propositions which are most nearly certain, namely judgments of perception" and goes on to say of them, "For these there is no 'method of verification,' since it is they that constitute the verification of all other empirical propositions that can be in any degree known."[87]

It is not at all clear how Russell can say that they "are most nearly certain," if there is utterly no way of verifying them. Furthermore, the idea of being "most nearly certain," rather than being certain, would seem to indicate some degree of uncertainty, and this would suggest the possibility of falsehood. Yet what does this mean, if there can be no verification or disconfirmation? An alternative would be to distinguish between propositions and perceptions. The proposition "this is red" is one thing and the perception of red is another thing. But, if so, then the relevant perceptions would be verification of the propositions, under certain conditions. Russell's difficulty lies in the implications of his view that perception per se is cognitive, and hence that the epistemological relation is ubiquitous to all experience. And, of course, it should be added that verification is not merely a matter of perception but pertains to a wider field of behavior.

Dogmatism may possibly serve the purposes of a religion, but it is a *reductio ad absurdum* of a philosophy, because it is the proof that what pretends to be an explanation is not an explanation. Moreover, if the premises rest upon dogmatism, so does the conclusion.

Generally speaking, experiences or activities, though they do not themselves constitute knowing, do constitute the ground for verification and justification of knowing. The exception consists of instances of knowing about knowing. The point here is not merely to state the argument that knowing is instrumental, but to state a condition which makes verification possible. Verification of knowing must have a source which is not itself in knowing, or else it would be circular, just as Russell points out. That source is the engagement with realities (transactions) required by the definition of the problem.

Reality does not exist merely to be known and does not consist merely of objects of knowledge, for reality is wider than knowledge, and there will always be more things in the world than there are in our philosophy, presumably, or in our science; neither is all life or experience merely an act of knowing or problem solving, even though it may be true that experience is suffused with meanings developed in all past activities *including past activities of knowing.*

The view of pragmatism is essentially an evolutionary one, and the pragmatist's conception of knowledge is not as something statically possessed, but as a function, as an act of knowing; the pragmatic view is that knowing is an evolutionary development of the methods even of lower animals dealing with their environment.

In their treatment of validity, many philosophers appear to believe that we must begin with some presupposed and unverifiable postulates. But such ideas are the products of armchair consideration. The infant presumably does not begin with epistemological or metaphysical hypotheses; he begins by acting on impulses, and, if he lives through it, he learns a good deal empirically in the process. The funded results of this learning are more or less reinforced or "verified" in the simpler phases of later experiences and constitute much of what is called common sense. This is the foundation of more elaborate learning. It is reconstructed in the light of wider experience, but it is not abandoned, except by those philosophers who would identify abstract logical structures with reality, and, in the process, reach the most skeptical conclusion. Struggling to achieve further the growth which has already been going on from infancy, men formulate more sophisticated proposals of basic postulates, and these are studied to decide whether they, in fact, succeed in opening up new possibilities. Therein lies their "verification."

But it should be noted that the verification which has already been going on does not rest on them. Mankind did not have to wait for Russell's earlier version of the inductive principle[88] before discovering that something was so. Man had found guidance in practice long before that.

Russell said that his inductive principle could not be proved,[89] and this surely must have been the case, because he later formulated quite a revised version, in his *Human Knowledge*. Yet no one is going to take the revised version merely on faith either, for men have learned that faith in this sense is unwise. I suggest that these proposals are methodological, and his revised version may be helpful and instructive. If so, that is its temporary verification.

The more complex biological act exhibits a means-end relation. Usually, our consideration of the earlier manipulatory phases of the act is concerned with their effectiveness, while interest in the final phases may lie in the consummatory. Knowledge is an outgrowth of the manipulatory phase of the biological act which intervenes between the stimulus and the consummatory phase. In Dewey's terms, knowledge is essentially instrumental. Yet to treat the earlier phase of the biological act as merely manipulatory or the later as merely consummatory is an abstraction: the manipulatory is also consummatory: it is affective as well as effective. Work may be arduous or delightful. One does not always fish merely for the sake of catching fish; he may fish for the sake of fishing. The kitten turns the mouse loose to catch it again. Similarly, the consummatory is also manipulatory in mastication or fondling, and it is instrumental in causing more remote results.

Thus, the pragmatist's view is that knowing exists for the sake of ends or values. To be sure, intelligence should be directed toward ends themselves to determine whether, indeed, they are worthy or may be improved. But, again, this does not mean that values are merely to be known or are merely subjects for scientific analysis, for to say so is self-contradictory: if values were merely objects of knowledge, they would no longer be values, even though knowledge itself may sometimes be a value. On the contrary, the development of the consummatory phase from simpler or lower levels into the great ends of life does require experimental intelligence or knowing, but for the sake of *having* values more worthy of being loved and cherished, more fruitful in reward. The view of the pragmatist is that intellect in action, actual thought or knowing, occurs in dealing with problems, and in any problem something is at stake which is an object of concern.

Life is not merely a problem. Activities go on, whether humdrum or in richer variety, without much difficulty. Problems occur within life, within a context of things which are not themselves problems. *Anything* of which we are aware, perhaps, may become a problem or problematic; nevertheless, it is not true that *everything* can be a problem. The very statement of any particular problem presupposes something given which is not itself a problem. When everything is a problem, the result is chaos, and, in the individual, a state of complete anxiety constitutes a breakdown and is pathological. However, Descartes' statement that he doubted everything was not pathological: it was merely false, for he should have doubted whether he doubted everything. More recent scholars have discovered the extent to which he carried over, perhaps unconsciously, what he learned in his earlier years from his Jesuit textbooks.

Problems are not pathological elements in life, even though some problems are concerned with the pathological. They are intrinsic to the business of living, because important things are at stake, including the development of things of still greater importance, essential to a better life.

Intelligence is said to be the ability to solve problems, including problems about ends. The function of intelligence, in the concrete sense of the word, is the inventive development of better ends of life together with the means of achieving them. As such, it is not something self-enclosed or operating in a vacuum; other means are necessary, such as the raw materials and forces of nature, including human nature, and a rich variety of activities, not only in addition to intelligence, but as a medium for intelligence. But intelligence has the peculiarly strategic virtue of being the most adaptable and dependable method of making new and effective use of what is available. As Lucretius says, it is not magic, for it is art. The more general consideration of intelligence is concerned with basic conditions which make possible the new and effective use of the available, for we are concerned with conditions under which men can live better lives and can deal with their world in more effective ways toward that general end. This includes the problem of developing better ideas of what is better.

II

Some Metaphysical Implications of the Pragmatic Theory of Knowledge *

There is nothing in experience that answers *directly* to the concepts or objects of science. Even though an empiricist might argue that a rationalist such as Descartes really derived his fundamental physical concepts, extension and motion, from experience, nevertheless, the empiricist would be forced to agree with Descartes that those concepts, in the abstract way in which they were conceived, are only "confusedly" represented in experience. Yet those concepts led Descartes into errors; for example, his theories on the conservation of motion could only be corrected by the further development of a new and more abstract concept, energy. Thus, instead of a causal world based on the conservation of motion, the result is an even more abstract causal world based on the conservation of energy. But whatever it may be that we would conserve as a basis for a logical statement of a causal system, causation has been understood since Hume to be other than a simple "given" of experience. Causation, on the basis of a conservative system, which is the only sense in which it can be expressed in physical laws, cannot be perceived, and there is nothing which compares directly with it, because there is nothing in experience to answer in any simple and direct way to its terms. For instance, the term 'energy' always "cancels out" and does not appear in the empirical conclusion.

If we may borrow the words, but not the thought, from another

*This chapter owes much more to George Herbert Mead than would be indicated by any set of footnotes. Nevertheless, I have been too free with the development to claim that it is a study of Mead.

philosophy, scientific objects, as distinguished from objects of ordinary experience, are "logical constructs," and language plays a vital role in the process. But I do not refer to a list of isolated linguistic "usages," for language is not autonomous, operating in a vacuum. Hence, the problem of scientific objects is more than merely linguistic; "tables" are still less so, but that is beside the point here. Some things may indeed be, in some sense, both objects of ordinary experience and scientific objects, but not, obviously, in the same respect. Nevertheless, we are here concerned with scientific objects as such.

From this the implication readily follows, as has been pretty generally accepted, that, if there is anything to answer *directly* and strictly to scientific objects, it must lie outside all possible experience; that is to say, in a transcendent and not in a merely transcendental sense. Quite a good deal of metaphysics hinges upon the supposition that things do exist, not merely outside of experience, but in another metaphysical realm discontinuous with that of experience, which answer or correspond directly to scientific objects; that the truth of science depends upon this correspondence; and that those things are indeed the only objective things. Now these suppositions seem to be perfectly gratuitous in the sense that there is no conceivable test by which the truth or falsity of the assertion of the existence of those things can be proved or disproved. That is to say, it makes utterly no difference whether they exist or not.

We do make hypotheses about things not directly observed, but the relation between the dualistic inner and outer worlds is not the same as the relation of ideas to their test in experimental research. Locke saw well enough the cognitive implication of this dualism when he defined knowledge as the perception of agreement and disagreement between ideas. Therefore, such an assumption of existence may not be necessary at all for science and is not necessary so long as the assumption makes no difference in scientific results. But one thing is necessary for science: that nature, including experience, must be such that science is possible. If there is an idea about which it is meaningful to say that it *may* be true, then some meaning of the idea must be stated in such a way that it can conceivably be tested; if it is to be said to *be* true, there must be a test for it. Then, since tests or experiments lie within experience, experience must be stated in such a way that tests or experiments are possible, respecting things that lie outside of experience.

Reality, presumably, reaches indefinitely beyond experience. But Kant distinguishes two senses in which things may lie outside experience, the transcendent and the transcendental. The distinction in Kant's treatment is not always clear and we are not bound to his views exactly, but his distinction is helpful for clarity. Much of nature may lie outside of any possible experience in any practical sense, like the center of the earth or the center of the sun. Nature reaches out beyond us into the minute and into the vast. But, in this sense, experience is continuous with some of the rest of nature, as Dewey said, and experience is sometimes extended in ways undreamed of in earlier times. Because of this continuity, hypotheses—concerned in their subject matter with what is not present in experience—may have many implications, some of which are for experience; and they must have implications for experience if the hypotheses are to be tested. But the transcendent world of Kant and the external world of the realist are not realms on which an enlarging experience may encroach. The external world is a disconnected realm forever barred, not only to experience, but also to confirmed hypothesis, as the analysis from Berkeley through Hume to Kant showed.

The Cartesian dualism of mind and matter persisted in one form or another because of the physical scientist's demand for a free field. The idealist-philosopher and the scientist of the nineteenth century were in two different fields. There could, therefore, be no conflict between them, although in this partnership the scientist dominated, for the philosopher eventually had to return to him.[1] While deduction was the method of the philosopher, the freedom of the scientist lay in his experimental method. Accordingly, the scientist maintained a world free from difficulties that would not answer to the scientific method. If the philosopher found paradoxes in the scientist's practice of taking experience generally, sometimes as objective and sometimes as subjective, the scientist shrugged his shoulders. He was getting results with methods that would have been even more paradoxical if synthesized with the Hegelian dialectic. What could not be subjected to experiment was, therefore, turned over to the philosopher, who was dogmatist-at-large.

However, in our century the philosopher, like the scientist, has more thoroughly grasped the significance of scientific method. At the same time, the scientist has been forced into the field that he had assigned to philosophy—that of consciousness; the field from which he had excluded consciousness became inadequate for scientific possibility. Nevertheless, consciousness has emerged in the scientist's field in a very different sense from what it had in that of the philosopher. Philosophic attempts to deal with the immediate data of consciousness have been, and are even yet excessively interested primarily in the "immediate" rather than in the "data." It is significant, therefore, that, as a problem of science, the field of consciousness has not appeared as one of abstractly immediate content, that is, of secondary qualities. Consciousness has appeared as a problem for the scientist in the failure of absolute entities. It has appeared as perspectives of consentient sets determined by their relation to so-called percipient events, as frames of reference involving observers, and as statements of results in terms of methods of measurement. And the concept of "method" here introduced marks the field of consciousness as definitely manipulatory in character, a notion that is further evident when one considers the function and importance of the laboratory in scientific achievement.

What in my estimation is important here is that the scientist as observer is much more than an individual to whom things are present, more even than an individual who can indicate things to others. Thus, various expositors of some of the phases of relativity, especially frames of reference, find need for "observers." But these are not necessarily the sort of observers in which we are interested; they do not make scientific observations in the sense of observation as it is considered in discussions of scientific method, and photoelectric cells could easily have been substituted for them. The point is that the scientist finds it necessary to organize data in terms of frames of reference in relation to each other. In short, the absolute world of the scientist, which he had constructed in the two previous centuries, has disappeared.

Consciousness is found in the actual organizing of perspectives, whether in terms of fields of force or of environment or of consentient sets or, more generally, of experience. The older parallelism located consciousness in the individual. But now consciousness is found in the reflective scientific activity of an individual already located in an experiential world. On the one hand, the environment is not merely a number of sensory attributes, or states of consciousness, nor, on the other, is it irrelevant to the individual. The individual is in a field of activity. And, just as Hume turned his back calmly upon his solipsism to play backgammon, so the modern psychologist begins simply by accepting the individual as living within the world, as also does his kinsman, the biologist. The psychologist of the juvenile court wants to find out what sort of a world the child lives in. The child may have parents that irritate him, but the psychologist is not interested in the absoluteness of irritable parents, neither in their status in an external world nor as mere states of consciousness.

It is said that a special wasp must bore into the flower of the Smyrna fig tree and carry the pollen. The wasp is an insect and the tree is a plant. There is, nevertheless, a short intersection of their biological histories. What the wasp or the tree does before or after pollination does not fall within the history of the other. But the man who cultivates the tree scientifically and imports the wasp is somehow involved in both histories. In being involved, he is neither fig nor wasp nor both. He is reflective, and their histories exist for him as matters of reflection. The wasp and the tree have no evident intention or purpose, though each is essential to the life of the other. To have such an intention, each of them would have to be conscious of what the other is about. If the wasp's activities respecting fig trees have arisen because the wasp is concerned about the propagation of fig trees, these activities would be fairly conscious. But actually, I suppose, the wasp acts under the stress of immediate circumstances. In the case of the grower, there is more than intersection of the two histories—the individual gets into the perspective of the other, and this is consciousness. It involves putting oneself in the other's place in point of reference. Logically, one can view the universe from the standpoint of a wasp.

The pragmatist has never followed the phenomenalistic analysis so characteristic of European philosophies, the attempt to reduce everything to passive perceptual elements, such as appearances or sense-data. There are numerous objections to such an analysis: (1) that it is an inadequate account of active experience; (2) that it takes perception to be the ultimate metaphysical foundation of reality; and (3) that the attempted reduction of "objects" to phenomena or sense-data mistreats them as though they were merely surface qualities rather than objects with an "inside" and a continuity of their own. On this ground, the idea that there could be "other minds" is not only a "problem," it is an anomaly.

The dualist philosopher, speaking before his fellow philosophers, may assure them that though he himself has a mind or self he doubts that they have, although he may generously say that he will accept their existence as a mere act of faith. He does not intend to be unkind: he is under the difficulty of keeping several different metaphysical realms coordinated. G. H. Mead advocates a position that implies not only that one becomes aware of one's own self only by the act of becoming aware of other selves but also that one comes to have a self only insofar as others exist in his own experience as selves. And in the words of Mead, the dignity of man is that when he calls upon himself, he finds himself at home.

Mead is concerned with how the "inside" of other things can come to be a matter of our experience, or how we could have any experience of the "insides" of other things. He finds that the problem is inherently linked with how we have any experience of our own inside, something which traditional philosophies had failed to accept as a problem but had taken for granted as something already given. Mead's answer is that this is an achievement of self-consciousness, where "self-consciousness" is stated in terms of the social act, as he defines that term. One can adopt another's attitude and this arouses a different attitude that is in response to the first.[2] There are two phases in Mead's analysis of the physical object of common experience: first, that it has an "inside" and, second, that it has the properties which it exhibits in manipulation.[3] Neither of these is reducible to mere phenomena.

The attitudes which have been mentioned are commonly in experience, but they are not to be understood as mere imagery, for imagery is too anemic to carry the full weight of the "what" of experience, even though it may be very definite imagery. These attitudes are motor in character, that is, sensorimotor. A picture may indeed be a definite image of water, but if it is "wet," it is so because we bring to the experience more than what is otherwise there. The source of what we bring lies in the countless activities of past experience, and as they are rearoused, they occur as inhibited impulses that constitute the meaning of the thing, but they are not primarily imagery. More thoroughly aroused and organized attitudes that are inhibited may constitute readiness to act and expectancies, and may exhibit the temporal character of the act, but they do not bring the future as such within the experience of the organism: these responses are not responses to the future, but to a present thing or situation.

There is, one may suppose, a fundamental difference between

the unreflective and the reflective attitudes. In the unreflective attitude, all items of experience are immediately experienced and, because they are directly there, do not require an "inside" or "something yet to be revealed." But the fact of principal importance is that, as such, they occur in a temporal order, though they have different dates in the act. If 'time' is understood in the sense of passage of events, time is definitely in everything, at least in everything outside the manipulatory areas. What exists directly within the experience of the organism may be said to be simultaneous with the organism and to lie in its "now." However, insofar as what exists in experience holds forth a "promise" of something further, it may be called a stimulus—something more than a mere physiological reaction. Thus we can have a situation in which what is "there" is not merely there, but holds a promise for the future. In distinction from the promise, the item is *surface*—it is qualitative.

We are not returning to consciousness as a secretion of content by the nervous system. Meanings do achieve expression as reactions of the organism, and obviously some of the conditions for the organization and continuity of action lie in the organism's structure. What we do with regard to the thing represents, in some sense, the overt expression of a motor attitude called out as a tendency to act in that direction. The item as a stimulus to activity arouses in the individual a terminal attitude which, in some degree, is definitely in the individual's experience. The terminal attitude is an aroused, prepotently motivated attitude, but one that is inhibited by the fact that it cannot be overtly carried out until near the end of the act. Being prepotently motivated, it dominates other attitudes and, in that way, organizes action. Hence, it institutes a means-end relation, although not necessarily a consciousness of that relation. As such, it may constitute something of a purposive act, but not in the old teleological sense, and neither is it necessarily a self-conscious or reflective act.

The continuous interplay between the complex and progressing stimulus and the response initiates, maps out, and controls the intermediate action or approach of the individual, so that the way of approach is dependent upon how he is going to take hold of things. The way in which one is ready to sit down at the table determines his approach to it. What the table is may not be in his consciousness at all. So long as one has the terminal attitude and nothing blocks his act, he does not feel called upon to make a judgment as to what the thing is. No alternatives are presented to him. The response is conditioned, determined, dynamic, and progressive. And this unreflective action, as in the case of instant decisions of experienced executives, is direct and often remarkably sure. Only reflectively does one seek out, among presented alternatives, enduring articles on the basis of which he may act intelligently. Reflection is the refusal to commit oneself immediately to one's intuitions. The reality that is "promised" lies ahead spatially and temporally. It cannot be said to be simultaneous with the organism: it belongs to the future. Rather, the terminal attitude initiates the act and gives a certain direction to intermediate acts. It is definitely in the experience of the organism throughout the progress of the act, controlling the way the individual approaches the thing and continually directing the process by which the culmination or end of the act is reached. Thus, the men with the moving van approach a piano differently from the way in which the musician approaches it.

The process described indicates a temporal control and unity in the act due to the terminal attitude. But if we act simply on this basis, we do not stop to see what is going to happen. The action determined by the terminal attitude does not carry with it a reflective statement of what the thing may be with reference to this situation. We are relieved of the necessity for, or inclination toward, stating what the nature of the thing may be. We have no hypothesis—we are not looking for a test. Possibilities and proposed acts are not considered, for the act passes directly through the manipulatory field to its consummation. We do not, under these circumstances, experience the future as existing now, for the experience of the future occurs only with the proposal of possibilities. When our action is directed by the terminal attitude, possibilities as such are not in our experience. Thus, in this nonreflective experience, the future is ignored. Its reality lies ahead in terms of the passage belonging to a spatiotemporal extension.

The process of acting upon the basis of immediate "promises" is conditioned and determined, though not predetermined. But the fulfillments are precarious and uncertain, for many tenets of experience upon which we act are unstable and hence undependable. Security can be attained only if we *stop* to seek out things in the present that will abide with us. So far as the things about us are stimuli, they initiate responses, some of which may be in conflict. But, since we can do only one thing at a time, one attitude or organized response must gain ascendency over all others with which it may conflict before it results in overt action. Thus, in a crisis, when there are several very strong responses that lead in different directions, action is greatly inhibited. This inhibition of the act gives one the opportunity to seek out the dependable in view of the future. So far as one stops to put himself into the perspective ahead, he has an experience of the future and he is reflective. It is, therefore, by continuing the act in the manipulatory area, rather than allowing it to pass directly to its consummation, that one affords himself the opportunity for reflection and the experience of the future.

I shall use the term 'experiential world' or 'world of experience' as an elliptical expression meaning the world insofar as it is present within our active experience. It might be called 'the perceptual world', but European philosophy, as well as its American imports, has made perception or its derivatives at once a kind of self-sufficient metaphysical principle and an exclusive function of a "perceiver" per se, and I fear that it is not possible to disengage 'perception' from that association. It will later be noted that perception, especially visual perception, which is so often used, is a rather late comer in the biological act, and, in any case, it is only one phase of this act.

The world in which problems arise or events take place is a world that is had, unlike a mathematical world of points and instants, or a logical world. It is only in the changing world of experience that one gets reality. Whatever else may be real is hypothetical. In this world, the "distance" of the thing is of a promissory character; and the distant thing is temporally, as well as spatially, separated from one. If one does not stop to think, if he merely acts toward what is there, then the reality not in immediate experience lies ahead, and he does not try to state to himself what the thing is. The bird pursuing the moth has the reality ahead of it. It is responding to a stimulus, the reality of which is there in its experience, but not as enjoyed eating. Distant things always lie ahead of us in terms of time and passage, which belong to extension. This situation just ahead is reality; it is what we seek, and we do not experience it as existing now. Liza crossing the river on the ice cakes reacts to the cake ahead as she hops from the one on which she has paused. The reality of the latter is there in her experience, but the reality of the cake to which she responds lies in her imminent future.

In reflective activity, one stops to put himself into the situation or perspective ahead. Hence, the sort of reality in which he is interested reflectively is referred to the past or to the future. The problem is how the future can be experienced, or in what sense the future can be imported into the present. That problem, as Mead[4] has pointed out, is how one gets into different perspectives; it is the problem of formulating a theory of the cognitive relation of the individual in his environment. The whole function of consciousness lies in the relation that is set up between the promise and the fulfillment; it occurs in the stoppage of the act that may intervene between the stimulus and the consummation. The assumption is that one controls conduct in relation to a stimulus, by regulation of the manipulatory process, and that this regulation is "social" in the sense that it depends upon the development of a self which is social, as Mead pointed out. It is self-control. If we do not reserve the term 'self-control' for the more dubious form of dogmatic moralistic inhibition, then any self-conscious control over our conduct is self-control.

If we have two acts which exclude each other with reference to the terminal object, they lead to conflict and inhibition. Direct action is stopped for a time, and there is, more or less, breakdown in habit. But this only gives one an opportunity for reflection. Reflection may, in fact, not take place. The stoppage may occur in lower forms. Thus the dog stops as the man prepares to throw a stone, but he does not reflect: another impulse seizes him and he turns in flight. However, this stoppage in the human individual is often used advantageously and is necessary for reflection. The wise man, unlike the beast that perishes, crosses his bridges before he comes to them. In the interest of the future, one seizes upon the interim to search all the now for possible traces of the permanent—for things which will remain constant with him and upon which he may depend. Reflection comes in the experimental activity of presenting oneself with selected elements that are alternatives or possibilities simultaneous with each other. That which is common to the conflicting elements gets into the experience of the organism and becomes the condition of the solution. In the direction of this solution, motor attitudes are called out as tendencies to act. There must, therefore, be a mechanism for thus calling out these responses, and it is primarily lingual in character.

Mead has given an exceedingly apt statement of this in his analysis of the "Significant Symbol."[5] A. W. Moore summed it up: "We know that language is not a tag attached to the results of abstraction but that it is a necessary part not only of the act of abstraction, but of the experience of an object and the existence of a self."[6] Communication is possible only in general terms, although it can refer to singular things. The individual thing in its uniqueness can be presented only in the immediacy of direct experience, which is not communicable—but the individual is not absolutely unique.

The ancient world dealt with generalizations, not as behavioral facts but as ontological entities, for ancient philosophers thought in terms of absolute agents. Among the warmest supporters of metaphysical realism have been lovers of mathematics and formal logic, whose concepts become very "real" to them. It is ironical that the further development of formal inquiry has called this doctrine into question in several different ways. There has been, for instance, the reduction of some systems to truth tables rather than postulates and the development of the theory of tautologies. Russell was shaken, as a realist, by his discovery that the eternal classes, inherited from the ancient and medieval worlds, were not necessary concepts. In his formal treatment, they can be defined in terms of properties or attributes, and definitions are principles of elimination.

The ancient attempt to deal with generalization and abstraction in terms of an ontological assumption of universals is a doctrine, like theological doctrines, which can neither be proved true nor proved false; therefore, I do not presume to prove it false. However, metaphysical realism must always face the keen edge of Ockham's razor, for it is a dead end that makes no particular difference even if "true" or assumed. It has in the past only served to mislead into unfruitful methods of inquiry, when taken seriously. I mention the problem of metaphysical realism only because it calls for an alternative theory belonging to fruitful methods of inquiry.

The alternative view which has been presented concerns the social nature of language as a development of behavior. If one can, when exciting another to act, excite in himself a tendency toward the same act, he is much nearer to being conscious of what he is about. It is not sufficient that the same function exists both in him and in the other, for these facts may be independent. Rather, in the cooperative act, he must identify his reaction with another, whether correctly or incorrectly, and respond to that reaction, using it as a guide of conduct. Such a complex act can be controlled only by means of gestures, particularly of the oral-vocal type, and this is communication. The individual must put his reaction into a form communicable to others and therefore to himself: the indicated object of the cooperative act is there for others as well as for himself. Consequently, he is capable of pointing out something to himself. In this sense, he is getting something that is *universal*. Here, interlocutory conditions obtain, and these conditions present the reflective object. But, although the situation is social in nature, and public in origin, it is not necessarily or always public.

We are interested, in this case, in the retroactive effect of communication upon the individual. Insofar as the individual in communication indicates things to others, he indicates them to himself, and, moreover, they exist for him as being objects for others. They are social objects. Forthwith, as things indicated, they exist for him as being "selected out"—as universals. As such, they are subject to manipulation, criticism, and elaborate technical development. In the individual, this is the means of presenting or of indicating to himself, in a universal fashion, the alternatives characteristic of the manipulatory area. This is the achievement of the reflective object. One turns it over in his thought and views it from all sides. In no sense is this foreign to the physical world, for the physical object lies in and is grasped in the manipulatory area. The timeless characteristic of a universal is that it is communicable to others and to oneself. In reflection, then, the permanent, static relations occur by which we import the future into the present or place ourselves in the perspective ahead. Hence, it is an abstraction from the passage characteristic of the world of experience.

In earlier thought, the ideal of science was stated as one of reducing passage to an instant, leaving a static world in which there is a distribution of compresent, timeless particles. In it everything is clamped down—the whole universe is simply an object establishing one perspective, which is to say, not a perspective at all, but an absolute world. Everything is an absolute object in external relationship to everything else. If we take the whole universe at an instant, then we have a world of things "simply located," in Whitehead's phraseology: things are simply what they are. If we can abolish passage and say that this is what the world is, then we abolish motion. We have the absolute world of Parmenides. There is no perspective, save that of God, and there is no time in the sense of passage of occurrences. Everything is what it is and where it is, regardless of its relations to everything else.

Bergson has insisted that if we turn to the psychical, we have a sort of extension or time different from the physical. In the former, the pulses of time are not commensurable. Things are continually entering and slipping out of experience. The processes of change that are going on are so identified with the content in the psychical that they cannot be abstracted or separated. At times, things hurry along; at times they drag. And the excitement or drag of an experienced thing is an essential part of it. This sort of process is not physical, according to Bergson. It is not abstract. Only if we kill the process, can we cut up its corpse into commensurable units.

What Bergson overlooks is that the process, the passage of occurrences, is not psychical, for it does not exhibit psychical properties. On the contrary, the stoppage of the process is the necessary condition for the psychical. Nevertheless, stopping the process is an essential part of the process. One has to stop to consider, to speculate, to grasp something that endures. This stoppage is not a destruction of reality; rather, it is a condition for directing reality. Were it merely reality that one wanted, any reality rather than some particular sort of reality, he could follow the stream, allowing it to dash his head against the rocks, and his place would be taken by the more fortunate. But, if one would direct reality, he must stop the process: it is in this moment of stoppage that he sets up the permanent space. We work out plans and patterns in an enduring world that is co-gredient with ourselves.

The instant, as employed by science, is not a pictorial representation of the specious present, for the latter is qualitatively variable and has a temporal spread. But the instant answers logically to the specious present as a cross section of change. The question is not, therefore, one of the reality of the instant as such which will have no temporal spread. It involves, rather, getting a durable hold upon the precarious passage that is essential to the world of experience. The term 'a world at an instant' is an ideal; it is a limit which is a logical construct. It does not involve honing the world to a knife-edged present, but, rather, involves a selection of the permanent. The actual selecting takes the form of manipulating what we have here and now in the laboratory, in the observatory, or in the field of research. This manipulatory activity is obvious in a multitude of guises: of measuring, of reducing the qualitative extent so that one can find simplicity, of finding the limits of series, of formulating a priori systems. Even in pure logic we must have rules of operation which may quite as well be called rules of manipulation. In a real sense then, the world in which we are reflectively active is the world that we are handling.

The world as an object of knowledge is an extension of the "now" or manipulatory area pushed out, just as Newton extended the falling weights, the swinging pendulums, and the rolling spheres of Galileo to the heavens. The distant thing, as an object and not as a mere stimulus, is an extension of the manipulatory area. How does the astronomer know what he tells us about those twinkling lights, as to their distances, their substances, their motions, etc.? He knows because he studies the light given off by a heated body here in his laboratory. He extends those ideas, thus developed, to the distant stars, just as Galileo extended his rolling spheres to the moon. And he modifies his views. At one time, quasars lay at vast distances even in astronomical terms. Now, he decides that some are not so far away after all. Of course, one may perhaps suggest that, at those outer reaches, the ideas of the laboratory do not hold true. But this suggestion, if taken wholesale, would leave the astronomer with nothing new to say. I say "wholesale," because he may for good reason modify some of the ideas. At least, the physicist has modified some of his ideas of gross bodies when dealing with subatomic particles.

This introduction of the future into the present is the establishment of co-grediency, and the stoppage represents the relation of the co-gredient objects to the percipient event. The distant or promissory character changes to simultaneity. Time as temporal passage is eliminated, and, with static objects of knowledge, we build a hypothetical world in which the objects stand to each other in a *logical* rather than in a *temporal* relation. It is only in a world made up of static instants, moments, or "nows" that we can have a mechanistic universe; but this is not the real world, although it is part of the modern world. It is, however, a real hypothesis for prediction and control. In short, the manipulatory area represents the world of things which, on the one hand, have ceased to be merely stimuli to immediate action, and which, on the other hand, stop short of the consummatory phase. Those things are objects of knowledge. When the physicist leaves his instruments in the laboratory and returns home to become a domestic animal, the beefsteak which he eats is not a swarm of atoms. It is no longer a *means* of chemical analysis; it is an *end* of human endeavor.

After all, it is the world with which we are faced and with which we deal that we wish to control. And science must return to this world of experience for its own validity. The hypothesis must be brought back to experimental data. The theory that an electron causes the saltatory motion of oil between two electrodes may or may not be substantiated on further test. But the oil is there in experience and does not need to be referred to consciousness. If the theory is discarded, the oil will remain to become the basis of, or to be taken into account by, another theory. In immediate experience, one is not presented with abstract universals or with mutually independent particulars.

In his attempt to return to the world the perceptual goods which have been purloined from it, the realist has, with surprising generosity, returned much more than was taken away. Thus, Russell burdens the penny with an infinite number of characters, shapes, etc. It is no longer an object but a clutter of renovated states of consciousness. The dualist has sought a content that is identical in all relevant perspectives, that is, irrelevant to any standpoint.[7] To shift the illustration of the penny to one that suggests problems slightly less trivial, whether we are talking of pennies or of dollars, we must say that wealth, for example, is nonexistent as a separate entity. But the scientist is not asking what is the reality of or behind perspectives; he is showing the means of change, exchange, or translation between them. If we ask what is meant by a dollar, the reply might be a Fisher dollar, a wealth of dollars in wheat, or credit on books: we get a formula of translation.

When we deal with reality, we deal with it in terms of consummations, whereas the realist seeks reality in an object outside the perspective, and one which he conceives to be indicated by the transformation equation itself. So far as we have a common object, we have a common perspective or an intersection of perspectives. For example, we say that the same thing has different values in different situations, or we say that a thing has one motion in one frame of reference and another in another frame. What is the meaning of this "same thing that is different"? Is there implied an Aristotelian substance and its accidents? Apparently, it is out of some such identity that the realist would create his absolute world in which there may be a distribution of perspectives, but in which also there is an insoluble problem of their relation to the absolute.

The statement of what a thing is must have a reference to the situation from which one starts. There is no reality-in-general or statement-at-large of an absolute. To seek such a statement is to seek a relation that is paramount, a *summum genus*. Such a conception lapses because, since medieval times, no one has been able to find any such paramount relation. One does not find given in nature an absolute time and space. The setting up of these paramount relations—religious, physical, and what not —has been social and essentially mythological. Of course, it is a simple thing to take one's own attitude as the absolute world. One may, for instance, adopt the coordinates of the fixed stars as a paramount relation, with the added advantage over Einstein's Special Theory that accelerations may be stated in such terms, and he might call this absolute space. Yet that was precisely what Berkeley exhibited as relative, over against Newton's absolute space.

The sense in which a thing is said to be the same entity having different values, or is said to be the same entity in different perspectives, is not a relation of substance and accidents, but is the sense in which a thing in one perspective can be translated into a thing in another. The world as being relative occurs in the perspective of the individual. That is to say, it is the world as related to him. That does not make it subjective. But one does not surround his own perspective by an absolute world when he relates it to another perspective. An organization of perspectives presents us with a larger and richer world.

We have all felt the egoism of other people who were unable to suppose that there are more things than ever occurred in their limited experience. But the significance of the disapprobation in the term 'egoism' cannot be very forceful if it means no more than that an acceptance of our attitude in substitution would be an achievement of the absolute. Neither can we expect anyone to act intelligently about anything with which he has had no contact in any fashion. The exhortation, then, is toward openmindedness and an outlook for exceptions, which are characteristic of a scientific attitude. Larger perspectives may be achieved, but not the absolute, unless one has recourse to "self-evident intuitions" or to some other form of dogma. An experimental or scientific attitude will not give it to him.

The scientist is interested in formulating some order between things as they occur in continuously broadened experience, including that of the laboratory, without questioning what is back of them in any ontological sense. It is significant that scientists do not frequently argue as to whether or not things exist corresponding to scientific objects, but whether or not such scientific objects are fruitful—on that basis, they are used or dropped. The objects of science are thus essentially functional and hence suggest that the theory of knowledge may be stated upon this relativistic basis.

The difficulty that I find in thus describing knowledge upon the basis of Whitehead's philosophy is that, for him, "objects" are antecedently in nature *as objects*. As eternal objects, they are absolutes by which he hopes to guarantee the order of nature. Man has long sought to find security in nature by putting some socially achieved object at the bottom of it to insure its conformity to human wishes, or at least its dependability. Were it not for God or Laws or Eternal Objects of some sort guiding nature along the straight path of order, nature would soon become chaotic. But there is, in fact, nothing to guarantee that any given problem, if it is really a problem, will be solved by the means at one's disposal. To cease the search for such an ultimate guarantee will not avoid all metaphysical problems; but it will avoid many prolix and dubious metaphysical speculations that have no other justification and enable us at least to define our problem in a more appropriate manner. Objects of knowledge, as distinguished from things that we find, are social achievements. They are not things that make nature go: they are things that enable a human organism to act, in some fashion, more effectively with regard to some observable things in nature. I would not even deny that an end of knowing may be to perceive order in nature. But it should not be overlooked that when the end of knowing is reached, then knowing is ended.

Things that occur in the experience of one individual differ more or less importantly from those that occur in the experience of others. On this basis, many have said that all experiences are absolutely esoteric. It would seem, however, that the social mechanism and its cooperative activities make possible the selection, presentation, and entry into the experiences of the several individuals, certain definite and relatively common objects. And these common objects make up the perspective common to that group. The participation of the thing in the "universal idea" or in the common world is social, and it represents the relation of the thing to the common world, which is an organization of perspectives.

In contrast to this, the difficulties and hopes of ancient speculation lay in the magic of a metaphysical participation. The physical science of that world had as its technique congruencies —geometry—which were brought within the manipulatory area naively, as a matter of course. Thus the distance perspective was ignored. This physics, however, was adequate for their mechanics. Problems like that of the heavens were thought to be solved if they could be resolved into geometrical forms. It is significant that those *forms* were not our *concepts*, which belong to the socialized individual, but were the essence, nature, and reality of the thing, just as Whitehead at once says that his eternal objects are abstractions and yet that they enter into the composition of things. Patent rights and copyrights, so far as they emphasize that the Idea is the property of the individual rather than of the group, would have been an anachronism in the ancient world. Thus, they came back to a dialectical content which endured for a statement of fundamental nature or ultimate reality. Ancient thought could find validity and reality only in that which was universal. Thought, then, had to see through the peculiarities of the individual to the universal. Because of this lack of attention to particulars, the ancients could not criticize their perspective and had no competent control over methods of observation.

Modern man, or the proponent of pragmatism at least, does not find reality in hypostatizing his hypotheses, but in his perspectives. As Mead says, "Data do not implicate persistent structure. They appear first of all as exceptions."[8]

[The] common world is continually breaking down. Problems arise in it and demand solution. They appear as the exceptions to which I have referred. The exceptions appear first of all in the experience of individuals and while they have the form of common experiences they run counter to the structure of the common world. The experience of the individual is precious because it preserves these exceptions. . . . They are the data of science. If they have been put in the form of common experience, the task appears of reconstructing the common world so that they may have their place and become instances instead of exceptions.[9]

Insofar as we date things of our common world, insofar as we seek the source of an idea, we must come back to the individual, simply because what escapes the individual escapes knowledge, but we are not speaking of an isolated individual. Facts are bits of biography—they get into the form of common experience only insofar as the individual reports them. As a theory progresses in acceptance, we no longer isolate parts as bits of biography. They become merged in the timeless monotony of textbooks that mislead elementary students of physics, as well as some learned philosophers, into thinking that truths have no histories. The scientist comes back to what he terms experimental data. From these, he constructs the formula or universal law. The disorganized "data" become organized "objects." Here he reaches the goal, perhaps, of ancient thought. But ancient thought was not willing to recognize the instrumental nature of the universal in relation to the individual experience; the constructed laws and objects are inventions, for they do not arise as descriptions. If one asserts that they are descriptions, it is always as an afterthought, for to treat these constructed laws and objects as descriptions is not to give an account of the actual rise of scientific objects and has no meaning in terms of scientific method.

If the theory of the social nature of thought, along the lines of Mead's account, can be accepted in a general way, then, according to Mead, the social character of universals and objects would seem to be suggested, to the extent that it can be shown how they arise in human conduct. An object is not merely something that is there, it is there *as something in common*, and insofar as it is something in common, it is a social object, and group activities organize around it. The attitude which the social individual takes toward the thing is itself a group attitude, for he has imported the attitude of the group into his own experience.

As has been indicated, the earlier instances of social activity constitute a cooperative public activity by which the individual acts as a stimulus, by his gesture, to call the attention both of himself and of another to the possibilities of a thing in its perspective. The success or failure of this attempt is the only test whether or not the possibilities in question are common. If the identification of the possibilities of a thing with the thing is its character, or nature, the result is that the character appears as the commonness of the thing to other perspectives; then the character appears to the individual as common to other perspectives. In this cooperative activity, an individual not only excites other individuals but also, by the same act, excites in himself the beginning of the act as a common or group act. In this sense, he is approaching something which is of the nature of a universal. He is responding to the item as if he were in the role of another.[10]

For the realist, the universal already exists as an eternal object. That is surely a simple answer to the problem of how we come to have universals; i.e., we already have them. But this simplicity is short-lived, for it involves, eventually, prolix metaphysical structures that seem impossible to relate intelligibly to events. The mysteries of "ingression" to Whitehead would seem

to be as great as were those of "participation" to Plato. When
the realist eliminates the act of knowing, in its social and experimental function, as the relation between his logical order
and the existential universe, there remains a gap impossible to
fill.

In the alternative position, the ontological status of universals
is that they arise in social activities. To designate this peculiar
function, they may be called "mental events." This function as
universals is precisely what distinguishes mental events from
other physical events. The assertion that universals have any
further status of a nonempirical sort is an ontological gratuity,
for it will account for no fact which cannot otherwise be accounted for.

So far as the problem of the universal has any relevance to
knowledge, it lies in the question, How does the individual consciously come to generalize his method of dealing with his environment? The position taken here is that universals occur
with the rise of common objects. The hen acts as a stimulus that
calls the chick to the worm. But we cannot assume that the hen
indicates the worm to herself; i.e., that she responds to the worm
as a common object. To do this, it would be necessary for her to
respond to herself in the role of another. The possibilities of
things do not at first appear in experience as common. A thing
is common insofar as the organism is able to indicate to itself
the possibilities of the thing in terms of the acts of the other
organisms in the group.

Man's achievement is that he can learn gradually to pick out
some of these characters and to manipulate them into new relations and organizations, rather than merely reacting directly
to them in their full, immediate situation. The dog recognizes
his master. But how? The psychologist may know, but the dog
presumably does not: he merely recognizes. Or it sometimes
happens that human animals have a feeling of recognition toward a place which they know to be quite new to them. The
psychologist may be able to explain this: he may note that there

are certain cues in the new situation similar to those in a place familiar to the individual. If the individual is not aware of the cues as such, then he does not know how he "recognized" that place.

So far as the thing is simply there in experience, it is not a universal: it is consummatory. Language makes possible the expression of dumb and mute experience in public and universal terms, not only for the sake of others but also for oneself. Present reflection is not responsible for the thing now appearing, nor is it responsible for the fact that some of the characteristics of the thing now appearing are more common and enduring than others. These characteristics cannot be put into the mind in any sense other than that reflection is responsible for—or indeed *is*—their selection, appropriation, and development as a basis for conduct. In that sense, things most surely are preexistent to mind. But the social mechanism, including language as a group phenomenon, allows the selection and entry of these common elements into the individual's experience as being common. These characters are the elements of social intercourse which may be carried on, not only publicly but privately. As far, then, as they may be selected and developed as common, they have the nature of universals and as such constitute the law of the group and are the necessary common guides of conduct which make the group a cooperative society rather than a gregarious herd.

Insofar as the thing appears in direct transaction, its being is so far directly revealed: whatever more it may be is hypothetical. Hence, science must return to the world of experience, but its method is temporarily to abstract, to stop the process, in order to seize upon certain characters to redirect the process. If one would not simply wait for the future to reveal the future possibilities of the thing, if one would anticipate the future, he must know what the nature of the thing may be upon which he may depend. In this sense, one reads into the thing a character whose full existence could be reached only at the end of a proposed act. This proposed act lies in a distant perspective, which is a future. The character, then, that he *now* gives the thing represents a possibility and is the importation of the future into the present. Obviously, this character does not appear in direct experience: it is of the nature of a group experience.

If we seek the origin of the universal, we find it arising in the public social situation, and we have pointed out that it is in manipulation and social cooperation that the community becomes a part of the individual's experience. Tools, instruments, means, etc., consciously accepted as such are common throughout the activity. Measuring devices are common, and it is in terms of them that the individual interprets his experiences, for he can interpret his experience to himself only as he would to another. The individual's experience can become common property only so far as the means of interpretation is common.

In Washington, there are a meter bar and a yardstick which are public property. The instruments, which thus enter the individual's experience, enabling his interpretation, belong to a social order, although they are not necessarily public. Later the individual may occasionally develop his own instruments of interpretation; but, if so, he will do it as a social being. When, however, we say anything is a yard long we relate it to a public social object, though, significantly, not to that object as distant— we do not, as a matter of fact, think very often of the particular stick in Washington, if the adequacy of our stick is not in question. The yard is generalized: the relating is an act of manipulation which ignores what is distant, in favor of contact. The yardstick that I have is equal to the one in Washington. I lay it on the thing that I would measure, as a means of public or private specification. The yard is then universal, belonging to the stick and to the thing measured. The congruency sets up an identity between them that involves abstraction from temporal distance. The world, then, that we build in the manipulatory area is a simultaneous world of congruency, a world of so-called primary qualities. What does not so lend itself is eliminated. Note that the universal as common is not a direct relation between two things, the stick and the thing measured. It is a social relation which inheres in the operation of translating brute existence into conceptual terms.

The reflective world built up in the manipulatory area abstracts from passage, which is essential to the world of experience, for it represents the abstraction of permanences. So far as we take these results of abstraction and hypostatize them, we get a world that does not appear in experience. We have extended the manipulatory area throughout the universe, and the consummatory phase in which values inhere must be put into some other realm. This is fundamentally the position of the so-called causal theory of perception. Because this theory is the result of a process of abstraction, which is at the same time ignored, there can be no intelligible relationship between the two realms thus set up.

The physicist does not get at the submicroscopic world in that manner. The physicist observes a minute globule of oil moving at certain speeds or multiples thereof. These different speeds can be stated in terms of energy and the differences in these energy levels are called electrons. It is obvious that the physicist is not experiencing the cause of his sensation. He could never get at the electron from any such starting point, for the sensation is abstracted from physical conditions. What he comprehends is the causal relation of the observed change in motion of the oil globule to other conditions, and he does this by measuring the energy of the moving globule. Such a method would be irrelevant if he started with a sensation which would admit of no physical terms.

If one understands scientific results, not as results of manipulatory processes, i.e., not as relative to method employed by the scientist, but as somehow already there, then one has absolute objects and, out of them, he constructs an absolute universe. What is there is simultaneous with the organism, and if the scientific world is there, it is a simultaneous world. So long as the physicist's interest in abstracted results led only to a very casual interest in his method, the nonexperimental character of this simultaneous world did not trouble him. However, the necessity for increasing rigor in results led him to a vigorous reconsideration of his method: he has found it necessary to state his results in terms of his actual methods of measurements. As P. W. Bridgman says, "This point of view, that the schedule of operations by which the symbols acquire meaning is as important a part of the physical situation as the relations which are found to hold between the symbols themselves, has a bearing on a very widely spread tendency in modern physics and science in general to see nothing as significant except the relations, and so to reduce all science to a kind of topology." [11]

What, then, is the nature of the reality of the object which is beyond the manipulatory area? So far as we state it, we state it as if we were at the thing and had it in a here and now. It is an extension of the manipulatory area; it brings the future into the present and eliminates temporal distance. Thus it is a logical world rather than a perceptual world, but, as such, it represents the universality of our hypotheses. These hypotheses must not be fossilized into eternal beings.

The world as we find it is not an implicative system. There is an intelligible sense in which we can say that an implicative or logical order inheres in the world, but not as direct hypostatization of scientific law. Rather, the logical system is the developed result of repeated application and use. In short, it is the sense in which the world comes to be understood. The cognitive function is an occurrence in the world in relation to which the world takes on new proportions. The function of the world in this way is only one kind of function, but experimentation consists of transactions as much as does any other occurrence. Experimentation is at grips with reality and, at the same time, universalization is an essential part of it, because experimentation is expressed in universal form. Even so, it can be said to be inherent in the world at large only hypothetically, and whether one universal form rather than another will be borne out is for the future to determine. To go beyond this is not so much to go beyond our understanding as to go beyond the nature of understanding. It is an act of faith which is hardly appropriate to the term 'realist' in its modern sense. There is no specific sense in which the scientist discovers laws: he discovers instances of laws; he discovers exceptions to law in the repugnant fact; but he formulates the laws. Thus the development of scientific law is not intelligible in terms of an asserted preexistent logical order in the world. Hypotheses *institute* logical relations between things, or, more strictly, between particular empirical statements of things. Things are thus *rendered* intelligible. The formula is, *if* the hypothesis be true, *then* the conditions imply certain results.

To some, the assertion that man creates the laws of nature is equivalent to the assertion that man controls nature at large. Except in the limited sense that the formulations of laws enables man to control some phases of nature, the inference is naive, for it is based on the assumption that nature obeys scientific hypotheses as citizens obey legal enactments. The two situations would be more analogous in their native instances. But, however that may be, the fact remains that the formulation of hypotheses does not coerce nature. Consequently, the charge of subjectivism or idealism is irrelevant. On the contrary, scientific exhortation implies a wariness for exceptions.

So far as things appear in experience as exceptions, the public or common world breaks down and must be so reconstructed that the exceptions become instances. This reconstruction is continually going on. We have a perspective that differs from that of any previous generation and consequently have reconstructed a somewhat different common world. There are revised editions of books in every field. When we ask for a history book we ask for the latest history, provided, I suppose, that it has been reconstructed in view of new but commonly recognizable data. In fact, only dogmatic institutions fail to accept this change as a matter of course and refuse to seek test and revision in terms of human experience.

The scientific attitude seems, therefore, to be one of setting up human experience—not, indeed, any experience, but carefully controlled experience—as the test of the common world. The common world is thus made to depend upon the perspective for its reality. Hence, we have arrived at the position in which the real world is a world of perspectives, and the common world of objects is hypothetical. The latter is a social achievement—the importation of the group experience into the experience of the individual. If, therefore, scientific objects are anything more than metaphysical dreams, they have reference, not to any realities that lie outside possible experience in the transcendent sense of the dualist, but at least to the observable things which constitute their tests. Scientific objects themselves have their reality just where they occur—in scientific method.

Following the pragmatic doctrine, we are attempting to "put" reality into the perspectives of the world of experience, while not denying hypothetical reality to a larger world, and to see what reality becomes in the process. We find that we must state the world of actual experience, not merely in terms of phenomena, appearances, or sense-data, but in terms of things—physical, psychological, legal, geological, economic, etc.—that manifest their reality in the manipulatory area. As far as the distant thing lies beyond our reach—beyond the manipulatory area—it is hypothetical. If what it promises is not borne out in the manipulatory area, it is illusory. And the manipulation signifies what we do in terms of the "promise." The worlds of the telescope and of the microscope are not greatly different from this, very much as if we were at the top of a skyscraper looking down upon the little "ants," and reacting to them as human beings of our own size. In the spatiotemporal world, this reality lies ahead: if we go down in the elevator we are "promised" association with individuals like ourselves. But it may be inconvenient to go down—by reflection, we bring the reality up into the present.

We want to know what the consequences will be of an act which we may undertake—we make a statement about the world in such a fashion that our statement will guide the formulation of specific acts and will indicate consequences that will be there in experience. The statement is hypothetical in that it is yet to be tested and reconstructed. It involves, nevertheless, a readiness to act, which doubtless would not exist with regard to the case at hand without reflection. It is an attitude of the individual's adjustment, properly called his consciousness, and is in terms of his acts. And the distant object makes explicit the hypothetical realities, insofar as it answers the responses of the organism. Note that what answers to "hypotheses that guide us truly" is not a cosmic "rational order" that mirrors the dialectic of our thinking; what "answers" are observable, eventual occurrences in nature that are denoted by the conclusions of the hypotheses. These explicit realities lie, not in a transcendent world, but in the perspective of the individual. They are there in their own right and do not need to be referred to consciousness; neither are they mere phenomena, appearances, or apparitions.

III

The "Nature" of Things

I

Whatever else reality may be, it is what it is in the transactions of the organism with things in its environment, for the metaphysical thesis here adopted is that reality is to be identified with transactions. "Things" in this sense are differentiations within transactions, for transactions are not purely homogeneous. Our statement of reality must, therefore, include what answers to the whole act, and the means-end relation emerges as an essential phase of the more complex biological act. This relation is an emergent in nature and cannot be referred to states of consciousness. The objects of ends are values.

The ancient Greek was at home in his world as the medievalist was not. Medievalism, in the European tradition, might be defined as the separation of the spiritual from the material, of ends from means, although the logic of this separation is not consistent and, perhaps, cannot be. Augustine sought his home in another world, because he found no value in this one. Modern man has returned home to the world. He is bringing values back to this world as in classic Greek philosophy yet seeking to avoid the confusion of means with ends which vitiated much of ancient thought.

In the same objective way that the organism finds food as a consummatory value in the world or else by art invents delicious new dishes, so man may find and also invent or work out other values in that world. We must state the nature of things in such a way that what we find in fact is also possible in our theory.

Although the view that I am adopting is a form of empiricism, nevertheless, I am not concerned with the analysis of mere presences or of appearances as such or of phenomena, for the actual situation is an activity, the immediacy of which is merely a phase. As isolated or considered merely in itself, it is an abstraction and one without meaning unless the act to which it belongs is taken into account.

Berkeley remarks, "The table I write on I say exists, that is, I see and feel it. ...."[1] I pass over the statement, 'the table I write on exists', as an analytic truism. Surely, too, writing on a table would ordinarily involve seeing it and feeling it. Moreover, seeing it and feeling it may be verifying conditions for some things that I say. Yet Berkeley's method is to reduce things to perceptual phenomena, so it is relevant to say that what cannot be passed over is any suggestion that 'I am writing on the table' is equivalent to 'I see it and feel it', for that is quite plainly false. When one is writing on a table, he is doing a good deal more than seeing it and feeling it. Writing on a table is not reducible to sense-data, and especially not to merely visual and tactual sense-data. Whatever Berkeley may mean, the view I am taking is that 'exists' is a general term for all the transactions which constitute the table, and that includes the transaction of being written on as well as being seen and felt. So it is pertinent to point out that writing on a table is not merely seeing it and feeling it; and yet it is this larger transaction, together with others unspecified, which in his own remark makes sense of "I see *it* and feel *it.*" Seeing, while it is itself a genuine transaction, is one thing and writing is another, even though they may be, in the given case, integral parts of a larger transaction.

I say that the larger transaction is required in order to make sense of the abstracted phase, because even the sense-data theorists are forced to begin their illustrations with "object words," and not merely that. As Berkeley's own illustration exhibits, we do not have merely static objects, but activities go on. Therefore, I am not adopting the restricted method of phenomenalistic analysis, or analysis of appearances per se. Nevertheless, there are appearances, as a concrete matter of fact. They belong to certain kinds of transactions among many other kinds. As isolated into mere appearances they are, however, abstractions.

The inadequate epistemologies of some philosophies deny the abstract except for tautologies, at least at the more abstract levels. But this omits consideration of many types of invented hypotheses such as were mentioned in chapter I. Berkeley remarks, "I desire anyone to reflect and try whether he can, by any abstraction of thought, conceive the extension and motion of a body without all other sensible qualities."[2] Whatever this may imply concerning our notion of realities in the concrete, one point is that it is just "by abstraction of thought" that we do "conceive the extension and motion of a body without all other sensible qualities." It is more pertinent for Berkeley, respecting the point that he is trying to make, to deny all abstract ideas. However, I do not wish to cover that ground again, but to note that, in introducing the word 'abstraction', it is necessary, I think, to inject the point that the dichotomy of empirical or concrete terms versus abstract terms is inadequate to indicate that there are different levels of abstraction. This dichotomy suggests an abrupt disconnection that poses artificial problems. On the contrary, the concrete and abstract at lower levels so merge that they are commonly confused. We readily speak of a particular as a "case" or an "instance," but these words imply generalization. And, in the other direction, abstractions are repeatedly hypostatized both in the common misuse of language and in traditional philosophical literature. The '-ness' and '-ity' endings supposedly are abstract, but people will nevertheless say, "Look at this redness." The metaphysics of universals is, I take it, a primitive theory of abstractions.

Any idea is something of an abstraction, and hence even a direct description, which is thus very concrete, nevertheless selects or abstracts certain features. But there are levels of abstraction; or, to state the matter in the opposite direction, some ideas are more concrete or more at direct grips with the realities of experience. S. E. Toulmin and K. Baier remark, "To describe Princess Elizabeth as 'heir apparent to the throne of England' is obviously to give a correct description of her." Perhaps so. But one might be tempted to ask, What does one look like when he or she is the heir apparent to the throne of England? And what change of appearance came over Elizabeth when she ceased to be the heir apparent? Since there are various levels, perhaps it is a matter of preference where we draw the line between the concrete and the abstract, but that should neither blur the genuine distinctions nor make them absolute. Surely, in the more extreme case, when we quite abandon consideration of any specific instance simply to manipulate significant symbols, for example in arithmetical or algebraic calculations, this is abstract in a sense that no direct description of specific cases may be, and it is more abstract than any empirical generalization based directly upon numbers of particulars.

As applied to fine art, especially painting, this same dichotomy of abstract art versus concrete or representational art is equally misleading and vicious. Representative art is also, though not equally, abstract, and while the *trompe-l'oeil* may be art in the sense of being the work of a good artisan or craftsman, it is usually not good art in the aesthetic sense. Not only is any representation more or less selective, but the mere attempt to represent or picture a three-dimensional object on the two-dimensional surface of a canvas is in some degree an abstraction.

So, too, any simple, direct description is the beginning of analysis, transformation, and abstraction; and generalization is essential to it. It may at this level be called "concrete," for it does directly denote features observed, but the act of pointing them out or indicating them also isolates them to some extent, partly by the mere failure to mention everything else in which they are submerged—one simply cannot mention everything specifically and in infinite detail. Dewey sought to overcome the theoretical difficulties arising from this, when the dialectical consequences are drawn, by using the term 'situation'. And then, too, there are degrees of directness of denotation. The assumed separation of connotation from denotation, while valuable as a distinction, is a relative matter.

It is no great wonder then, that, rather than the absolute separation of the concrete and the abstract, there is a confusion of the two. There are repeated claims, for instance, by Husserl, that phenomena or appearances—and such elements of appearances as colors—present "essences." According to Santayana, only "essences" are directly given to "spirit" or consciousness by perception or thought, and he says explicitly that "an essence is observed,"[3] and "the experience of essence is direct; the expression of natural fact through that medium is indirect."[4] Similarly, Whitehead makes green into an "eternal object." However, if no patch of color is the same all over, it would seem that the universals have indefinitely multiplied; hence, Russell at one time introduced "point events." The fact is, however, that we call the whole patch "green."

So far as these views treat immediate presences as directly presenting essences, I take them to be illegitimate hypostatizations of abstractions, offensive to genuinely realistic or objective thinking. Sheer immediacy is just what is not essence; it is not and per se has no essence; it is unspeakably peculiar. Immediate qualities may come to have essences, but they are not themselves essences. However, as I shall note later, we do identify things with their natures, for thus they are objects and are intelligible. We do this so readily that Russell can claim that 'this is red' or 'redness here' is well nigh infallible on the grounds—and this is the questionable point—that it refers merely to what is present. Ayer, who at first denied that any empirical proposition could be conclusive or purely ostensive, later recanted and claimed that such propositions as Russell mentions above are conclusive, and for the same reason, that they refer only to what is present.

I must confess, however, that I have long since given up the attempt to convince my wife that I am infallible on anything. When I say, "This is blue," she is just as likely to say, "It isn't either. It's aqua," or some other outrageous thing. To say 'This is red', is indeed not to refer merely to a present thing, but to compare it with other things not present. Nothing could "refer" solely to mere presence except the merest vocal or other gesture, such as yelping or pointing one's finger.

Russell analyzes the expressions, 'this is red' or 'redness here' in terms of propositional functions. That is to say, as has been noted previously, the logical atomism of Wittgenstein and Russell created a metaphysics of entities called "facts" which were to answer to the propositional function of symbolic logic, '*Fa*'. As Urmson says, "Russell called the universal elements in facts components of those facts and the particular elements he called constituents of the facts."[5] Thus in the propositional function, '*Fa*', the '*F*' was supposed to name a characteristic or universal while the '*a*' named a particular, which took the place of the old use of 'substance'. Actually, the very idea of a universal should indicate that the reference is not merely to the present, although, as we have seen, others would not accept that view.

The transactions of the organism are located among and continuous with other transactions that constitute reality. Transactions are events or occurrences, and if these and only these are realities, they will exclude certain other views, such as the view which has taken properties to be realities. Unfortunately, for the sake of both brevity and conventional expression, I shall use language which suggests that such is the case. This seems to be convenient in order to avoid cumbersome language, but it necessitates an explanation here and now of what is meant.

We must distinguish between the transactions of a thing and its properties. Transactions are particular occurrences while properties are more or less general. The transactions are the realities. We analyze transactions and the very terms of the analysis constitute generalities. If one asks a chemist what he is doing, he may reply, "I am determining the properties of copper." Of course, that expresses the significance of what he is doing. Actually, he is not working with copper but with one piece of copper, and he is finding out what it does. Yet his very language states the matter in general terms.

Analysis, being linguistic, is generalization and may be stated in terms of properties that are more or less general in a variety of ways: they may be general characteristics of the particular thing, or they may be general to many things of a kind. But concrete analysis, as distinct from concern with abstract relations, is directly concerned with transactions, and thus we may speak loosely of the transaction as giving or constituting the properties of things, but that is not an exact statement. Strictly, properties are generalizations, and they do express the nature of things. But there are no realities, I take it, to answer directly to generalizations, for realities are particular. Strictly speaking, there are no general things. But generalizations themselves are realities emerging in behavior and so have direct connection with other realities, especially in the case of more concrete generalizations.

Things are experienced actively prior to reflection and abstraction, and this experience involves particular things in particular situations. The psychologist deals with generalizing responses—that is to say, similar responses to similar things—and habitual responses. In this way the object is in a sense hypothetical, for it may seem to involve expectation in some sense, although the merely habitual act is thoughtless. But mention of the hypothetical is reading into the situation something that is not there. There is no identifiable hypothesis, concept, or essence as such in the situation. The response is direct. We directly perceive and deal with trees, for there is a buildup of responses to the particular familiar thing. These are generalized responses in the sense that they are carried over from repeated experiences with the thing. And there is also the similar response to the similar kind of thing.

Moreover, our terminology is misleading. Not only is there no hypothesis, idea, or concept necessarily existing in the situation; neither is there any necessary dualism of object and responses in the actual situation. The attempt to treat objects and responses as separate things is to create imaginary entities. There are transactions, and the transaction constitutes both what the object is doing and what the organism is doing.

Of course, the familiar thing may surprise our habitual or generalized response. A trickster will do an unusual thing which quite obviously astonishes us. But astonishment is not reflection, although it is a reaction to a sudden frustration of the habitual response. Later, we may say that we had thought the thing was a such-and-such, but the fact is that we may not have thought at all, for there was no question. We merely interacted with the thing in a habitual way that was unexpectedly frustrated.

If a man has thrown a stick at a dog once or several times, the dog may respond to that man by cringing or by aggressive behavior. The man has meaning for the dog, and the meaning consists of an aroused attitude or initial phase of an act on the dog's part, carried over from a past situation, whether or not the act is inhibited so that it does not pass on into the full overt act. That is to say, the man has meaning for the dog even on occasions when he does not throw a stick, for it may react to him somewhat as it did when he did throw the stick. This meaning of the man is a characteristic of the man for the dog, for it arises in a transaction between the two. This meaning constitutes generalization, as the psychologist uses that term. The generalization may belong to that man or it may belong to all men, as far as the dog is concerned.

A qualification needs to be made here. The psychologist finds the processes of generalization and differentiation to be phases of the behavior especially of higher animals, including more basic human behavior. There is an important difference, however, between the generalization that the psychologist is talking about, and the verbalized generalizations which are used in logic textbooks: 'All men are mortal'. Yet the two types of generalizations are related in important ways. At the level of animal behavior which the laboratory psychologist is often considering, generalization and differentiation are matters of behavior reactions which do not constitute analysis but constitute a condition for analysis. We may say that a man has a certain meaning for a dog or that the rattle of a feed bucket has a meaning for a domestic animal, even though the animal is not aware of meaning as such. In this case, it is we who analyze. There is no mechanism at his level, such as language, by which the animal may indicate meanings to himself and so be conscious of them as meanings.

But this prelinguistic level, whether in man or other animals, provides the foundation for analysis and the approximate conditions for its validity. Thus, verbalized generalizations may seem merely to report what is already there. But, apart from the universals of the realist, which stem from a simple correspondence theory of truth, we do not find generalized realities to answer to generalized expressions. What answers to the generalization are the particularities which are there as instances. The case would seem to be all the more clear in respect to generalized relations. At any rate, at least one thing is obvious: to talk in terms of generalized relations is not to talk directly in terms of specific events or transactions. They are scarcely to be confused.

The supposed physical properties of things—mass, length, and time—are generalized relations. Of course, the earlier and traditional concept of mass located it "in" the thing, and this idea was reinforced by the notion that "mass is the quantity of matter." Mass was absolute, except where problems forced a recognition of the concept of "relative mass." But "mass" is not a primitive idea in the experimental or laboratory sense, for the laboratory definition of mass in terms of acceleration is decisive; mass is relational. Actually, some say that "mass," at least in theory, is abandoned in favor of "energy." Perhaps this exaggerates the significance of the mass = energy equation, but mass still remains relational.

It is often overlooked that abstraction is inventive and, consequently, abstraction is often treated as mere extraction. This mistake would hardly be made except that, at its earlier and more concrete levels, abstraction is selection.

Selectivity is characteristic of any transaction, and so it is pointless to attempt to make it the basis for a denial of reality—either the denial of reality to what is selected or to what remains unselected—in a particular transaction. 'Selectivity' means that some features of the situation are relevant to a certain matter and some are irrelevant. If a man is shot with a gun, what difference does it make to the physiological results whether the gun was blue steel or chromium-plated? Indeed, in many situations, it involves considerable study to determine just which features are relevant and which are not. The fact, then, that an organism is selective—that is, that it reacts to some phases and not to others and reacts differentially in different ways to different features—is nothing new per se in nature. One chemical may react to light while another does not.

The foregoing remarks may be made more pointed by reference to the slogan: what cannot be measured does not exist. It would seem unnecessary to enlarge upon the reasons for the bias toward measurement. They are of very great importance. But in that slogan, the selection of features that readily lend themselves to quantitative expression and to the mathematical and logical manipulation which such expressions make possible is carried to the extreme of becoming a metaphysical doctrine of the "nothing but" sort: one that is both questionable and dangerous—dangerous in the only sense that anything *is* dangerous, namely, that it puts values in jeopardy. This is my major concern, but here I invite attention to its questionable character.

The expression, 'what can be measured' may mean either of two different things: what can be measured now, that is to say, at some given period of history; or else what can be measured in some vague future, infinitely extended. Respecting the first meaning, it may be noted that many things are now measured to which attention was hardly given in earlier times, and to

which no thought was given that they could be measured; and
it is entirely possible that this process will continue in the future.
The slogan, in these terms, would suggest that what we cannot
now measure does not exist. It is not a very plausible view; perhaps it may be saved by being translated into the optimistic
view that things do exist that cannot now be measured, but they
will all be measured in the future. This turns out to be the second meaning noted above, but it renders the slogan innocuous
and useless, and it could not easily be shown to be probable.

There is also the question whether what is measured is to be
strictly identified with the relevant qualitative situation. It would
seem that hot, warm, tepid, cool, and cold are qualities not obviously identical with degrees of temperature, although more or
less related. Apart from the relativity of hot and cold which
Berkeley noted, note also that there is a difference between
taking a nice warm bath and scalding to death and that this is
more than a matter of degree. Actually, the two—hot or cold
versus degrees of temperature—belong to and so are selected by
different operations: sticking one's hand into the water or reading
a thermometer.

Perhaps the slogan, that only what can be measured exists, is
so blatantly false when put baldly that to take it seriously would
be rather pedantic. I would not mention it, except that it seems
to me to underlie, in an unexpressed way, certain thinking. The
selection of properties or features of objects solely on the ground
that they readily lend themselves to quantitative expression may
be very good for some purposes, but, nevertheless, is a reckless
disregard of what is of vital importance for other purposes. It is
now beginning to be tardily and not sufficiently recognized that
the selection of problems for attention, and of the ways of viewing problems, largely on the ground that they lend themselves
to computerized methods—ignoring problems which do not—is
unfortunate in general, especially in dealing with human situations. In many cases of human affairs, attempts to describe in
quantitative form would provide only misleading pseudoexpres-

sions. Indeed, for many purposes, the accounts of the poet and the artist, both terms being used in their broadest senses, may serve far better than those of the scientist.

I come now to a point which is of more technical philosophical significance. The slogan in its misleading aspect is, I think, involved in one meaning of that ambiguous term 'material object' which is so frequently and so casually used by analysts, not to mention the realists who preceded them. In one meaning of the term, 'material object' may indicate merely a thing that has physical properties, whatever other properties it may have. This would seem to be unobjectionable, for reality is not compressed into the straitjacket composed of the concepts of physics. Since the term 'material object' used in the same sense involves no denial of properties that may be expressed in terms not limited to a particular discipline, it may be applicable to things of ordinary experience in their full richness.

There is the other meaning of the term 'material object' that is often intended—the meaning which takes for granted in an unexpressed and concealed form the slogan that what cannot be measured does not exist. It is that there are things that have—and have only—physical properties; that is, they are exhaustively described in terms of physics and answer simply and solely to the concepts of physics. The seventeenth- and eighteenth-century material object of the external world was of this sort, for the primary qualities of Locke answered to the needs of the physicist, that is to say, the physicist of that day. This traditional notion reappeared in the twentieth century in the philosophy of realism and, with less elaboration, in contemporary philosophical discussion. Such a "material object" is the diaphanous "object of knowledge" that, in competition with reality, is indeed "all sicklied o'er with the pale cast of thought."

I am suggesting that selection, however valuable, never tells the whole story. The alternative, indicated by that remark, is not that the whole story can be told, but rather that there will always be more than can ever be told. The measurements that the police take for the purpose of identification do not say all that there is to say about a man, and, indeed, there is more to him than can be said. If an art museum wishes to ship a huge painting, it may be concerned with the weight, size, fragility, etc., but that is hardly an evaluation of the painting. Or, again, the director of the museum must make judgments of the paintings that he buys, but he cannot make such judgments by using a computer, which means that if he were sufficiently influenced by our computer civilization to become so enamored of computer methods as to consider only such features of paintings as may lend themselves to computer expressions and ignore all others, he would not be more rational but more insane, just as he would be if he were not to use such methods when available and relevant.

Respecting levels of abstraction, the constructed nature of things may be of two or more types: objects of empirical generalizations and, again, objects of more or less abstract hypotheses such as do not directly describe anything observed. We say that combustion uses oxygen, or again, that the electron may be defined in the terms of quantum mechanics. The statement of the natures of things is always in some sense abstract, being expressed in terms of characteristics or properties which, at the most concrete level, are directly generalized from actual occurrences. When we say that this horse is herbivorous, or that horses are herbivorous, we are ascribing a characteristic to this horse or to horses, and, similarly, when we say that this man is a swimmer. We ascribe such characteristics even though, as a matter of fact, no horse is always eating and, in any actual case, he could not possibly eat it if there were no "herb" available to eat; and swimmers do not, as a matter of fact, swim without water.

With the emergence of new organisms, some things that already existed may come to be eaten. This fact is not to be referred to "states of consciousness." We might express this fact in a short way by saying that those things become food. But I propose that it should be correct to say neither that they become food nor that they were always food, for either illegitimately injects a temporal expression into a logical relation. The things *are* food. The occurrences are generalized in the form of characteristics and express the nature of the thing.

It is frequently the case that we speak of the essence of definition as specifying properties that the thing must always have. Then, if we fail to recognize that properties are generalizations, as distinguished from actualities or events, we may think that it is implied that there is always something observable or actual denoted by the property. But the idea that something is a property or characteristic does not imply that events of the kind signified by the generalization are always occurring in the history of a thing. We may classify some trees as deciduous and define a deciduous tree as one that drops its leaves in the winter. But the tree obviously is not at all times dropping its leaves in winter—in summer it is not dropping its leaves in winter. The carnivore is not always eating meat: sometimes it sleeps. Nor is an explosive always exploding. The general statement is the tautology that any event will occur when and only when the conditions for its occurrence are present, but we nonetheless generalize the property.

Precisely the same reasoning is applicable to qualities which are often called secondary qualities. Copper oxide is green. In the actual case, it is a transaction which occurs under certain conditions. It "greens," just as the German says that it does. But green, or, better, greenness, is a characteristic or property of the object copper oxide irrespective of whether anything with eyes capable of seeing color is looking at it. Thus, we properly ascribe that characteristic to it in the Precambrian age, and it is as nonsensical to raise the question whether there were organisms in that age with distant receptors which noted color as it would be to deny that a thing is a hammer just because it is in a tool chest and is not hammering, or to deny that a thing is an explosive just because it is not exploding.

I am taking the position that there is a significant meaning in saying that a thing is red or green irrespective of whether it is being seen by anything at the moment. But the question is, What is that significance? The point would be that ascribing a characteristic *is* expressing the significance or meaning. In the concrete case, a thing will be red or green only under certain conditions. We do not hesitate to label something "explosive," although it is not exploding and obviously could not possibly explode except in conditions under which it will explode. (Tautologies are not false.) Thus, to label it "explosive" is the intelligent thing to do and we treat the object with respect. Indeed, the public law may require a label, and such a law is not nonsensical. Yet the label would perhaps be unnecessary if the explosive nature which it ascribes were something we witnessed. Moreover, this object has never exploded and it may never explode, if destroyed in a nonexplosive way. If it is so destroyed, there can still be no denial that it was explosive. On the contrary, perhaps it was destroyed because it had become an unusually dangerous explosive; a slight shock might have set it off.

One thing which traditional realism and the doctrine of essences prove as a matter of empirical fact is that colors, for instance, are just as much subject to generalization and abstraction as any other occurrences. This much is true, regardless of the metaphysical interpretations which those philosophies give to it.

To meet the need for some discriminated terms, I have been using the word 'thing' in the sense of an existential thing which need not be a well-defined object. We may have an instance in which something exists, but is noted only to the extent that it excites our interest or curiosity. Something is there, but what is it? In this situation, when we ask what this thing is, we do not have an object, at least in the sense of a defined or delimited object, or in the sense that I am using the word 'object'. At the simplest level, it is something of which we are wary; at more cognitive levels, it is an unknown. When a thing acquires meanings, it is an object, in the sense that a meaningful thing may be said to be an object. But we are aware of the object, not of the meanings per se, for the object is unanalyzed, and it is not there as a mere phenomenon, because it has an "inside."

An account of the genesis of meanings may find that they arise out of activities of any sort. Thus, they may arise out of activities which are transactions with the thing, or, again, out of activities which are imaginings, or the two together, not to mention other activities, such as the social. Meanings which do not lead to frustration of action, including thoughtful action, may be unquestioned, and so these meanings constitute the unquestioned object. So far as they arise in actual transactions with things, they cannot be relegated to some other metaphysical realm, and there is no general ground for calling them into question as being "projected," however misleading they may be in the particular case; for what a thing does under one set of conditions may not be what it does under another set.

Ordinary experience involves the presence of objects—trees and houses, for example—insofar as they are involved in our activities. Some philosophers seek to present these things as structures of sense-data plus meanings. That would not be an adequate statement of the activities going on, but that difficulty is not the point here. Rather, the point is that the analysis is not relevant to the familiar and unquestioned objects with which we are actually engaged in ordinary experience, because analysis belongs to a thing that is in question and which is, therefore, not present as an object. Indeed, one might ask in that case, What is it? Or, of course, there may only be something about the object which is in question, so that, to that extent, the object is only partly defined.

The analyst can employ his general doctrine of sense-data only by putting all objects in question, and his excuse is the fact that we can question anything. But that does not mean that we are questioning everything, and there is no sense in which everything is in question. Thus, the analyst himself cannot present his problem in such a way that it will make sense without opening with "object words." Such philosophers are confusing quite different functions. The familiar trees of ordinary experience are objects, but that was sometimes not the case in the static trench warfare in the forests of France in World War I, where camouflage achieved a high state of art. Great amounts of shelling produced many jagged tree trunks and these were imitated in papier-mâché for the benefit of snipers and observers. The question then might well be, What is that? There is no definite object, and, hence, what is there must be stated in terms of data.

All generalizations may be put into the form of hypothetical statements, and modern logicians would treat all generalizations as pseudocategoricals. But it would seem that some statements that are general in form may refer to particular facts. For instance, 'All the men who were at the Alamo were killed'. Moreover, when generalizations are so overwhelmingly guaranteed by experience that they are emphatically taken as unquestionable, they readily take on the guise of the categorical. Thus it seems to be merely a theoretical technicality to say that they are hypothetical; it signifies the bare possibility that a question might be raised. But it should be noted that to say that a statement of the nature of things is hypothetical is no denial of its truth.

An historic view would indeed locate the nature of the thing in the thing itself, although sometimes the view was that the nature or essence was logically or even metaphysically prior to the thing. I suggest that there is some sense in which the identification of the nature of the thing with the thing is significant; namely, that it is thus an object.

We do identify things with their natures. The fact that we may arrive at the nature of a thing by judgment is no denial that the judgment is true, nor does it give the judgment a merely subjective status. We are not going back to a mentalism in which ideas are referred to a mind. We do, however, need a name for such distinctive behavioral functions as ideas, and we may as well use the distinctive term 'mental'. Ideas may be hypothetical, but they are or may be genuine hypotheses respecting what the thing is; and, in the case of objects of ordinary experience, they are behaviors directly engaged in the transactional process of working with things, guiding our dealing with them. The separation of the concept and the object occurs in the unexpected or in disconfirmation and, to that extent—but only to that extent—we have no object. There need be no total breakdown. In the confident act, we are engaged with unquestioned objects. An experimental judgment, which is one arrived at by working with the thing, is in part a product of the thing; while, at simpler levels, meanings are still more directly developed.

It is one view of phenomenalism that no conjunction or disjunction of sense-datum statements, however complex, entails the existence or the nonexistence of a certain material object. The plausibility of this view I take to be an illusion of abstraction, for certainly, insofar as we abstract from objects, as the sense-data concepts do, then we do not have objects. I take no responsibility for the special meanings of the terminology 'essence', 'sense-datum', or 'material object', for one need not accept the metaphysical presuppositions of the phenomenalist. If I should use the term 'material object', I would mean by it anything that has material properties, whatever other properties it may have; and the material properties would not be merely appearances.

I suggest, however, that the hypothetical object, including its continuity, may be such that its definition does imply that, under certain circumstances, it will do certain things which, under further circumstances, are readily observable; and this is a condition for asserting its existence. This still does not entail the existence of the hypothetical—for that would be affirming the consequent—but it would entail some probability, however slight, that the hypothesis is true. That is to say, if the thing does not do what is thus implied under those circumstances, then whatever else it may be, if anything, it is not the object thus defined; and if it does do what is implied, then the hypothesis is at least to that extent confirmed. I still think that there is a furnace in my basement. It helps to explain the peculiar noise that I hear at times and the heat that soon issues from the registers, and the fact that when I decide to go down into the basement, I see it.

The formula that if x has done y, or is very similar to other things that have done y, then x is the sort of thing that does y, and so, in that sense, that is its nature, may be trivial. But it is the basis of an alternative to the view that would transfer some or all characteristics of things to some other realm, either external or subjective. Certain additional categoricals are required: first, that sometimes conditions exist under which x does y; and further, that sometimes y or some effect of y appears. Potentialities are not fully expressed without stating the additional conditions under which they become actualities. Thus, per se, they are abstract, and, apart from those conditions, are not even real potentialities. In other words, things have potentialities under some conditions that they do not have under others.

Thus, we do identify the nature with the thing, for it must not be overlooked that the hypothesis nonetheless states something about the thing. The hypothesis is an invention, but inventions are not made out of nothing. I am saying that a hypothesis can be true; I am not saying that all hypotheses are true. It arises at least in part out of conditions involving the thing that are prior to and wider than the difficulty that is the occasion for reflection and formal deliberate hypothesis and which provide the conditions for confirming the hypothesis, if there is to be any confirmation. The behaviors of animals, including human animals, with respect to things with which they operate are transactions which constitute to an extent the reality of those things. Further, with respect to the familiar things with which the animal has had much experience, the habitual response is a product of what the thing has done. To that extent, that is what the thing is.

II

I wish to investigate the nature of things, or the sense in which things may be said to have a nature. The nature, of course, has been said to be the essence or definition: as such, it is universal, and, in that connection, the point which I shall wish to develop is that the nature or definition of a thing is a "logical construct," if I may borrow the words of another philosophy, without borrowing the thought. This is perhaps most obvious at the more abstract level. Tables, as objects of ordinary experience, are not logical constructs; but things as objects of knowledge, especially scientific objects, may very well be considered to be logical constructs, in an intelligible sense.

Dewey and A. F. Bentley suggested that, historically, there have been two basic types of explanation, and they proposed a third.[6] The first is called explanation by self-sufficient principles; the second, explanation in terms of interaction; the third, which Dewey and Bentley themselves proposed, is explanation in terms of transactions. I shall use this as a sort of framework on which to hang what I have to say.

The view of the ancient world was that reality is absolute. The search was for an ultimate source which could only be identical with itself: as such, what is real or what is ultimate reality and what does not require explanation neither comes into being nor passes away. Anything else requires explanation. The implication is that this ultimate reality, therefore, is one, eternal, uncreated, indestructible, unchangeable, motionless, and indivisible; without variety, multiplicity, or alteration.

Aristotle might be taken as the exception that proves or tests the rule, for his empiricism threw him into conflict with the Parmenidean Way of Truth, although Aristotle's empiricism is not all that there is to Aristotle. He certainly paid his respects to Parmenides as he did to all his predecessors. Of Melissus and of Parmenides he says, "Their premises are false and their conclusions do not follow."[7] And, again, in another place he says that "to believe them seems next door to madness."[8] But, elsewhere, he gives a more balanced and more perceptive view: "However excellent their theories may otherwise be, anyhow they cannot be held to speak as students of nature. There may be things not subject to generation or any kind of movement, but if so they belong to another and a higher inquiry than the study of nature."[9] Aristotle's own study of nature led him back to this "higher inquiry." Thus, this doctrine of ultimate reality is the Ptolemaic center around which Greek philosophy orbited from Parmenides (5th century B.C.) to Plotinus (3d century A.D.). The intervening centuries brought many changes, including the greater part of the rise and fall of Greek civilization.

Parmenides and Plotinus differed markedly in many respects. Parmenides was naturalistic and logical; Plotinus was religious and mystical. But in the respect that I have mentioned their views were very much the same. Parmenides saw that if reality was of this nature, then the world of our experience is a complete illusion. There is no variety. There is no multitude of individual things. There is neither change nor motion of any kind. Nothing moves, nothing comes into being or passes away, nor is there alteration of bright color. Both Emile Meyerson[10] and those of the pragmatist school have pointed out that this was the result of the identification of reality with a logical system, and pragmatists have argued that it signified the fallacy of that identification.

Plato and other philosophers of the time did not proclaim the consequences as unqualifiedly as Parmenides did. But they were mostly sympathetic with this deduction in a variety of ways, for it is an implication of the hypothesis that reality is absolute. Some, less willing to accept Parmenides' view, set out to save the appearances of things. Motion cannot be a real property of the absolute, but somehow motion had to be grafted onto the changeless absolute: they did so with the doctrine of unmoved movers. It is a self-contradictory notion which neither Plato nor Aristotle could state to his own satisfaction. The doctrine of *actus purus* notwithstanding, the simple logic of the matter is that an eternal object is a timeless object, and a timeless object cannot act; it cannot do anything at all. When Whitehead speaks of his "eternal object" ingressing into an event and, more particularly, of its ingressing into one event and taking on a mode of location with respect to another event, he is literally talking nonsense. The eternal object cannot have any conceivable relation to temporal events, as such, as Plato at one time saw. Later, in the *Timaeus,* he did attempt a solution, for in his terms he could not escape the problem.

Motion or change of any kind is an excrescence in an absolute world, for an absolute world is a static world, a mere "is," as Parmenides and Plato said. If motion is nevertheless to be introduced, there must be special principles or first causes by virtue of which things are kept going, for, as Aquinas said, "Whatever is in motion is moved by another." The concept of explanation by self-sufficient principles is the logical consequence of the essentially static view of nature plus the empirical observation that things do move. The syllogism is as follows: all moving things, if nothing moved them, would naturally come to a standstill; but they do not come to a standstill, so, something must move them. This something is ultimately the static absolute and so it is self-sufficient, for it requires nothing to move it and requires no further explanation.

The ancient world proposed a variety of unmoved movers which were essential in order to introduce motion into or maintain motion in an otherwise static world. Thus Plato defined the "soul" as that which moves the body, and Aristotle must have either one or else fifty-five gods to keep the fifty-five wheels of the astronomical universe in motion. He remarked that Democritus lazily refused to explain motion. Apart from gods and souls, other self-sufficient principles, some of which we call "forces," were made responsible for change by various ancient philosophers. There were forces of condensation and rarefaction, or, again, of attraction and repulsion, not to mention others.

Note that here the concept "force" was not used to signify a change or analysis of change, but something outside the change which brings the change about. It was a first cause; it was an agent in an absolute sense. So, too, the words 'force' and 'energy' are often used in the present world in much the same sense; i.e., as if they denote self-sufficient causes. Again, Newton spoke of force being impressed upon things. Russell tells us that the external world is made up of a "distribution of energy." I do not connect these two views, for, possibly they cannot be brought together, except negatively. The concepts of either view, at least if taken literally, cannot be treated as an abstract analysis of an actual change or transaction.

The static, absolute object involved the mystery of being an absolute agent, and this *was* a mystery, for it was contrary to the intelligible view of Newton that for every action there is an equal and opposite reaction. In more general terms, causal relations are relations between events, and thus causes and effects are events. This provides the grounds for the further analysis of events in terms of variables which express change. But the static, absolute, and eternal object was not an event.

The doctrine of absolute objects, which was so much a presupposition of the ancient world—and later times—is explicit in such divergent philosophies as those of Democritus and again of Socrates or Plato, who would not deign even to mention Democritus. Both Plato and Democritus are said to have used the same illustration with the same conclusion. When I am well, the wine tastes sweet; when I am ill, the wine tastes bitter. What is notable is the conclusion which then is assumed to follow: therefore, the sweet or bitter taste cannot be taken to be a real property of the wine. It is not a real property of the wine because it depends upon me and my condition.

Well, then what would be a real property? By contrast, it would be a property which a thing could have irrespective of any other thing. Now a property which anything may possess irrespective of anything else may be called an absolute property. And a thing possessing such absolute properties may be called an absolute object. Democritus in his atomic theory enumerated properties assumed to be of this type. As the illustration respecting taste would indicate, the absolute properties do not include what

Locke was later to call secondary qualities, such as color, odor, sound, or taste. On the contrary, Locke found that primary qualities "may be called *real* qualities, because they really exist in those bodies."[11] Of course, Locke's view may lead us to raise a question which Berkeley could very well ask, How can a "sensation" in the mind "resemble" a "power" in a body? It will be noted that all that was actually proved about the taste of the wine was that it was relative. What seems to be overlooked is that if the cupboard was bare and there was no wine at hand then there was no taste, either sweet or bitter. The interesting point is the immediate inference; namely, that since the property is relative the property is not a real property. Later, Berkeley adopted this same form of reasoning, for he was concerned to deny both "the absolute existence of sensible objects" and "the absolute existence of unthinking things,"[12] and for the same reason, as he said.

I would like to give some attention to the specific arguments, because a critic, Haig Khatchadourian, to whom I shall refer more extensively later, expresses the view that I misunderstood the argument. My view is that the argument for subjectivity was based on the more general argument for relativism, in distinction from absolutism; namely, whatever is relative is subjective or unreal. Thus Lovejoy says, respecting judgment, "The objectivity belongs to it in virtue of its asserting something which is not relative to a standpoint, the subjectivity in virtue of its asserting something that is relative."[13] He goes on to develop this thought.

Physicists . . . usually begin by insisting upon the equal 'rightness' of the differing judgments of length, shape, *etc*. . . . This equal rightness, it turns out, means simply the equal wrongness of all these judgments, their epistemological subjectivity. . . . Eddington . . . gives an answer. The proposition is '*true* but it is not *really true.*' And this somewhat oddly phrased distinction signifies that the proposition 'is not a statement about reality (the absolute), but is a true statement about appearances in our frame of reference.'[14]

Khatchadourian's view is that the argument for subjectivity was based on the *premise* that the things in question are relative to perception or to mind. Note that none of the arguments that I have so far quoted make any explicit reference to perception or mind. Some might be interpreted that way, although that is not the explicit premise; but others have no such relevance. Note further that the following arguments are not *based* on relativity to perception or mind, although they *conclude* that perception is subjective, which is precisely my point. For instance, the following argument does refer to mind, but in the conclusion, not in the premise, and that point is crucial.

Thus Berkeley says, "*great* and *small*, *swift* and *slow*, are allowed to exist nowhere without the mind, being entirely relative, and changing as the frame or position of the organs of sense varies."[15] Obviously, the premise from which he argues is the relativism of "great and small," etc., to the "changing frame or position of the sense organs" which may be stated and which is indeed stated below in physical terms, "several miles distant." His point seems to be that relativism leads to contradictions, and so the things cannot be real and so, he concludes, "are allowed to exist nowhere outside the mind." More elaborately, in a dialogue between Alciphron and Euphranos he argues this point by using as an illustration one that had been employed by Descartes,[16] not to mention the earlier skeptics:

Euph. Look, Alciphron, do you not see the castle upon yonder hill? . . .
Tell me, Alciphron, can you discern the doors, windows, and battlements of that same castle?
Alc. I cannot. At this distance it seems only a small round tower.
Euph. But I, who have been at it, know that it is no small round tower, but a large square building with battlements and turrets, which it seems you do not see.
Alc. What will you infer from thence?
Euph. I would infer that the very object which you strictly

and properly perceive by sight is not that thing which is several miles distant.

Alc. Why so?

Euph. Because a little round object is one thing, and a great square object is another. Is it not?

Alc. I cannot deny it. . . .

Euph. Is it not plain, therefore, that neither the castle, the planet, nor the cloud which you see here are those real ones which you suppose to exist at a distance?[17]

I shall not raise the problem invited by Berkeley's remark, in his terms, that he had been *at* the large square building, "several miles distant," but go on to quote another of his arguments, one that he adapts from Locke.[18] It makes explicit what he takes to be a contradiction.

Philonous. Can any doctrine be true that necessarily leads a man into an absurdity?

Hylas. Without doubt it cannot.

Phil. Is it not an absurdity to think that the same thing should be at the same time both cold and warm?

Hyl. It is.

Phil. Suppose now one of your hands hot, and the other cold, and that they are both at once put into the same vessel of water, in an intermediate state; will not the water seem cold to one hand, and warm to the other?

Hyl. It will.

Phil. Ought we not therefore, by our principle, to conclude it is really both cold and warm at the same time, that is according to your own concession, to believe an absurdity?[19]

Hume carried forward and summarized the logic of the argument of his predecessors:

The fundamental principle of that philosophy is the opinion concerning colors, sounds, tastes, smells, heat and cold; which it asserts to be nothing but impressions in the mind, deriv'd from the operation of external objects, and without any resemblance

CARL A. RUDISILL LIBRARY
LENOIR RHYNE COLLEGE

to the qualities of the object. Upon examination, I find only one of the reasons commonly produc'd from this opinion satisfactory, *viz.*, that deriv'd from the variations of those impressions, even while the external object to all appearance, continues the same. These variations depend upon several circumstances. Upon the different conditions of our health: A man in a malady feels disagreeable taste in meats, which before pleas'd him most. Upon the different complexions and constitutions of men: That seems bitter to one, which is sweet to another. Upon the difference of their external situation and position: Colors reflected from the clouds change according to the distance of the clouds, and according to the angle they make with the eye and the luminous body. Fire also communicates the sensation of pleasure at one distance, and that of pain at another. Instances of this kind are very numerous and frequent.

The conclusion drawn from them, is likewise as satisfactory as can possibly be imagin'd. 'Tis certain, that when different impressions of the same sense arise from any object, everyone of these impressions has not a resembling quality existent in the object. For the same object cannot, at the same time, be endow'd with different qualities of the same sense, and as the same quality cannot resemble impressions entirely different; it evidently follows, that many of our impressions have no external model or archetype. Now from like effects we presume like causes. Many of the impressions of colour, sound, &c. are confest to be nothing but internal existences, and to arise from causes, which no ways resemble them.[20]

One could have a field day analyzing many details of the logic of these arguments, but I wish to emphasize only one point. Before that a brief comment will be adequate, I trust, to signify an alternative view: that if we do not already assume a dualism of mind and external objects, then the question of an impression having "a resembling quality existent in the object" does not arise. However, the main point is suggested by what is perhaps the key argument; namely, the remark, "For the same object cannot, at the same time, be endowed with different qualities of the same sense." Perhaps the criteria of reality may be:

(1) No property P of an object *a* is a real property of *a* if evidence used to ascribe P to *a* is matched by evidence to ascribe Q to *a* when "P" and "Q" are contraries.

(2) No property P is a real property of an object *a* if the presence of some other object *b* is a necessary condition for the presence of P.[21]

Possibly, the assumption is that this is guaranteed by the law of contradiction. Yet, as Aristotle stated that law, "The same attribute cannot at the same time belong and not belong to the same subject and in the same respect."[22] However, a relativist could make the obvious point, that the conditions for the law are not satisfied in any of the quoted arguments. If to a cold hand the water is hot and to a warm hand the water is cold, that, most assuredly, is not "in the same respect," but constitutes different conditions under which the water is hot or cold. The relativistic standpoint, just mentioned, is that things are functions of specific conditions. In this connection, only on the doctrine of absolute properties are the arguments of Berkeley and Hume rational. Lovejoy gives us a more recent expression of this absolutism: "I am unable to understand what is meant by one and the same area being two shapes, or to conceive how an area can be sensibly circular without also being geometrically circular."[23]

The properties which Democritus assumed to be real properties were those which a thing may most plausibly seem to have in and of itself, irrespective of anything else: size, shape, hardness, motion, and number. They are, therefore, absolute properties, properties which could be thought of as confined within the boundaries of the thing, although a question might be and indeed was raised respecting motion. Notably, the list did not include weight.[24] This was precisely because weight was recognized to be relative. As Democritus said, there is no absolute up and down. The Epicureans, who took over Democritus' general views, presumed to correct him in this respect, and it was because they assumed that there was an absolute up and down that they could reintroduce weight as a real property. With greater wisdom, Newton, following Gilbert, substituted the concept of mass, yet one which he in turn assumed to be absolute along with his absolute space and absolute time.

III

A pragmatist like Mead could note that the properties which Democritus ascribed to the atom were exactly the properties which answer to the hand, not indeed to a mere touch, but to a process of handling or manipulation. Size, shape, hardness, motion, number, etc., are essential to grasping. These properties are exactly those that a person could distinguish in an object if he holds it in his hand behind his back. Democritus was describing a manipulatory object, and in this relativistic and transactional interpretation, weight could be reintroduced, ceasing to be a notable exception. But that is not the interpretation that Democritus gave, for he was seeking absolute properties; and so weight had to be excluded.

Ordinarily, one thinks he is getting down to reality when he has something tangible—when he can get hold of something. The common use of the word 'grasping' for understanding has a literal, although limited, basis. At more elementary levels, anything has that sort of reality which it exhibits when one has it between his thumb and fingers: that is where one tears the thing apart to find out what it is and makes use of the familiar tool.

The root meaning of 'tangible' is 'touch', and touch is closely allied with grasping. However, if touch were the important factor, we would be faced with a curious problem, for touch has been taken to be as much a sensory quality as is color, sound, or taste. Yet also, touch has been said to be peculiarly the final test of reality for every doubting Thomas, for touch involves hardness or resistance. Moreover, touch or contact has been taken to be the basis of explanation: if properties are confined within the boundaries of the thing, then there is something mysterious about action at a distance. But say that this billiard ball is moving because another struck it, and the mystery is solved. The fact that equally mysterious factors, such as elasticity, are involved, is apparently irrelevant.

Yet a point is overlooked. Grasping and holding and manipulating are not merely affairs of touch, for what is at the tips of the fingers may escape: grasping or holding involves resistance, size, and shape; and it is these qualities which have most often been associated with matter. The Democritean atom was something that a small man might have got between his thumb and fingers. This distinction drawn in favor of grasping rather than touch indicates that manipulation is basic to the meaning of what things are. The importance of the hand in man's development has been noted often enough and the operational account of meaning, in some sense, may be considered to be accepted in psychology. The hand, then, establishes a manipulatory field that intervenes between the stimulus and the consummatory act. To return to *the more primitive meaning of matter* is therefore to return to *the more primitive means of finding out what things potentially are.*

As "matter" the thing has possibilities; it is something to be manipulated, investigated, and used. The determination of its possibilities is the determination of its nature. The material thing is manipulative and instrumental, and it belongs to the intermediate or mediating phase of the act. The material exists for the sake of something. There is, however, a further point to consider. If one places the thing and the actualization of its nature in a temporal order with a temporal distance between them—I mean a real process of the passage of events—he has got inevitably to reintroduce consummatory qualities, not indeed in all the world, but as part of the world, and especially of objects of active experience.

Aristotle's qualitative physics involved the introduction of consummatory qualities in all the world. But as soon as the physicist began employing experimental method, he started building his system in terms of manipulatory concepts that per se had no place for the qualities of Aristotle's world. The physicist was a doer rather than a contemplator, and he declared his independence of Aristotle in emphatic terms. The "nature" in which he was interested had action as its prime assumption, rather than rest, and looked forward only to more action in which the result is always identical with the antecedent—*ex nihilo nihil fit*. Matter and nature were thus identified, making the consummatory qualities mere epiphenomena or subjective vagaries. Coincident with this, perhaps, was in general a certain puritanical pride in refusing to consider human enjoyment and "consumption" as having any meaning for science, for the scientist took pride in being impersonal. Science was the extension of the manipulatory field intervening between stimulus and consummation.

So far as a quality simply occurs or appears in experience, let us call it consummatory. It is only when we are concerned with its significance that we may properly call it a datum or a fact, for those are logical or epistemological terms. If we would not wait for the future to reveal the further characters of the thing, if we would *anticipate* the future, we must know what the "nature" of the thing may be upon which we may depend. In this sense, we read into the thing a character or nature whose full existence would be reached only at the end of a proposed act or an indefinite number of acts, and thus the character is not consummatory. Any such proposed act lies in a distant perspective which is a future. The *character*, therefore, that we *now* give the thing represents in that sense *the importation of the future* into the *now*; or, if we ignore the temporal relation of the thing to the future events in which it will more fully reveal itself, saying here and now the thing has this nature, we ignore time. Obviously, this character does not appear in direct experience.

Consider a simple object of ordinary experience. If we have a small six-sided block, and if we look almost directly at one of the faces, the corners of that face may appear as nearly right angles, but the corners of the other faces that we may see will not. The eye has the thing in perspective and the corners are not interchangeable directly. But we have instruments with which to measure them, and which belong to a social and public order. With the square and the rule, we try each corner and edge. Congruence is set up in this manipulatory act, and we ignore the successive character of the operations, saying that the angles or sides are simultaneously equal and interchangeable. The result that we get, therefore, does not appear in any perspective, nor is it directly compounded of perspectives. Russell's method of getting the "real" penny as a sum of an infinite number of "aspects" of perspectives is simply not what we do. We have not followed his method of getting all possible views of the block, from every point of view and far and near. Neither do we restrict ourselves merely to viewing. What we get is the result of congruency in manipulation.

Present reflection is not responsible for the qualities that now appear in experience, nor is it responsible for the fact that some of those now appearing are more common and enduring than others. But the social mechanism of the individual, as stated in the previous chapter, makes possible the selection and entry of these common elements into the experience of the individual *as common*. The commonness is established in the identity set up by the manipulatory act. We get the nature, or "inside of the thing," or "what the thing really is," therefore, in manipulation, because there we have congruence and hence identity with the thing. We now say that the block is a cube. The cube is a mathematical object. As such it is the inner nature of the block, made up of those characters which appear as identical in manipulation. All else are mere surface qualities.

We are concerned with the nature of things because we can and must deal with things proleptically. Intelligence is foresight and strategy. Our future depends on things or on what they will do. If our reaction is to be appropriate, our preparation and the measures by which we act must take into account the nature of a thing: we must have respect for it. In that sense, the independence of the thing with its nature is a necessary presupposition. The nature of the thing is not merely an idea of our own or a matter of subjective whim and caprice. Locke indicates the independence of the thing by the word 'substance'. But, whatever else may be said, the implication is that the independence is not absolute, for we can change things. Locke founds the independence of the thing on the fact that we cannot change those things merely by a subjective "mental" act. Thus, I am stating the presupposition of relative independence, not as a correlative or opposite to something "mental," but as a presupposition which arises from the necessity of dealing with things on their own account, as a condition for dealing adequately with them.

So far as our concern with things is limited only to a few possibilities, the character of the thing is very concrete in meaning. This object is a hammer, though it may not be hammering. A more reflective concern does not limit the possibilities of a thing to a few ordinary experiences, carried over directly from the past, because deductive processes lend themselves to an indefinite number of new possibilities under varied conditions. We now get a conception of the nature of the thing, which is an *abstraction*.

We are concerned with the nature of things in order to know what they will do; but that is an elliptical statement of the matter, for it is conditional or, as has been said, relative. Strictly, the case is not that its nature will imply what the thing will do, but rather what it will do under certain conditions. It is not a Leibnizian monad which has its whole future within itself absolutely, to be unrolled. Its future is there as possibility. That is to say, once more, that its nature is not metaphysical but logical.

When we ask what a thing is, i.e., what is its nature, we wish to be informed of some character that does not appear in immediate experience, i.e., what it will do or what will implicate what it will do. So far as "what it will do" is readily and simply specified or described, the answer is concrete, although it is not a description of what we now have in a present experience. However, at a more thoughtful level, we may want some idea of the character, that will indicate to us what it will do under various possible conditions. This is abstract. As Whitehead says, "The shape of a volume is the formula from which the totality of its aspects can be derived."[25] Again, if we see a blue liquid and inquire what it may be, we do not wish to be informed that it is a blue liquid. We already have its surface qualities, so to speak. We want to know its nature—its inside. If we are told that it is a hydrous copper sulfate, or if we are given a formula and if that has any meaning for us, we may be satisfied. To the chemist, this is an organization of meanings or possibilities, stated in logical terms, that will give rise to deductions or conclusions under certain conditions. The hypotheses find their use in calculations.

So far, then, as we read the future possibilities into the thing as its character or nature, we say we identify the thing. The reality of this nature would exist in our perspective only at the end of an indefinite number of proposed acts. But we say here and now, "This is what the thing is." Insofar as we hypostatize a "present" character, then, time is eliminated and we have a simultaneous world of what Whitehead called objects in simple location. We verify the length, breadth and thickness of the block by successive acts, but we say the cube has these simultaneously. The elimination of time, or the future as such, means that having the nature of the thing is not an actual awareness of the indefinite number of future possibilities, but the organization of modes of action that would find their expression in some particular future. One may compare Whitehead's suggestion:

I do not hold Induction to be in its essence the derivation of general laws. It is the divination of some characteristics of a particular future from the known characteristics of a particular past. The wider assumption of general laws holding for all cognisable occasions appears a very unsafe addendum to attach to this limited knowledge.[26]

Perhaps we do not actually think of the object as a result of operations, simply because we could not carry these operations always in mind. An indefinite number of activities are readily forgotten, although they may be in some sense preserved as an "apperceptive mass." These countless inhibited acts constitute the meaning of the present object: they are what the present thing is. Thus, we turn the object into a thing-in-itself.

At a more sophisticated level, we have a more conscious process in which the nature of the thing is expressed in abstract terms. One may speak of the energy of a moving body. If we define kinetic energy as $\frac{1}{2}ML^2T^{-2}$, we use the concepts M, L, and T, which refer to results of measurement, all of these results being obviously a statement of the relations of the body of other things. If, then, we denote these relations—i.e., $\frac{1}{2}ML^2T^{-2}$—by the word 'energy' and proceed to treat energy as a "something" enclosed within the boundaries of the thing, we have contradicted ourselves. At a still more abstract level, energy is found as an integral. Thus, the location within the boundaries of the thing of our abstractions which indicate the possibilities of the thing in relation to other things is hypostatization. If we built a world out of such objects, we then have extended the manipulatory area throughout the universe, creating a world that does not appear in experience, and we would perforce have to create some other realm that our consummatory qualities may inhabit.

We have already noted that, besides weight, one other of the absolute properties of Democritus was brought into question in the ancient world because of its inconsistency with the static view: that property was motion. In a negative way, Parmenides and Zeno had the logic of the argument on their side, as the modern world has confirmed to the extent of eliminating absolute motion. The absolute object cannot have motion as an absolute property. If reality is to be equated with the absolute, it cannot move.

Similarly, in the eighteenth century, Bishop Berkeley successfully attacked Newton's doctrine of absolute motion, which Newton had concluded from observations or experiments, whirling water in a bucket. Newton had noted that the question whether water will go up the sides of the bucket was not relative to whether the bucket was turning or not. Berkeley explained that the occurrence was relative, for it was relative to the great masses of the fixed stars. Of course, the bishop had ulterior motives; he wanted to glorify God, so made matter relative in order to make God alone absolute. But Russell remarks that the bishop was not at his best when he argued that just because scientists and mathematicians are sometimes as muddleheaded as theologians, therefore theologians are more correct than scientists and mathematicians. However, Berkeley's more remote aim is beside the point here. His great variety of arguments, adding up to the conclusion that all earthly matters are relative, makes him foremost among the moderns, although they may not be relative in the way that he would have them.

Most philosophers rejected Democritus, although the early modern world returned to him. Philosophers more often stated the absolute object in terms of ideas, forms, universals, essences, or natures. Plato sought to avoid stating things in terms of the contact of Democritus: his alternative was a resort to other absolute entities, the way of Ideas. One outcome of this was the Ptolemaic system, which involved not merely the simple question whether the earth rather than the sun was the center of the universe, but the more philosophical question whether the astronomical world should be stated in physical rather than in merely mathematical terms. Maimonides raised the still-debated historical question whether the latter was adequate.

The idea of the absolute object was expressed in the notion of substance; that is to say, in the sense that "the whole may subsist of itself," as Locke puts it. Thus also, Descartes says, "By substance we can conceive nothing else than a thing which exists in such a way as to stand in need of nothing beyond itself in order to its existence."[27] This view of the absolute object belongs to Descartes' more general distinction of the absolute from the relative, of which he was quite conscious:

> I call "absolute" whatever contains in itself the pure and simple essence with which we are concerned; such as all which is considered as independent, causal, simple, universal, unitary, equal, similar, straight, or as having other qualities of this sort; and I call "the absolute" itself that which is the simplest and clearest of all, and which we can therefore use in solving further problems.
> And the "relative" is that which, while having the same nature or at least participating in it to some degree, is secondary in that it can be traced back to the absolute, and deduced from it by some chain of reasoning. But, in addition, it involves in its conception certain other things which I call "relations," such as whatever is said to be dependent, resultant, compound, particular, multiple, unequal, dissimilar, oblique, and the like. And these relative things are the further removed from the absolute, the more such relational qualities they contain in subordination to one another. We are warned in this rule that all these things should be distinguished, and that their connections with one another and the natural order among them should be observed, so that we can pass from the last to the most absolute by traversing all the other steps.
> In this respect, the secret of the entire method consists in the fact that in all things we diligently note that which is most absolute.[28]

The doctrine of the absolute object, then, was stated in terms of "substance." Aristotle remarked that it is "of substances that the philosopher must grasp the principles and causes."[29] Spinoza could define the absolute object more exactly in his definition of substance. Substance is that which is in itself and is conceived through itself. If one recalls his lengthy controversy with Boyle, one might feel that nothing could be further from a description of what the chemist actually does than Spinoza's definition, if the chemist is concerned to find out what a substance is. For what he does is to put the substance into relation with other things. There is no sense in which he merely conceives it in itself and through itself.[30] He notes what it does under the circumstances.

What the substance does is a transaction involving other things. Eventually the chemist does state the nature of the objects, and this statement of their nature is not merely a direct empirical description of the transaction. But neither is the transaction nor observed chemical reaction merely incidental. Rather, he must eventually develop a statement of the nature of the objects, in such ways that he can use it to implicate the transaction. This implication is a logical relation. As Hume points out, it is not an observed or empirical relation, and consequently the statement of the nature of the object is a logical statement. It is indeed a logical construct, as Russell and other older analysts would say. Because it is not a directly empirical statement, it is not a direct description of an antecedent object. Rather these hypotheses gather around the observed transaction to constitute their meaning or to constitute a logical analysis of the transaction in relation to other transactions. However, we shall consider the transactional view later.

IV

The idea of interaction has come to be fundamental, and thus taken for granted, in the language of modern thought. In a number of ways, however, it retains some of the most questionable speculations of ancient thought. One thinks of the interaction of mass particles, of a magnet and iron filings, of organism and environment, of perceiver and perceived, of subject and object, etc. The very mention of these pairs of opposites is sufficient to bring sharply to one's attention that the interactional theory sets up or readily incorporates dualisms as a presupposition even though, a priori, these dualisms may not seem necessarily implied. The doctrine of opposites is not, of course, an invention of the interaction theory, but a carry-over from the ancient world.

Furthermore, if one begins with the idea of interaction, one presupposes objects which enter into the interaction, but which are antecedent to it. What might be confused with this is that, also, from the transactional point of view, as one considers any particular transaction, he has objects already defined in terms of previous transactions providing a sense in which we can speak of objects entering into the transaction. Such objects, however, have not been defined in terms of the transaction under consideration (unless it is a repetition) but are to be redefined in its terms. Thus they may not implicate that transaction at all or in all respects, for it may be a posteriori.

It would seem obvious also that one cannot assign any actual causal relation to hold between objects prior to their interaction. Thus they are, in that respect, isolated and independent. But such a position leads to difficulties, equally obvious. For instance, how can one speak of the interaction of organism and environment as if they were antecedently independent? However, I pass over this in order to emphasize a further point, for I am more concerned with the more general difficulty which arises with the next assumption.

The explicit assumption of the interaction theory is, I take it, that when two things interact what occurs is a result of the nature of the things which enter into the interaction; and, indeed, the very nature of the interaction will depend on the nature of those things. That is to say, inherent in this view is the notion that the specific or peculiar result of the interaction is what it is because of the natures of the objects which enter into the interaction. In other words, the objects which enter into an interaction must antecedently have a nature by virtue of which the peculiar result is produced. It is the meaning and implication of this assumption to which I wish to give attention. One may thus say that something is bought and sold because it is a commodity, that someone sells because he is a seller, or that someone buys because he is a buyer. The implication is that somehow or other these things are antecedently a commodity or a seller or a buyer: a sale, which is a result, occurs because there is something which antecedently has the nature of being a commodity; and there is something which antecedently has the nature of being a seller; and there is something which antecedently has the nature of being a buyer, and when all these things bump together, there is a sale, and one can then supposedly understand why the sale occurs. This view, if taken literally, runs into the difficulty of implying self-existent things which in interaction react in ways which must be an expression of virtues or natures antecedently inherent within the separate things. Therefore, while the concept of interaction is in many ways a reorientation away from the Aristotelian object, toward an emphasis upon relations between things; nevertheless, it has to retain the Aristotelian account of inherent nature by virtue of which the particular kind of interaction results. This is mysterious.

There has been a conscious attempt to get rid of the ancient doctrine of "virtues"—for example, the idea that ether would put one to sleep because of its soporific properties, or the explanation of how things can be known, by saying they already contain within themselves the principle of intelligibility. Realists are still carrying on this epistemological account in terms of metaphysical "forms," "universals," "eternal objects," etc., which antecedently inhere in things and render them knowable, retaining the notion that universals constitute principles of intelligibility. Composing a list of illustrations would have the disadvantage of presenting ideas that are so much discarded and, at any rate, so uncommon in actual use that the general problem may seem to have little significance. After all, "universals," in the metaphysical sense, "eternal objects," etc., are in any explicit sense confined to the esoterica of philosophical (or theological) literature. Rather, I wish to deal with matters of customary thought. Perhaps I may be forgiven if I seem to dramatize a bit.

Lest it be thought that I am going a little overboard in stating the implications of the interaction theory in terms of the doctrine of virtues, I shall attempt to clarify the point by drawing a distinction between two things that are often confused. This may be developed in terms, let us say, of a supposed answer to Hume's axiom that whatever is distinguishable is separable and whatever is separable may occur separately. The supposed answer is, for example, that a fire will inevitably burn, or a fire necessarily gives off or projects heat. Giving off heat is necessarily connected with fire, and so it would be impossible to have a fire without its giving off heat. Significantly, in one sense all these things may be true, but in that sense they do not answer or contradict Hume, and to suppose that they do is to misunderstand Hume.

One hot August day I walked into a furniture store and saw a fire blazing in a fireplace. I rather dreaded passing by it. The anticipation of feeling the reflected heat that must be coming from it was repulsive. Of course, the sophisticated reader is already far ahead of my story. He will say that most probably there was no fire; it was just one of those clever displays—perhaps unusually clever. He might even imagine my naiveté in other things, for instance upon watching the magician sawing the beautiful lady in two. But this last, I should say, is not exactly the same thing. One may see a head sticking out of one end of a box, and legs sticking out of the other end, and the magician sawing down between—clear down. One does not actually, however, watch the saw go through the beautiful lady, for that it does is an inference. Whereas, I actually saw the fire: it is my critics who insist upon inferring that a fire gives off heat. Of course I saw a fire. I have seen many fires in fireplaces, although nearly always on rather cold days, and this fire was exactly like any other fire that I ever saw, as nearly as I could discern. The point is that, taken as a direct description of actual experience at the moment, the statement 'I see a fire' is as accurate a description in that case as it ever was or could be in any other apparently similar case. I am quite sure that, according to Russell, on that occasion people would have been caused to shout "Fire."[31] If anyone has ever exclaimed, "I see a fire," the chances are that what he saw did not differ in any marked way from what I saw. So, as a matter of empirical statement, in any sense that anyone ever saw a fire, I saw a fire—and it did not give out any heat.

There will be those who, with perhaps a bit of pity for me, will insist that I did not see a fire—I was plainly mistaken. But whether with pity or disgust or with a cold impersonal attitude, they will insist that I did not see a fire because what I saw was not a fire. It could not possibly have been a fire because I have admitted that it did not give out any heat.[32] I think, however, that quite possibly I have a right to complain at this point that this argument of my opponents is confused and circular. How could one ever prove that there are fires which do not give off heat, unless one observed fires that did not give off heat? But my opponents simply will not accept my observation on that point. They evade it by a definition: if it does not give off heat, it is not a fire.

That is to say, there are two different things involved here. First, there are matters of direct observation of what, from baby-hood, any commonsense person has learned to denote by 'fire'. The word 'fire' merely denotes a common class of things that he sees. And then there is a concept "fire" which by definition necessarily implicates giving off heat. Obviously, if 'fire' is so defined, then a priori no one will ever see a fire that does not give off heat. But that merely begs the question.

For countless generations the people of Europe had seen swans, and every one of them had been white. So, all swans are white. Why would one say, No cows are purple? I suppose it is because no one ever saw a purple cow. But there came a day when someone got off the boat down in Australia and there was a black swan looking him straight in the eye. Yet if that man had had the resourcefulness of my opponents, he would have been equal to the occasion. He would have looked that *thing* right back in the eye and said, "You ain't no swan."

I have chosen the negative case as an illustration because it most clearly shows the distinction between the perceived thing which may be denoted by the word 'fire' and the defined concept "fire" which expresses the nature of fires. But it is the positive case with which I am more concerned precisely because it so readily permits confused identification of the two. In the positive or confirmed case, a nature is read into the antecedent. This nature is legitimately logical but it is not existential, or causal in an existential sense. Causally, a thing does not give off heat because it is fire. To mistake this nature as something existential (to suppose necessary connections between things) is occult. It ascribes virtues to things.

The idea of antecedent virtues which is implied in the interaction theory should not be confused with the question of antecedent conditions. Of course a man may, antecedently to selling, proclaim himself to be a salesman. He is indicating as a present fact his willingness and desire to sell. A company may hire him and call him a salesman. All that is a matter of antecedent conditions and of ordinary observation, so I could not say that there is anything occult about it. But if he does not sell, the company will probably inform him that he is no salesman, at least not any longer. The matter of antecedent conditions is often amenable to observation either directly or indirectly whereas there is no sense in which virtues are observable, any more than was the Aristotelian natural tendency as something antecedently existing. One may sometimes identify the minute sprout in the bean seed, but this is not in any exact sense the Aristotelian form in its teleological function, however much the two were nevertheless sometimes confused.

What I have been saying is that the general difficulty with the interaction theory is one that stems from its thesis that the result of the interaction is a product of antecedent natures in the objects that interact. These antecedent natures cannot be identified with antecedent conditions of an observable nature, şince there is no sense in which such observable antecedent conditions, of themselves, imply what follows. I mean, there is no sense in which we can deduce logically a later consequence merely from a direct description of observed conditions. The most that we can directly observe in conditions prior to a result are simply antecedent conditions. This is a tautology, and Hume makes a point of it. What the doctrine of antecedent virtues does surreptitiously is to read back into the objects retrospectively their future so that in some vague sense they are already what they are going to be. These antecedent virtues are occult.

V

The virtues and powers are thus arrived at by a posteriori method but are then treated as though they were a priori with respect to the results. This is quite legitimate provided that the distinction is not confused. The a posteriori methods are empirical and existential. It is they that come to grips with reality. The a priori methods are inherently logical and hypothetical. In some sense of the word 'essence' or 'nature', the philosophers have always been right—essence is necessary for intelligence. I suggest that the two are not alternative methods of inquiry; they are both phases of any very well-developed inquiry. It is a noted fact, one that is recognizable in logic, that propositions may be ambivalently shifted back and forth between being empirical, existential generalizations, if their terms are empirically defined, and being hypothetical and definitional expressions. Dewey makes a good deal of this shift, and Wittgenstein remarks, "What counts today as an observed concomitant of a phenomenon will tomorrow be used to define it."[33] Does the statement 'Men are rational animals' express or presume to express a categorical and existential fact about men, or is it an a priori definition? The fact that it may be either creates confusion in the ranks of logicians. But logical relations are not to be confused with temporal and existential relations.

As James said, the implication is that reality is not to be identified with a logical system.[34] The moment one identifies his logical system with reality, which is to say, makes his logical system into a metaphysical system in any complete sense, he is faced with mechanism. The only alternative in this case to necessary connection or determinism is chance, for all things then either have a necessary connection—which is a logical connection—or else there is an absence of such a necessary connection—which is a chance relation.

The attempt to define a causal relation as regularity of sequence will not do. A necessary connection may imply regularity of sequence, but regularity of sequence, in the sense in which it must be taken, does not imply necessary connection. Regularity of sequence is an empirical conception and can go no further than observation, except as it may lead to habitual expectation, as Hume says. Regularity of sequence is an observed regularity, always confined to a finite set of observations. It does not claim to state any more than what has been observed; and, in the broad field of nature, that is little enough. It implies nothing.

Its lack of implication is illustrated, I think, by considering the meaning that it would give to its opposite, which, for want of a more precise word, we may again call "chance." The opposite of regularity is irregularity: that would define 'chance' as belonging to a set of cases in which when we have A, then B sometimes occurs and sometimes does not occur. However, this does not provide for the possibility that what has been a regular sequence within a given set of observations may be only a chance relation. The very calculation of probability implies this. And research workers find often enough that when a set of data has provided regularity of sequence, some later set may be quite different.

The opposite to asserting that things have logical relations is neither that they are illogical or irrational, nor that they are all matters of chance, but rather that they are nonlogical. For logical relations are between propositions and not between things. It is equally nonsensical or meaningless, therefore, to speak of things either as being related logically or as violating any logical relation.

Whitehead wars against mechanism. Nevertheless, his eternal objects ingress into the underlying activity and make things what they are. But the question arises, What selects these eternal objects that will ingress? If the eternal objects which have already ingressed select those that will follow, he has mechanism willy-nilly. His solution is to introduce the "indeterminate." Hence, there is an arbitrary factor: chance, or, as it is often called, "God,"[35] which is thus "the ultimate irrationality."[36] Later, without undue ceremony, 'God' ceases to be the name for this arbitrary fact and becomes "the supreme author of the play," something that does the selecting.

I have spoken of "identifying" a logical system with reality, or making it into a metaphysics in a "complete sense." As White-head says, "The aboriginal stuff, or material, from which a materialistic philosophy starts is incapable of evolution."[37] Re-translated into what I am saying, if one starts with what supposedly answers to the concepts and postulates of a mechanical system which has only the primitive ideas of M, L, and T—for mass, length, and time—he can never make it spell "life," and, if one identifies reality with this logical system, then, theoretically, life is impossible. So, of course, we need God to do some miracles. Indeed, this has repeatedly been taken as a sort of proof of God's existence. Descartes was quite correct about logical systems: you cannot get any more out of them than what you put into them. But this does not deny that when one has new and more complex conditions in reality, new things will emerge; that is to say, something *different*, not necessarily *more* in the old terms. To say that we cannot deduce life from a logical system of M, L, and T is not to say that life may not emerge from the actual materials we have at hand, under certain conditions. The identification of the two is a misleading fallacy.

In speaking of logical systems, we must distinguish between formal logic or mathematics, and what may be said by using logic or mathematics as a language; that is, the expression of things in logical and mathematical terms and the formulation of those ideas into systems of logical or mathematical relations. We must distinguish, on the one hand, between purely formal systems—which are not even logic at all because they are so far uninterpreted—and, on the other, logically formulated systems, such as one having the terms M, L, and T. The former may be a two-valued system for which interpretations have been given, or a five-valued system for which no useful interpretation has been formulated. But it is the latter type with which I am concerned. Any interpretation is a selection, although it is not merely a selection, but a development. Thus the attempts to deal in general with ordinary language from the standpoint of an interpreted two-valued system of logic are often incredibly naive and dogmatic. This is no denial of the value of formal systems: some of them are powerful instruments, but not as a model for ordinary language or for showing what ordinary language is or ought to be, anymore than mathematics is. These "ideal languages" are not even autonomous like any vernacular language. They must return to the common language in order to state rules which make any sense at all and, more than that, to get an interpretation.

A selection is nonetheless a selection. It is more than nothing. And mechanical systems, as far as they go, are not necessarily false, as the Romantic would have it. What needs to be emphasized is that what the selective mechanical system fails to mention is not thereby rendered either nonexistent or irrational.

No transaction, even though treated as a result, can be identified in all major respects with its antecedent conditions. The empirical properties of water are not in all respects identical with empirical properties of hydrogen and oxygen. In that respect the relation of the transaction to its actual antecedent conditions is nonlogical. It is an emergent or, to use the older term of the pragmatist, it is a novelty. Descartes' axiom holds for logical systems: there can be nothing more in the result than there is in the cause. Again, in the modern view, logic is a tautology or identity. There can be no novelty, in this sense, in a logical system. But objects of knowledge are logical constructs, and constitute a logical system. Therefore, realities cannot in all respects be identified with objects of knowledge. Of course, when things do function as objects of knowledge, that is as genuine a function as any. In any case, let us say that the virtues and powers constitute the character or nature of the thing. But if the character or nature is attributed to the thing antecedently, then it does not denote anything subject to observation. This, then, is the difficulty.

From the point of view of a transactional analysis, the difficulty is resolved because the definition or character of the thing is taken to be abstract and is not descriptive. It is the formulation of a concept which is logical in import and not metaphysical. Its concrete or existential references are to transactions. The transactions arise from antecedent conditions but are not results of objects, for they define the objects insofar as the objects are relevant. We do have objects antecedently defined, but their definitions are the results of prior transactions and do not necessarily implicate the present ones. They are, at the most, analytical results of antecedent conditions and need not implicate the present or future results in any logical way. The natures of objects are defined in terms of the transactions, and their character is expressed as a hypothetical and abstract statement from which may be deduced in some respect what will occur. If we use the word 'causal' in the sense of a temporal process, then the *conditions* belong to a causal and existential process. But the *natures* of things do not. They are logical constructs and have an implicative function, which is a logical relation.

There is an ambiguity respecting cause or causation. 'Causation', before Hume, meant a necessary connection between things; but, with Hume, it became schizophrenic and split in two. It continues to mean necessary connection, but, in that case, it is a logical relation and not a temporal relation between things. In this sense, causal relations may be stated in the form of differential equations. Or, on the other hand, it also means a connection between things which are temporal, but in that case it is not a logical relation and is not a necessary connection. When I speak of causes in this sense, I am indicating it by speaking of cause in a temporal or existential sense.

Leibniz and, again, Russell sought to introduce the identity of logic into the reality of passing events through the concept of continuity, and Russell uses this concept of continuity to define causation.[38] We do find continuities in nature in an empirical sense, and abruptions can be treated as a relative matter, as Leibniz says. The views of Leibniz and Russell have one merit, that they take changes as something given to be analyzed. They do not, in the first instance, deny change. Yet the point of their argument is that, if we take antecedent conditions and results closer together, they are more nearly alike. The limit of this "process" is an identity. There is an identity if we conceive of change at an instant.

The instant is an infinitesimal and it scarcely need be remarked that it is beyond the empirical. It is "metaphysical," in the transcendent sense of that term, for not merely is it something too small to be caught by the naked eye or by the microscope, but it is beyond all possible experience. However, it is in this metaphysical interpretation that Berkeley's destruction of the calculus remains unanswered. For the mathematician's answer to Berkeley is in terms of a theory of limits. Yet these limits are of the nature of abstractions and are not metaphysical. It is the very point of the reply to Berkeley that the limit is not something to be reached but something implied. For if the limit is reached, then $dx = o$; and the sum of zeros is zero, as Berkeley says. But rather, as dx approaches o, the approximation of the area under a curve approaches the expressed area which is taken as the correct area.

However, there is a greater howler in the argument. For the nature of the analysis by means of the differential equation does not at all take antecedent and consequent closer and closer together, because there is no separate description of antecedent and of consequent, nor any stated relation between the two. Rather the equation integrated is an expression of the relation between variables, and not the relation between any particular antecedent state and a consequent state. That is to say, the pictorial and metaphysical interpretation of the process of integration of an equation as though it were a process of bringing antecedent conditions and consequent results closer together is not, in any sense, the logical implication of the theory of integration interpreted as a theory of limits. Confusion seems to arise from the fact that if some value is substituted for a variable in a differential equation, then some other value is implied, and these values may be said to describe a particular state. Other values describe other particular states. But the limit is not a value to be substituted for a variable. When Berkeley did so, he was mistaken. Yet he was quite consistent in doing so if the limit is metaphysically interpreted as a component of the series.

Once more, then, the howler is that an expressed approximation is confused with an expression of an antecedent condition. A statement of antecedent or of subsequent conditions may be a description of observable properties, or of what can be observed in the structure of the thing, either what shows externally or upon dissection. This is the anatomy of the thing under observation, and does constitute a part of the conditions for what the thing will do. But what the thing will do is neither a part of the anatomy of the thing nor can it be directly deduced from the observed antecedent conditions because the two cannot be equated or may not be reducible to common terms without the intermediation of some theory. The theory is an hypothesis that institutes logical relations between statements of conditions, and it states the nature of the thing in question.

If we have a steam engine, we may have a fireman who can operate it well. He knows to feed fuel to the firebox and to keep water at a certain level in the glass. He knows his engine and the series of connections between the blazing fuel and the turning wheel. Expanding steam is created which enters a cylinder and pushes the piston back and forth as valves open and close. The piston is connected by a rod to a crankshaft on the end of which a wheel is well and truly fixed. Thus there are connections between things, as matters of empirical fact; although, in indicating connections, I have sometimes mentioned objects, such as pistons, rather than events which constitute causal interrelations, merely to shorten the illustration. Yet, between the blazing fuel and the turning wheel, whatever other connections there may be, there is no logical connection. They are qualitatively different, having nothing in common. There is no sense in which they are commensurable.

If, however, the engineer analyzes both the blazing fuel and the turning wheel into energy units, they are thus rendered commensurable. Indeed, he may then discover something that the fireman never suspected. The fireman may think of his well-tended engine as running at full efficiency. Or if it is old or worn, it may not pull as well as it did. He compares the engine with itself when it was new or with a similar engine. The engineer, however, may discover that, even if the engine is new and well tended, not more than 20 percent of the energy created by the fuel is being delivered at the wheel: there is an astonishing 80 percent loss. Yet the energy does not merely cease to exist; the conservation of energy requires that it escape somehow.

I am not concerned with the astonished fireman, but with the formulation of an energy system as a logical system for analyzing the function of the engine. Of course, the energy system was not created merely to analyze steam engines, much less a particular steam engine. It is a general theory and has a

far wider application. Its even more startling results and vast
success have given it a high prestige value. Hence, one tends to
identify reality with the energy system, and to relegate the steam
engine as the fireman knows it to subjective states of the individual's mind or brain. Thus Russell says the external world
is a distribution of energy.

We wish to state the nature of the thing in a way that will
render what occurs logical. The realist's theory that truth is
"correspondence" leads him to assert that all truths are descriptions. But we do not merely describe things, we *invent* hypotheses as to the nature of the thing, so that these, together with
particular propositions, will implicate what will happen. The
hypothesis is invented—because it is not direct observation—and
the implication is a logical function, not merely a descriptive
one. It is the function of such an hypothesis to institute logical
relations between descriptions: the hypothesis renders things
logical. So the statement is an abstraction rather than a reality.
On the contrary, if we state the nature of things in terms which
implicate what will occur, then, as experimental research goes
on, the statement is revised in the light of what is observed to
occur. What is observed is settled fact which may outlive various
hypotheses. The scientist is continually revising his theories of
the nature of things in terms of observed occurrences which are
transactions. His objects are thus reconstructed. This point is
of major significance in one respect, for it emphatically settles
the question as to which is the reality that must be accepted as
such. It means, too, that we do not, in the first instance, find
the natures of things within the things. We first find out what
happens or occurs.

Confusion between ideas and realities is not solely confined
to patients in mental institutions. There are many illustrations,
for instance the idea of "time reversal," in which such an abstract object of knowledge as time is confused with the passage
of events. In this case, some scientists conclude that historical
processes—time in the sense of the passage of events—are prob-

ably reversible precisely because certain equations are invariant upon the replacement of t by $-t$. Watch a projected film run backwards. If the film shows a steam engine, one sees smoke pouring into the smoke stack and coal leaping to the fireman's shovel from the firebox.

The astronomer calculates a solar eclipse on May 28, 585 B.C., exactly as he would calculate and thus predict any future eclipse. His method is the same, whether for past or future, but the passage of events is not "reversed." What he denotes is a reality that might have been seen by any shepherd boy. But, as a scientific object, it is a matter of theory. The relation between past or future calculation is a logical relation.

The transactional statement of the case is that things are what they do. Then one may say that things do what they do because of something, but the word 'because' is ambiguous. It may denote either a logical relation or a causal relation in the existential sense. In the logical sense, if we know the nature of the thing or what it is, we may use that, together with other premises, to deduce what it will do; and we say that it does what it does because it is the nature of the thing to do so. But that is not a causal explanation—in the causal sense, things do not do what they do because of what they are, in the sense that they have such and such a nature. The empirical fact comes first: they are what they are because of what they do. What they do is denoted as a transaction involving other things as well. The concrete realities are the transactions, not antecedent, self-existent objects. The characters, natures, or essences of objects are logical constructs. If, then, we define the natures of objects in terms of transaction and then read back the defined characters of the objects into them antecedently, we are confusing a logical relation with an existential process, making it illegitimately into a metaphysical description. What I am saying could be stated in older terms: the nature of a thing is indeed its essence or definition. But those terms must have functionally cognitive meaning. They are not in all cases prior to the thing nor do they cause it to do what it does.

To develop further the point that the "character" of the thing is abstract, we may consider, with Ryle, the brittleness of glass. If we say that the glass shatters (under certain conditions) because it is brittle, we are making a deductive, a priori statement. If we say that it is brittle because it shatters, we are making an inductive, a posteriori statement. The relation of brittleness to shattering is a logical, not a temporal, relation. Actually, we assume a given piece of glass is brittle although it has not shattered. That is its meaning, and we are wary and handle it carefully. The *idea* is that it is like other pieces of glass which have shattered. We may be led to believe this by its observable conditions, its hardness, for instance. We recognize it to be glass and not clear plastic. Thus we do attribute supposed characters to particular things because they are like other things which have performed in certain ways. We buy a copper wire, not because the wire that we buy has ever conducted electricity but because copper is a good conductor.

At the beginning of section II of this chapter, I said that I wished to investigate the nature of things, or the sense in which things may be said to have a nature. In that the nature can be said to be the essence or definition of the thing, it is universal and a "logical construct."

There is a further consequence which I wish to mention but not develop, since it would be something of a digression. It is that if we metaphysically identify these logical characters with reality in any final and existential sense, then we have created a world out of logical objects and, hence, we have created or conceived of a purely logical world in which there can be no place for values or for the poetical. In that case, values and poetry must be relegated to the realm of superstition or of subjectivity. But all that is a matter to be developed later.

To return to the main point: if we speak of an interaction

between objects, then we assume that in some sense they are already, antecedently to the interaction, what they will be in the interaction, for the assumption is that it is by virtue of what they antecedently are that they interact as they do. Therefore, if we speak of an interaction between an organism and an environment, we assume an antecedent independent status of each. To be sure, some meaning may be given such words in a relative sense. We may think of an organism being transferred from one environment to another. But neither organism nor environment is any longer the same, more or less, for they act differently. Rabbits were transferred to Australia and starlings to the United States. The outcomes were not such as were predicted. For the newly introduced organisms behave in different ways when they are introduced into a new environment, and there is an answering adjustment throughout the environment. In any case, it does not make sense to speak, in general terms, of the interaction of organism and environment. We cannot in general define 'organism' and 'environment' independently as absolute entities. The organism is not an absolute mass particle in an environment of absolute space and time.

In particular, food is a key biological concept. Its relativity is obvious, for we cannot determine whether anything is food merely by close inspection. We must find an organism which can utilize it in its digestive processes. Using the interactional theory one may think of the ox and the tiger as being in the same environment, i.e., as being in the same meadow. On the face of it, however, the ox and the tiger do not have the same environment, for the environment of the ox includes the tiger, and the tiger is not food for the ox. The grass of the meadow is food for the ox while it is something for the tiger to slink through. It is the transactions thus denoted which define the relations and the nature of the objects. The ox does not eat grass because it is herbivorous; rather, it is herbivorous because it eats grass.

Clerk Maxwell, cited by Dewey and Bentley, came to the conclusion that he was not really concerned to analyze the magnet and the iron filings. He was analyzing an electromagnetic field of transactions. He does not state the transactions in terms of the magnet, he states the magnet in terms of the transactions.

Psychological accounts are especially vitiated by the interactional terminology, for it presupposes, in a dualistic fashion, antecedently separate entities—a subject and an object—as the given subject matters of analysis, and this subject-object dualism has infected much of philosophy. On the contrary, the psychologist is primarily concerned with certain transactions which constitute a field of behavior and which may indeed serve to define the nature of the subject or of other conditions so far as he is concerned with them at all. The older language of interaction required postulation of a subject with magical powers called a mind. Its powers were of the nature of magic because it was something *sui generis*, producing results by virtue of its own nature. The modern psychologist is not concerned with any such object. He is concerned with distinctive functions—functions so distinctive that they may be denoted by a distinctive term 'behavior' and, still more distinctive, 'mental'. He might be concerned with how these functions arise out of other functions, but he is not concerned with them as products of magical objects.

The substitution of the word 'brain' for 'mind' misled many people into thinking they had gotten rid of magic, because the brain is an obvious piece of anatomy. Yet in the interaction theory it was but the substitution of one bit of magic for another. After all, the primitive Indian did magic with natural or observable objects such as painted sticks and feathers. Somehow or other, the brain produced, by magic, things called sensations out of physical events. For those who considered themselves more sophisticated, the brain ceased to be the seat of the mind or soul, but it became the seat of consciousness. The confusion between the term 'brain' as a magical term and the term 'brain' as an anatomical and observational term might be noted if one adheres more strictly to its observational characteristics. What one finds in the brain, as a matter of observation, are neurologically connecting pathways, such as may serve to make possible more highly organized activity. He may find these connections to be very complex and perhaps to include feedback or other complications. As such, the brain mediates behavior; but he does not find anything labeled "sensorium." Thinking is no more a product of the brain than it is of the hand, except that the brain is a strategic center, much like a telephone central. Similarly, others treat the hypothalamus as a magic producer of emotions. The modern lover will, presumably, tell his girl that he loves her with all his hypothalamus. But I judge that no intelligent girl will be willing to settle merely for a pulsating hypothalamus.

The interactional language provides a dualistic split in what the psychologist is talking about, which is both artificial and misleading. The Gestalt psychologists, for example, fell afoul of this traditional dualism, setting up gestalten on the part of the subject to answer directly to gestalten on the part of the object. However, as one psychologist remarks, we still have no good transactional language. For the time being, at least, we must talk one way and think another. In that respect, we can sympathize with Francis Bacon's concern with language, at the beginning of modern times, when old language proved inadequate for new ideas.

We have noted that, in the transactional theory, the realities are the transactions. Objects are defined in terms of transactions and constitute an analysis or the meaning of the transaction. This does not imply that, prior to an analysis, the transaction is an undifferentiated plenum. On the contrary, the differences that are observed to exist are the grounds for the analysis. Because the development of this point is more relevant to the next chapter, I leave it until then. One conclusion, however, which I shall draw from that development and which is relevant to this chapter on the nature of things, is, for instance, that it is meaningful to say some things are red, whether anyone is seeing them or not. Neither is it suggested that we come to any transaction without the defined objects of previous transactions. This could only occur in the completely naive experience of the newborn infant, but that is speculative and is not the point here.

Having summarized the transactional view, I should like to mention its application to the problem of perception, especially visual perception, but, again, leave it for later development. Interesting applications of Dewey's transactional theory have been carried out in an elaborate experimental analysis of perception by a group of ten psychologists. While it would be too much of a digression to survey the report of this work, I would like to refer to it in passing. It presents astonishing perceptions brought about by control of conditions other than the "subject" and "object" and makes emphatic the inadequacy of the dualistic subject-object conception. Under carefully controlled conditions, a human hand is seen to be of enormous size, or a boy is seen in direct visual comparison to be much larger than a man, for they are viewed in what appears to be a normal room, but is not. In still other cases, cards which are actually attached to frames are "seen" to move independently of the frame. These, it should be said, are matters of direct perception, not mere inference as when a magician on the stage seems to saw the woman in two. Of course, it need hardly be said that the point of the experiments is not to produce startling results, but to analyze perception. Perhaps the briefest statement of the significance of these experiments, for our present purpose, is contained in a few sentences by one of the group, respecting the theory of the experiments: "The institute demonstrations . . . provide a systematic means of examining . . . problems of visual perception, and out of this examination there has been developed a systematic formulation . . . which is neither solipsistic denial of reality nor a postulation of its independent existence. This basic theory is one which has elsewhere been called 'transactional.'"[39]

It would be too much of a digression to permit a reasonable exposition of these elaborate and systematic experiments. Therefore, I shall apply this analysis to much simpler illustrations of visual perception. But since I wish to extend the analysis to qualities and values in chapter V, a good deal of repetition would be involved. Hence I reserve the further analysis of perception to that chapter.

IV

The Location of the Object

I have chosen the title for this chapter, not because I think that it is particularly definitive or self-explanatory, but because it suggests reference to Whitehead's idea of "simple location,"[1] without necessarily being bound by his precise views. As Whitehead expresses those views:

To say that a bit of matter has *simple location* means that, in expressing its spatio-temporal relations, it is adequate to state that it is where it is, in a definite finite region of space, and throughout a definite finite duration of time, apart from any essential reference of the relations of that bit of matter to other regions of space and to other durations of time.[2]

It is my point that "simple location" in this sense is a fallacy if taken, not as an abstraction, but in a metaphysical or existential sense.

I refer to Whitehead's statement because I would like to consider two views, one of Russell and the other of Whitehead, which apparently seek to state the nature of objects in such a way as to avoid that fallacy. I do so in order to state by comparison a third view which has something in common with them in this respect, but which differs from them in some basic ways. In general, this third view is largely Mead's. However, before I compare their views, I would like to consider the view of objects against which Russell, Whitehead, and Mead react, or at least which presents a sharp contrast both to their views and to the one that I wish to present. In this connection, Russell has, in fact, at least two very different views.

When Democritus assigned the properties of size, shape, hardness, motion, number, etc., to his ultimately real thing, the atom, he assigned these properties as absolute, not as functional, properties. We may reinterpret them as functional in a variety of ways. For example, according to Mead, they are, in the first instance, properties of *manipulation* in the root sense of that word. They are not merely properties of control but of control in the most direct way, control by the hand. Size, shape, and hardness—or resistance—are of special significance for grasping and manipulating. Thus, the physical object has been defined in their terms. The hard surface lends itself to getting hold of the object, and it provides the object's boundaries. Thus the boundary was stated in the foregoing terms, and all the properties of the object were located within its boundaries. However, since these "basic" properties were thought of in other than functional terms, they were not taken to be merely some functions among others.

The ancient doctrine locating all properties and functions of the thing within its hard boundaries or its spatiotemporal limits has been carried over into the modern world by the dualist philosopher, and by the materialist as well, who presupposes this doctrine as a criterion for what is a property of the thing. Thus, Hobbes was concerned with whether the sound was "in the bell." Locke says that the primary qualities are in the thing, and 'in' presumably means within its boundaries. But what are the boundaries of a star such as the sun? A scientist might write, "When astronomers examine the sun with a solar telescope, its edge appears sharp, as if it marked a definite surface. This apparent surface is in fact a transparent, though highly luminous, layer of gas about two hundred miles thick, called the photosphere. From it comes most of the light we get. Outside the photosphere lie two other layers—a region of flamelike outbursts of gas, called the chromosphere, and an almost endless outer atmosphere called the corona."

The question would be, then, What are the boundaries within

which the qualities are to be located? Certainly we do not have any hard boundaries into which one may bump. Lovejoy writes, "An experienced datum is conceived as epistemologically subjective if it is not assumed to possess, and therefore to be capable of exhibiting, any 'intrinsic' quality or relation which the intended object of knowledge has within its own spatio-temporal limits."[3] Khatchadourian repeatedly takes this criterion for granted without question in criticizing my views. "If we hold that perceptual qualities are not in objects, it follows that they are located in the percipient. . . ."[4] "Perceptual qualities . . . cannot be a property of both the percipient and of the cognoscendum, since that would mean that they are located both where the cognoscendum is located . . . and also where the percipient is located. . . ."[5] "The crucial point is whether or not an effect can be 'in' the remote relatum in the same way as it is 'in' the proximate relatum."[6]

Contrary to the foregoing views, the criterion which I was and am using is that a property belongs to a thing if it is a *function* of the thing. Its properties may be "in" the thing, in the sense that they are identified with its "inside," or its frame of reference or perspective, but that does not presuppose an irrelevant function such as a hard surface. Rather, any function that may be relevant defines the boundaries or location.

The ancient view, that the properties of the thing must be located within its skin, was taken to imply that causal relations must therefore be stated in terms of contact. But that conclusion would seem to be outmoded as being inadequate to modern science, which has come to state its concepts in terms of distance functions. True enough, motion could be conceived to be exchanged at the point of contact. However, if an event or transaction is to be stated as a function of a set of conditions, this would be a statement in terms of some form of field theory. Energy systems are stated in terms of field equations. New instruments for investigating the expanded universe give rise to new objects of knowledge. Of particular significance is the fact that the various new instruments, like light rays or electromagnetic forces, have something peculiar in common—they involve distance relations, rather than contact.

The concept of absolute mass which Newton substituted for the older concept of absolute weight could again be identified with the thing enclosed in its hard boundaries. "Mass is the quantity of matter," F. S. C. Northrop loved to reiterate, invoking at the same time the axiom of the conservation of matter. Weight may then vary with the relations of the thing, but mass does not. Nevertheless, at the surface of the earth the two can be numerically identified and so, within convenient ranges, the mass may be determined in the pan of a balance where and when it is at rest.

The view was also propounded that if a force is impressed on the thing then it will be accelerated, and for the given and determined mass the acceleration will be proportional to the force. Yet it turned out that at very high velocities, this relation does not hold. One assumption can save the relation, and that is to bring into question the doctrine of absolute and constant mass, by assuming that the mass has actually increased, an increase expressed by the ratio of the square of the velocity of the thing to the square of the velocity of light. However, this new value of the mass belongs to a distance relation, for it cannot be got at rest in a pan; it is relative to velocity, and there is no sense in which the velocity of a thing can be stated in terms of the boundaries of the thing, for velocity is a distance relation.

But the properties with which Democritus was concerned could, at first glance, be interpreted to inhere within the skin of the thing. These properties lent themselves to measurement in simple ways at early stages. There was the hard ruler of a certain size and shape; and, because it was hard, it could be laid on the hard object end over end to guarantee commensurable units, and in contact with the object, its enumerated results were identical with the dimension of the object. Hence these properties in their simple terms made possible the earliest development of science. Although there was some early modification from more limited commonsense concepts, and, later, these concepts were fundamentally modified in many respects, still, they provided a very convenient gradient for the developing science. Resistance became generalized in early modern science. Leibniz defined the reality of the thing in terms of resistance. The term meant not merely hardness or resistance to what would penetrate, or more fundamentally, to what would occupy the same place, but resistance to change of the states of rest or rate of motion or direction of motion. Thus, the concept of inertia was developed from resistance.

Thus, the idea that the properties of the thing lie within the boundary of its hard surface lent itself to certain forms of simple measurement, i.e., size and shape. If we measure the length of the sides with the rigid ruler or try its angles with the right square, we bring those instruments into contact with the object. But the measurement of the distance of ships at sea was not possible by means of a ruler laid end over end to the ship. It required surveying or distance methods rather than contact. These methods provided a triangle inaccessible to the contact ruler. Yet logic reduced the inaccessible triangle over the sea to a similar triangle that was on firm land where a ruler or chain could be laid. Thus, the former could be interpreted as having its meaning in terms of the latter, and the interpretation or transformation was by means of logic or mathematics. Euclid could "prove" the congruence or equivalence of two triangles by picking up the one eternal triangle and placing it on and in contact with the other.

Not everything in experience provides a hard surface: a fire does not, neither does a cloud or fog. One may conceive of some sensitive device that would show resistance, but the cloud has feathery edges; it thins out. So does the supposedly hard and polished surface, although in minute or microscopic ways.

The micrometer must exert a certain pressure, leaving a dent, negligible, to be sure, but nonetheless real. Thus the hard surface is not as fixed as it might seem. It is not absolute.

It has already been suggested that the view that all the properties of the object are located within the boundaries defined by a hard surface leads to difficulties. There was early recognition of the obvious difficulty presented by action at a distance in the case of the lodestone and the iron. If all properties constituting the object are to be located within its hard boundaries, as thus defined, then all intelligible causal action must be brought back to contact with the hard surface. But the older attempt to reduce all causation to contact is entirely inadequate to the possibilities of modern science.

Locating all properties within the object's boundaries does not lend itself to measurement of all properties of the object, for example, luminosity. Luminosity may be measured in terms of candlepower, and that means foot candles. In these terms, an expression such as 'luminosity at the object' would be meaningless, unless it loosely signified luminosity *near* the object. Luminosity can have no meaning in the sense of zero distance or contact, for luminosity, in terms of foot candles, is, in simple conception, measured by comparison with the light of a standard candle, reflected from a screen one foot from the candle. This is evidently a distance function, not a contact function: it must have some distance in order to *be*, and greater distances of a cosmic order would necessitate a spatiotemporal concept of distance. The same thing is true of all radiation functions, including gravitational and electromagnetic attraction. My point is not that things must come to be stated in terms of distance functions, but that such functions provide a very different metaphysics from that generalized merely from contact.

Furthermore, not all things, even physical things, can be defined in terms of an object rigidly enclosed in a hard boundary. Thus a sharp distinction has been taken for granted between physical objects and events, or between structure and function.

In this sense, an explosion is not a physical object, as ordinarily conceived, but an event.

Still another point to be taken into account, as it was not in the ancient conception, is that any properties are relative to conditions, at least so far as any particular realization or occurrence or actual instance is concerned. Modern science states that things occur as functions of specific conditions; they occur in a field or situation or under certain conditions. The same thing applies to any attempt to state precisely the nature of the thing, namely, the measurement of its properties, for the measurement is relative to a specific set of conditions. This situation establishes a frame of reference or perspective or what, in special cases, are called "spaces."

However, the earlier view, insofar as it recognized a causal relation, had to define it in terms of the resisting object, that is, contact. Motion could be exchanged at the point of contact. Ancient thought, however, could go no further than defining contact in terms of the point-instant, for Zeno was unanswerable. The ancient could not define the point or instant in any intelligible fashion. He had to accept them, like all his objects of knowledge, as ultimate results, not as results defined in terms of an ongoing process. For the Pythagorean, the point was an ultimate reality. He must simply ignore Zeno.

The infinitesimal calculus of the modern world has succeeded in defining the point or instant in terms of a series which is interpretable in some cases as an ongoing process. Zeno would have had a field day with its earlier statement, as Berkeley, in fact, did. However, the general idea has proved susceptible to correction by the theory of limits. This new instrument of knowledge released thought from the resisting object, for it had found a language for dealing with change; and change, so far as the physics of the time was concerned, was a spatiotemporal relation. In a certain sense, Descartes had already united change and geometry, for he could express acceleration graphically. He hoped, in fact, that physics could be reduced to geometry, and

he almost discovered the calculus. Though the idea of acceleration or of deceleration can in some sense be expressed both
algebraically and geometrically, it can only be analyzed by calculus. One can solve the algebraic equations for certain points,
but this method cannot deal with the motion going on at that
point, for it cannot deal with the whole process in the sense in
which the calculus may integrate or differentiate the algebraic
formula for the whole path. With the integral calculus, new
concepts emerged, especially the concept of "energy," which
provides a constant to be "conserved" along with matter.

Motion is a distance relation, not a contact. It cannot be stated
in terms of points and instants, as Zeno showed, unless points
and instants are defined as limits. Thus the "new language," as
Plato called it, which can deal with change, or, at least with
motion, has also become the language, par excellence, for dealing with the new instruments of the physicist—all radiation or
distance phenomena. It was the calculus which made Maxwell's
field equations possible, equations which do not describe the
bounded object, but electromagnetic fields. One may say that
the field itself is the object, not the magnet; or else that the
nature of the magnet is stated in terms of the field.

The ancient static view stated causal relations only in terms of
contact; nevertheless, the moon is not in contact with the tide.
Action at a distance was an anomaly for the ancients, especially
because all consummatory characters that belonged to the distance receptors and were of a distance nature had been eliminated; the "real properties" were within the boundaries of the
thing, i.e., confined within the space occupied by the hard-
bounded object. Similarly, the action of a thing was bounded
by its surface. Zeno's argument that motion itself was then impossible simply had to be ignored.

The calculus avoids or resolves the paradox of action at a
distance, for it is the language for expressing distance relations
and for analyzing transactions. In that sense, it can analyze
cause-effect relationships having a spatiotemporal spread. Men,

of course, did not suddenly drop their older point of view, but interpreted the new in terms of the old. Carrying over the doctrine of the absolute object, they interpreted the integral calculus in teleological terms, where the end value seemed to be laziness, or the principle of least action as stated by Maupertuis. That is to say, the question was posed with teleological significance, How could the thing in some sense foreknow, upon starting a path, that one path rather than another would be the path of least action? However, the calculus provides no such conception, it provides instead an integral for the equation expressing the whole transaction. Stated in another way, the "principle of least action" is merely a misleading way of saying that the curve of best fit is found by the method of least squares of divergence.

The developing analysis of the modern world was creating concepts expressing relations having nothing to do with confinement to the boundaries of a thing. The resisting object is no longer the essential thing, and hard matter evaporates into the distance property, radiation; the everlasting atom explodes, and the eternal Idea becomes an hypothesis. Things become events, occurrences, transactions which are analyzed as networks of cause-effect relationships that know no antecedently prescribed bounds but reach as far as ever they may.

Differential equations have been said to be the expressions of causal laws, an interesting and notable idea. If so, it is all the more significant to point out that differential equations never express a proposition in such a form as, "Entity A is the cause of entity B." Neither do they express relations between antecedent and subsequent events, but rather they express relations between continuous variables, which are interpretable as the analysis of processes or as transactions. The idea of an entity, per se, causing something is either an extremely elliptical expression or else it belongs to the older doctrine of the absolute object.

Distance, of course, had always been recognized and could be conceived as a relation between absolute objects, although this created the problem of empty space. But another implication emerged from Maxwell's equations, in the form of the constant with which Lorenz and Fitzgerald could greatly simplify those equations. It was this constant which Einstein later interpreted as a transformation equation between frames of reference. The transaction involves different perspectives and can be stated in terms of their intersection.

The question of the location of the object may be raised in reference to Russell's argument for a dualism, by which the world of experience is relegated to a mind or else to subjective or private mental states located in a brain. Russell introduces the notion of the location of a star several thousand light-years away, in order to state an epistemological argument that the sensory content present when "we see the star" is subjective; he concludes that we do not see this distant star at all. In the intervening light-years between the star and our sensing it, it could conceivably have ceased to exist. Thus, according to his argument, it is implausible to assume that at the end of that long physical process the mind snaps back to the star like a stretched rope and somehow grasps the actual star. The concept of the location of the star, which appears to be presupposed in that argument, is that the star is wholly and simply located within a boundary called the circumference of the star, whereas what is seen is an event wholly and simply located in a brain, and that the two locations are separated by several thousand light-years. Since the two events are wholly separate and distinct, the event in the brain is not the star and is, therefore, merely subjective.

I would now like to turn to a very different analysis of the object, also posed by Russell—for example, a penny—as a "logical construct." Russell's theory of logical constructs appears to be a metaphysical view, or so I have assumed. But the later view of "reduction" by the logical positivists and analysts is different, so they claim. They attempt to avoid the show of metaphysics by becoming Pickwickian. A typical positivist would say, "When I say that a table is a logical construct, I do not mean that the table is a logical construct. Oh, no! What I mean is that any sentence in which 'table' occurs can be translated into a set of sentences in which 'table' has disappeared." The sentences would be about sense-data or sense-contents. Yet, however "linguistic" these statements may seem, Ayer, for instance, all too frequently betrays more metaphysical yearnings, as when he remarks on "the failure of some philosophers to recognize that material things are reducible to sense contents."[7] But Russell's view, with which I am concerned, is explicitly metaphysical.

In this analysis, the penny is a collection of all its "aspects," each of which occurs in a "perspective." I turn to this view, not merely because it is an alternative to Russell's theory of the star, but because it is a serious and studied attempt to state a form of relativism in terms of the realistic analysis. Russell thus states the problem:

Given an object in one perspective, form the system of all objects correlated with it in all the perspectives; that system may be identified with the momentary common-sense 'thing.' Thus an aspect of a 'thing' is a member of the system of aspects which *is* the 'thing' at that moment. . . . All the aspects of a thing are real, whereas the thing is a mere logical construction.[8]

Again, "Thus a thing may be defined as a certain series of appearances, connected with each other by continuity and by certain laws."[9] Russell continues, "Starting from a world of helter-skelter sense-data, we wish to collect them into series."[10] It may be noted that sense-data are sensations.[11]

In these terms Russell raises the question of "where a thing is." His answer is, "We formed a straight line of perspectives in which the penny looked circular. . . . We can form another straight line of perspectives in which the penny is seen end-on. . . . These two lines will meet in a certain place in perspective space, i.e., in a certain perspective, which may be defined as 'the place (in perspective space) where the penny is.'"[12]

Even if the object as Russell has constructed it is a logical construct, this is no proof whatever that the objects of ordinary ex-

perience, the everyday pennies and tables, are logical constructs,
for there is no evidence that they are constructed in any such
way. Things become objects in ordinary experience in that they
arise within the varied activities (transactions) into which the
organism enters. And these are not primarily logical. The view,
then, that I wish to present contrasts with Russell's in several
major ways.

Russell, of course, attempts to correlate his view of perspectives with his dualism; however, as I shall indicate, I think the
correlation is not entirely successful. His "one all-embracing
perspective space" represents the external world and he has
defined the location of the object as an intersection of lines of
perspectives in that perspective space, whereas he defines perspectives in terms of "appearances."[13] While, according to Russell, some perspectives are not perceived,[14] nevertheless, the
"sensation of seeing a star will be one of the events which *are*
the brain of the percipient at the time of the perception. . . .
from the physical point of view, whatever I see is inside my
head."[15]

My first objection concerns Russell's location of the object at
the intersection of lines of perspectives. This location is not
consistent with his statement that it is the aspects that are real.
If it is the aspects that are real, then the real thing is not located
at a point. Perhaps we do sometimes speak loosely of the moon
as being located at its center of gravity when we mean that it is
located with reference to its center of gravity. But if we landed
on the moon, we would say that we were at the moon, not a
thousand miles away from it, although we would be more than
a thousand miles from its center of gravity. Now, Russell may
by definition give any Pickwickian sense he wishes to his words,
'the location of the object'; however, in any direct sense, a thing
is located wherever it is. Thus, if the aspects are real and constitute the object, then the object is located wherever its aspects
are. Pennies are where you find them.

My second objection concerns Russell's concept of "lines of

perspectives." I suggest that perspectives are related to each other according to transformation functions by which a thing (or aspect) in one perspective is identified with a thing (or aspect) in another perspective. These transformation functions are not necessarily merely a matter of lines, if indeed there is any sense in which they are at all. One cannot line up the "aspects" which belong to different perspectives. Certainly the transformation equations between Einsteinian frames of reference are not matters of lines. If or when the transformation functions are not matters of lines, then Russell's concept of lines of perspectives is meaningless. Thus Russell speaks also of "correlation by similarity" between perspectives,[16] but the relation of similarity per se is not a relation of lines between perspectives, nor does it guarantee lines. One who is at the same distance from two pennies might find an aspect of one to be more similar to an aspect of the other than to a later aspect of the first, if the distance changes. It may be, of course, that Russell would appeal to the infinitesimal of continuity, but I do not see that this would answer the point. And, anyway, mathematical infinitesimals are not matters of perception or appearance.

It seems likely that Russell assumes that the relation between perspectives is a matter of lines, which would give plausibility to his assumption of a superspace or "one all-embracing perspective space," which, however, also reintroduces the old absolute space. My view would, in this respect, be more nearly that of Leibniz in locating space and time *within* the monads, and not in relations between monads. Of course, Leibniz is not consistent when he attempts to adapt this view to the traditional soul-body relation, for he speaks of the body as a cluster of monads. At any rate, other transformation functions between perspectives are not spatial functions and do not suggest Russell's "one all-embracing perspective space."[17] I suggest that his "one all-embracing perspective space" is itself a logical construction.

The greatest difficulty with Russell's view is his location of some perspectives in the head[18] or brain.[19] If the appearances are in the head, and successively in it, then how could one possibly form lines of them or lines that would intersect in an absolute "perspective space"? The point is that Russell's perspective theory and his traditional mind-matter dualism do not work together. They are alternative views. By the logic of his view, this peculiar head or brain would seem to be a region of his one all-embracing perspective space, or a region of his superspace, as it would have to be for a perspective to be located within it. This, of course, would not be a head or brain that anyone ever saw or could see. That this is so is confirmed by a further very odd conclusion: if aspects are located in a brain and if all things are merely collections of aspects, then all things are located in one or more brains.

Russell, later recognizing a difficulty of the location of the visual world in the brain, says, "I do not think that my visual percepts are a 'portion' of my brain; 'portion' is a material concept. . . . Observe that a 'portion' of a brain is a set of points (or minimum volumes); an event may be a member of certain points (or minimum volumes) that are members of the brain, and it is then said to be 'in' the brain, but it is not 'part' of the brain. It is a member of a member of the brain."[20]

I am not quoting Russell for the sake of accepting his analysis or his solution, but merely to indicate his recognition of the problem. Is a table in the brain in the same sense in which a neural impulse is in the brain? Russell now avoids saying, in an ordinary spatial sense, that percepts are in the brain, much less that they *are* the brain.[21] He avoids saying, in an ordinary spatial sense, that percepts are *in* the brain, by defining 'in' to mean 'member of'. Although this is a key point of his metaphysics, Russell carefully avoids saying what he means by 'member of'. Yet, evidently, 'member of' does not have the sense in which a leg is a member of or a "portion" of a body, for he denies that his visual percepts are a portion of his brain. Neither can 'member of' mean 'among'. That is to say, if a board is in a house, it may merely be one board among all the other boards, or a member of the set of boards that go to make up the house. But, in that sense, the board again is a portion of the house. However, Russell has denied that his percepts are a portion of his brain. Again, consider the "set of points" which Russell says is a portion of the brain. Now any of the points (or minimum volumes) would be a member or would be among the other points. If so, it too would be a portion of the brain. In that same sense, if the event is a member of the set of points, it too would be a portion of the brain; but Russell has denied this.

Perhaps, however, he was using the term 'member of', not in a physical or existential sense, but in a logical sense. Thus one of the points is a member of the class points, or it is a member of a more restricted class defined to mean 'points in a certain area of the brain'. Actually, I do not understand how a class could be a portion of a brain, but, at least, it would surely be the case that 'member of' in the logical sense of that phrase does not mean 'portion of'. 'Portion of' is transitive. A portion of a portion of x is a portion of x. And if 'member of' means the same thing, it too is transitive. But 'member of' in the logical sense is intransitive. Hence, Russell would seem to be using 'member of' in the logical sense. If so, such a use is a straight-faced confusion of logical concepts with existential relations or entities, although, doubtless, his solution is consistent with the view that objects are logical constructs.

At any rate, the membership relation—in the sense of a logical relation—is between a member and a class; this does not express a spatial relation and so, of itself, has nothing to do with spatial location; members of the class of things that are sodium may be located anywhere in the universe. Even though, by a particular definition, the members of a class may be defined by some physical property such as location, the relation of the member to the class is not itself a physical property such as location. Membership, in the logical sense, is not a physical property of any kind.

The idea that the percept is "a member of a member of the brain" seems only to add to the difficulty, since the membership relation is intransitive, from which we can only draw the negative conclusion that the percept is not a member of the brain. But the fact that a particular brain is not a class would lead more directly to the same conclusion. In any case, the idea that percepts are located in a brain is evanescent.

I have suggested that the interrelation between perspectives is stated by the transformation functions which may hold between the perspectives. But the nature of the transformation functions would not identify a perspective as a whole (if indeed that means anything) with a region of another perspective, and thus there is no meaning in which the one would be located in the other. A perspective is not a region. For instance, it is a space, not a region of space. Rather, a thing in one perspective may be *identified* with a thing in another perspective, by appropriately respecting relations. Indeed, perspectives are identified by means of relations. Thus, the table I see would not be identified with my brain, but with the table I use or with the table someone else sees, or with the table that reflects light, or with the table I saw a moment ago from another angle. In ordinary matters, this identification is effected in the adjustment of common activities, rather than by abstract equations. The perceptual and manipulatory objects of common experience are not logical constructs, as reflective or scientific objects would be, but they do mediate perspectives and constitute identities or intersection of perspectives. In any case, the table is not in the brain; and because of the *identity* of things in different perspectives, I do not ordinarily sit down to two tables at once, as Russell says he is accustomed to do. There would, moreover, be many more perspectives than just two. Hence, once more, his dualism is irrelevant.

I have mentioned the identification of a thing or aspect in one perspective with a thing or aspect in another perspective. Berkeley denies the identity which is thus asserted. He remarks, in the character of Philonous: "Strictly speaking, Hylas, we do not see the same object that we feel."[22] There is a sense, of course, in which this is a truism. Thus, it may very well be that, strictly speaking, no two views, even of the same thing, have exactly the same content. However, Berkeley's metaphysical intent is too heavy a burden to place on this truism. That is to say, Berkeley cannot use the truistic sense to prove something quite different, ruling out a question which is sometimes no trivial matter. For instance, on going through unfamiliar mountainous country, one may genuinely question whether a mountain that he now sees among others is to be identified with one that he saw some time previously from far back on the trail. But he could not accept a dialectic that would prove a priori that no such identification is possible. Moreover, in the same way, one does identify the thing he hears with the thing he sees. A ventriloquist may deceive us, but in that case, it makes sense to say that we are deceived, whereas on Berkeley's view, it does not. In short, the question whether we see the same object that we feel is one which must be settled for the particular case.

Khatchadourian has presented some views directed against the identification which I have mentioned.[23] In terms of his dualism, he reiterates that "the perceptual object itself is considered to be numerically distinct from the *cognoscendum*, the causal object, for reasons some of which we have already mentioned."[24] Khatchadourian, like other dualists, is using this argument for numerical distinction in an attempt to establish a metaphysical subjective-objective dualism, and criticizes my account for not taking "into consideration the metaphysical implications of the causal action resulting in these qualities."[25]

It should be rather obvious that numerical distinctions, even if proved, do not establish any such metaphysical dualism. However, at present I am not concerned with the dualism but only with the numerical distinctness supposedly proved. His point is to show that "the object from which the causal chain is assumed to have started" is considerably removed from the final "transaction."[26] The purpose of the detailed argument by which he attempts to demonstrate this[27] is to show that an indefinite

number of objects participate in the causal chain A-B-C-D-E
between A, the object called the *cognoscendum,* and the final
transaction involving E. Thus, he indicates this indefinite number of objects in the causal chain of A, B, C, D, E. He wishes to
say that property e which appears at E, the end, must be a property of E and cannot be a property of A.

His "more important" point is that "the view that causation
is a transaction in which the generated qualities belong to both
the transacting terms (assuming for the sake of simplicity that
they are only two) *does not as matter of fact entail the position
that in a causal chain the qualities arising at the end of the chain
belong to the first term. . . ."*[28] Of course, Khatchadourian's a
priori argument in this particular respect and in his own terms
is quite correct when he concludes that it does not entail that e
will be a property of A. I never said that it did; I did say "as the
particular case may be."[29] However, on the next page he goes
much further (the causal chain here is A-B-C): "Thus, there is
no way in which we can conceive e to be a property of A."[30] Thus,
as these quotations indicate, his conclusion has grown. He first
says that it is not entailed that e is a property of A; now he goes
much further and asserts that e cannot be a property of A.

However, I suggest that his conclusion is not entailed either.
Rather, it may be quite possible that the introduction of intermediate causal transactions does not necessarily prevent e from
being a property of A, for it need not be transmitted as a rigid
and unmodified bundle. When the astronomer photographs a
distant plant, star, or galaxy, there are many intermediate transactions. What he gets is upon analysis identified with different
things or transactions. There is the spectrum from the distant
star, though perhaps shifted toward the red end; there is the light,
perhaps bent out of its path while passing the sun or other
great masses; there is the boiling atmosphere of our earth, con-
tributing its effects. Or again, suppose we have a friend whose
voice we have come to recognize in face-to-face situations. Then
we talk with this friend by telephone, clear across the country.

We may still recognize his voice. Now, as Khatchadourian at first says, it may be a priori improbable that we should hear a voice which in any sense belongs to our friend, when one considers all the intermediary devices in operation. To overcome this improbability, indeed, requires a great deal of human ingenuity and maintenance. But, surprising as it may be, just that result can be accomplished because my friend, speaking, is one of the causal factors in the situation.

A problem raised by this causal chain theory is that it makes an indefinite number of things to be the causes of the perception. This renders Khatchadourian's view meaningless in the sense that whichever one of the innumerable causes it is that he designates the *cognoscendum* has, as starting a causal chain, it has no more significance or distinctiveness than has any other of the causes in the process. On his own argument, it may even seem that, being farthest removed or among the causes farthest removed, it would have the least significance. Thus the argument overplays the point and defeats itself; it leaves no meaning to the simple correspondence of a particular physical thing or *cognoscendum* with mental states in a brain.

Khatchadourian has other a priori arguments which are still less plausible, I think, but perhaps their correction may throw more light on the matter. He says that if the quality e at the last term E is to belong to the first term A, then it must belong to all the intermediate terms. In his words, he asserts, apparently by a priori intuition, "that if qualities e are to belong to A, they must belong to B and C, since all these terms stand in the same logical relation to e as A does (i.e., all are indirect causes of A)."[31] I do not understand the point of the parenthetical remark and so will ignore it. It could be a slip, a momentary identification of the *cognoscendum* and the object of experience, which, in the terms of his argument, would be a confusion. However, his general point is, I think, that if quality e at the end of the chain is to be said to belong to A at the beginning of the chain, then it must be said also to belong to the intermediates, B, C, and D.

The fact is, however, that some things that we hear long distance we identify as our friend's voice and there are also noises that we distinguish from his voice. An expert may recognize the various noises, clicks, and hums as belonging to various devices in the causal chain of instruments, whereas we who are not experts can only identify certain of the things among those that we hear as being our friend's voice. That is to say, we do not at all indiscriminately identify all the properties with everything in the causal chain, as Khatchadourian would have it. And in Chapter V, "The Metaphysical Status of Qualitative Things," I shall attempt to show why this is the case. One important fact to be noted about these identifications is that, while sometimes they are incorrect, nevertheless, they are also often corrigible. According to Khatchadourian, they are always incorrect, a priori.

Of course, so far as the metaphysical argument of the dualist is concerned, it makes no difference whether one is talking with a friend long distance or face-to-face if the latter means anything in dualistic terms. In either case, according to the dualist, all the elements of experience are merely subjective states of mind or of a brain. From the opposite point of view, I, too, agree that it makes no difference. Yet the dualist often states his argument in terms of the *cognoscendum* being "far removed" from the perceiver, just as Khatchadourian does above or as Russell does in respect to the star. Just how this interpolation of more and more physical things is a greater proof of subjectivity of the end result is never made quite clear.

Khatchadourian, from the standpoint of the dualist, is trying to make the contents of experience so much a matter of absolute immediacy as not to require any mediation, and to restrict experience to that condition. I suggest that, while the eyes and other instruments may be the condition or—in the broadest sense—a cause of seeing, they are not thereby the cause of what is seen. Galileo observed the moon with a telescope, and some of us see only with our spectacles things which we at one time could see without them. So far as I can observe, there is no difference between the familiar things that I used to see without spectacles, for instance the small print of a book that I have had for many years, and what I now see with them.

My view is rather different from what Khatchadourian has presented, for it is one of organisms in direct transactions with things, and a transaction is not confined within the circumference of a point. It has extent. Khatchadourian's general position, similar to Russell's point about the star, seems to be that the transaction into which we enter is far removed from A, so that nothing that we have can be in any direct sense a property of A, but I suggest that this is in point of fact not the case, however one may account for it or fail to account for it. In a long-distance conversation, we do not talk to the telephone we hold in our hand, nor with the wire or other instruments that lie in between. We talk with our friend. The telephone is a means by which we converse with him. And all the warm, unique quality of his voice and his spontaneous reaction to what we say is there in our experience. Thankfully, we are not locked in the solipsism of the dualist.

Looking through the family album, I come upon a photograph which I show to the children. "This," I say, "is a picture of grandfather." But Khatchadourian corrects me. "Not at all," he says. "Photographs are produced by cameras, not by grandfathers. Even though the grandfather may have had some place in the long chain of prior events which led to the photograph; nevertheless, any property of the photograph would have to be ascribed to the camera or even to some later stage in the chain; for all the properties of the photograph were produced by the camera or by the later stage."

Of course, I am not sure that I have represented Khatchadourian correctly, for perhaps he would not talk at all about photographs being produced by cameras but about states of consciousness or perceptual qualities produced by the brain (or mind).[32] But he does argue that if any such property were to be attributed to grandfather it must be ascribed to the intermediate stages in the chain, for instance, to the camera. I suggest, on the contrary, that there is no such thing as photographs in general or consciousness in general to be produced. Rather, a photograph in particular is a photograph of something in particular and a state of consciousness in particular is consciousness of something in particular; and what they present in particular cannot in all respects be reasonably stated to be properties of or ascribed to the camera or brain (or mind). Whatever Khatchadourian's theory may be, if it cannot ascribe some features of the photograph to grandfather, the theory is ipso facto irrelevant.

I do not apologize for my repeated reference to matters of fact, for I do not accept the limitations of the linguistic analyst. It is characteristic of my view to suggest that if we have an epistemology that does not *confine* itself to linguistic analysis and the attendant generalities of a priori plausible reasoning, but is sufficiently empirical to attend to actual cases of scientific analysis, as constituting examples of knowing, then more fruitful results may be possible. Perhaps the following account of the earliest examination of the first photographs of Mars will illustrate sufficiently what I mean.[33]

Speaking of these photographs a scientist said, "You'll notice each of the pictures shows a dark spot in the lower right corner. We've definitely determined that this is something in the equipment. That's our problem: to tell what's on Mars, and what's in the collection system." He added, "Remember we are trying to distinguish details on a planet we've never seen." Scientists at the Jet Propulsion Laboratory put together transparencies of Mariner 4's first two pictures of Mars, and a W-shaped dark area twelve miles wide overlapped. "We knew then," said Dr. Bruce Murray, "that it was a valid photograph of a feature on Mars. We knew then that we had something to map." An hour later a computer verified that a bright spot in the spacecraft's third picture was also undoubtedly a feature of the Martian surface. Named 'feature B', it is an unknown object about two miles across.

Note that whether the scientist may be observing something on Mars is for the time being in question. But it is a genuine question. Is the evident datum to be referred to Mars or to something else? Thus it is not a question to be resolved by a priori generalities one way or another as a matter of antecedent metaphysical reasoning, but rather something to be studied item by item, according to the relations which each has.

I am not beginning with the presuppositions of questions which dualists raise, but with what seem to be the facts of the analysis of given transactions. We do not have a world of mere data. The existence of such a world is a myth, and such a world would be chaos. Infants aside, we each have some objects already present in the situation, in terms of which the particular problem is stated in part and the data analyzed; but as far as there is something there and yet we do not know what it is, or do not know what it is in some respect, we do not, to that extent, have an object. One may, however, have or obtain data, and with that he may construct or reconstruct the new object, utilizing still other objects that are fairly well known, indicated by the "object words" in the above quotation, such as 'Mariner 4'. One could not, by mere inspection of the data, make any sense of it. Such things per se are not, in any genuine sense, data at all but supposed mere presences. They occur in a situation of known objects by which one reconstructs objects in question. Maps of the old Mars are in existence, showing canals, seasonal green areas, and polar caps, but little detail. Now, in the manner illustrated by the quotation above, new maps will be constructed, possibly without canals. Some of the data are indicated by the words of the quotation, 'dark spot', 'W-shaped dark area', 'bright spot'. Data, then, lie in what Mead called "the betwixt and between." They are to be absorbed into the new object; but, for the time being, the data lie between the old Mars—the old object—which is gone, and the new Mars—the new object—which is not yet in existence. There is, for instance, the datum named 'feature B': "It is an unknown object about two miles across."

The activities of an organism are transactions, and many of the organism's activities are experiences. As experiences occur, they are not, in the first instance, analyzed—for they do not come already analyzed. To note various phases of experiences is, to that extent, to analyze them, but this is not a concern with mere immediacy as such. One may be concerned with the obvious relations of things experienced. One may be concerned with the thing of experience as a function of any of its elements: the organism, an object already identified like "Mars," or conditions.

Once, while driving a car all day, I suddenly noticed a sharp, clear, continuous ringing. It sounded much like a power saw. The question was, Is this just a ringing in my ears or is it coming from something in the neighborhood I am passing through? I could not settle the issue by merely examining the ringing sound itself, only by such relations of objects as I could establish. Obviously, if it was a quality or property of something in the neighborhood, as I drove my car on at fifty-five miles per hour, it would soon fade away.

I may see an apparent spot on the wall because of a previous conditioning of the retina caused by looking at a strong light. Another spot may have been caused by an object which had previously been hanging on the wall for some time, but is now removed. And the two spots may look very much alike. I do not distinguish between them either by direct inspection or on the basis of a subjective-objective dualism. The conditions for either of them are equally physical, but they may be different conditions which are distinguished because the spots behave differently. For instance, one spot moves as I turn my eyes and the other does not. One seems larger as I look at the wall from a greater distance, while the other seems smaller.

I am not concerned with the analysis of mere presences or of appearances as such or of phenomena. The actual situation is an activity, of which the immediacy as such is merely a phase. As isolated or considered merely by itself, it is an abstraction, without meaning unless the large act in which it has its actual locus is taken into account. The essential feature of Russell's analysis is that he defines his perspectives solely in terms of appearances. This leads to at least two difficulties: (1) he therefore has made "appearance" the basic concept of his metaphysics and hence the basic function of the universe; (2) he has destroyed the unity of the object.

The attempts by Russell, and by Whitehead, to make appearance or perception the basic metaphysical principle of reality are most peculiar. Perception, and especially visual perception (to which they make primary reference), is presumably something which has arisen rather late in biological evolution. I can only hazard the guess that this peculiar notion has been brought about by preoccupation with the epistemological problem, and with that problem as the realist states it, namely, in seventeenth- and eighteenth-century terms. Nevertheless, it still remains the case that the question of *how* we know is not identical with, even though related to, *what* we know or surmise. Especially, in any view outside of outright idealism, the process of knowing or of perceiving in particular is not constitutive of the universe, except, of course, that it is one of many functions in the universe.

Russell destroys the unity of the object by blasting it into a countless number of aspects or appearances. That is to say, it evaporates into the perspective of other things. Russell fails to provide a sense in which the object itself establishes a perspective. Russell's point of intersection of lines of aspects will not serve this purpose, for his aspects all face the other way or belong to other perspectives, those of hypothetical viewers, and there is nothing beyond their facade. Any real thing, as Mead points out, must have an inside. Whitehead recognizes this when he remarks: "There is thus an intrinsic and an extrinsic reality of an event, namely, the event as in its own prehension, and the event as in the prehension of other events."[34] I cannot, however, agree further with Whitehead because he ties his view in with the realist's metaphysical baggage of universals or eternal objects;

also, because the model of his concept of perspectives, like Russell's, is perception. So, I shall return to Russell. Before that, however, I would not like to leave the notion of unity merely in terms of the abstract notion of prehension.

When I refer to the unity of the thing, I mean, first, an actual unity and not merely a formal unity. An instance of a formal unity is a class; for example, the class of all things that contain iron atoms. The members of such a class are presumably scattered over the universe. Sometimes the members of such a class are called a "collection," but usually they are not collected. Such classes do not constitute entities.

In using the word 'actual', I refer to actions, occurrences, events, or happenings, rather than merely definitional constructs. By 'actual unity' I mean the case in which some of the actual functions of a so-called part are mutually affected by other things or parts. In this sense, the relation may be called "organic," and a number of such mutually related things may be called an "organism," as Whitehead called them, as did earlier philosophers. However, if we say with Leibniz or Whitehead that all actual things are organisms, we risk the danger that such an expression may suggest the primacy of biological organisms as models of such a notion. On the contrary, I would ask what is the more general meaning of saying that biological entities are organisms. To avoid the implication or suggestion that biological organisms are paradigm examples of realities or actual things, I suggest a more general definition of a unity or whole. The sense in which an actual collection is a unity or a whole is the sense in which it has actual properties (not merely formal properties) which cannot be attributed distributively to its elements.

While Russell does say that there are perspectives that are not perceived,[35] nevertheless, he says that the perspectives are "private," and he goes on to define 'perspective' in terms of "appearances,"[36] which are invariably spoken of in terms of seeing. I do not mean that Russell would, if pressed, necessarily restrict aspects to visual aspects, but it is quite clear that vision is the model for his metaphysical structure, and he nowhere mentions anything else, so far as I know. Still later, Russell is even more explicit: "A thing may be defined as a certain series of appearances connected with each other by continuity and by certain causal laws."[37]

Similarly, the metaphysical doctrine of the logical positivist, stemming from Kant, makes phenomena constitutive of things, the word 'phenomenon' presumably meaning the same as 'appearance'. Such views seem to be held by idealists, and things become mere apparitions with no insides. I suggest that the terms 'sensation', 'appearance', and 'perception' are inadequate to serve as ultimate metaphysical terms or as models for metaphysical structures. A metaphysics must include all functions.

There is also the hypothesis of the continuity of the object, which is a problem for the phenomenalist. Though Berkeley had God as the last resort in this connection, that is no answer to the problem, for there is no tree in the Quad for God to keep his eye on. God merely has his own "ideas." While scientific hypotheses are most frequently about unperceived things, the ordinary continuity of the object is not merely a metaphysical view, it is the common guide of ordinary experience and so integral to ordinary conduct that few would think of it as an hypothesis. That my furnace is in my basement is not merely a metaphysical dogma but a working hypothesis. Moreover, in any problematic situation, the idea or hypothesis is always about something not present.

In another place, Russell denies the generality of the idea that "a thing is real if it persists at times when it is not perceived...."[38] However, a series of disconnected events, whether perceived or not, may be real enough, yet it is questionable in what sense they would together constitute "a thing," rather than several different things. We have noted in the previous quotation that Russell defined 'a thing' as a series of appearances connected by such properties as continuity. Yet, if a thing consists merely of appearances, what connects them when there are gaps in the series? When the thing is dissolved into aspects or appearances in *other* perspectives and has thus lost its unity, then its continuity becomes unintelligible. Any metaphysical view must provide for the continuity of things.

The use that Russell makes of the term 'sense-data' to indicate the basic elements of his object emphasizes its sensory or phenomenal character. Russell might, in some sense, demur, for in one phase of his philosophy he felt that sense-data were neutral. But as I have noted, he came to identify sense-data with sensations.[39] At a later time, Russell said, respecting some data, that "a 'public' datum is one which generates similar sensations...."[40] To be a sensation and to generate sensations would seem to be quite different things. But mixing together Russell's changing views can only produce confusion.

At any rate, "neutral" or not, sense-data are evidently abstracted elements of a sensory process. This is emphasized by the contrast which we have if we substitute the more general concept "transaction." Transactions—or occurrences—are not, in general, stated in terms of sense-data or of sensory processes. Moreover, the use of the term, 'data', suggests a cognitive function which is irrelevant to a general metaphysics of objects, except upon an idealistic basis. The term 'data' might be relevant so far as a thing is a scientific object. As a scientific object, it may indeed be a logical construction, although not "a mere logical construction"; but this is not a general or metaphysical conception, except for idealism.

So far as any actual penny is concerned, it is not something merely sensed—it is handled, it works in candy machines, it reacts to acids. No one of these functions is general either, nor is any specific function; still, by the same token, they are not reducible without remainder to the function of sensing, or to things which merely exist as sensed. Indeed, sensing is presumably merely a phase of a larger biological act. Russell's argument might have a more superficial plausibility if his illustration were a star rather than a penny, for a star's most obvious effect on the earth is visual. Even that illustration would, however similar, be subjected to criticism.

Perception is a latecomer in the biological process. Vast numbers of biological organisms survived before they could see objects; that is, they maintained life long enough to reproduce. Perhaps the living thing, prior to visual perception, had some slight degree of visual sensitivity as a foundation for later development; indeed, distinctive reaction to light is found in some chemicals. The organism's development of distance receptors was doubtless a great aid in opening new possibilities. The main point is that the development of visual perception intervened in a process that was already going on. Perception is and always has been primarily an instrument of conduct—the psychologist loves illustrating how relative it is to the interests of the organism.

A brief reference to the phenomenologist may serve to make these remarks more pointed. Though Merleau-Ponty's thesis of "the primacy of perception" belongs to philosophic esoterica, it may elicit two comments. First, it is a general characteristic of the attempt to make any term all-explanatory, to the degree that it is broadened out of all usual meaning. Accordingly, Merleau-Ponty extends the term 'perception' to cover "unconscious perception," to which he gives great attention. Although he also sometimes confuses the term 'conscious' with the term 'self-conscious', I shall not follow up that point. The point here is that, whatever the status of subliminal stimulation, it nevertheless raises a question as to the meaning of "phenomena" in any such connection. Yet, however broadened the term 'perception' may become under the logical pressure of its inadequacy, the chief examples of perception are those of seeing and hearing—more especially seeing—and they are taken to be the paradigms of perception.

My second comment is more particularly related to the general point that I have been making. It is that such perceptual functions cannot be intelligibly isolated from the larger context of the organism's activities which are already going on, except in the abstract and isolated speculations of philosophers. Any number of experiments show, indeed, that an animal's own activities change what it sees and hears. Laboratory experiments that tamper with the feedback loop, which provides an intimate relation between perception and the more inclusive activities of the organism, show that it is a key to developing and maintaining perceptual adaptation and orientation in advanced mammals, including man.[41] However, the way in which Merleau-Ponty brushes behavior aside as being merely "motion" indicates a lack of interest in the literature of that field.

There should be no objection to anyone's placing a limit on his problem or confining himself to particular questions. However, the preoccupation of philosophers with the functions of distance receptors to the extent of confining the whole field of epistemology to that function, and moreover, to the extent of creating a whole metaphysics or theory of reality out of that function, can have no plausible foundation.

Russell's account of the penny has a major characteristic which I have been considering and which appears to be most questionable: the model for his concept of "aspect" is perception, more particularly, vision. Similarly, Whitehead seeks to generalize perception into a metaphysical conception, at least in the form of "apprehension." He introduces a considerable quotation from Bacon which begins, "It is certain that all bodies whatsoever, though they have no sense, yet they have perception." To this Whitehead adds, "I believe Bacon's line of thought to have expressed a more fundamental truth than do the materialistic concepts which were then being shaped as adequate for physics."[42] Later, Whitehead continues his development from this point of view: "The word *perceive* is, in our common usage, shot through and through with the notion of cognitive apprehension. So is the word *apprehension*, even with the adjective *cognitive* omitted. I will use the word *prehension* for *uncognitive apprehension*; by this I mean *apprehension* which may or may not be cognitive."[43] "The actual word is a manifold of prehensions."[44] "The realities of nature are the prehensions in nature."[45] It seems quite clear that it is only in terms of the idea of perception, taken as a model for metaphysical generalization, that Whitehead could speak of an object, for example, green, whether eternal or not, being "at *A* with a *mode* of location at *B*."[46] The latter phrase would seem to be most clearly modeled on the function of distance receptors.

It would be a digression here to consider the realist's metaphysical baggage of eternal universals, except to offer briefly a negative point respecting "mode of location." The point is not only that the doctrine of universals is of no aid in this connection, but, rather, is a confusing element in at least two ways. First, there is the difficulty in conceiving that an eternal or timeless and absolute object could—as a temporal matter, in a particular instance—take on a special reference or "mode of location"; or secondly, more in general, that it—as a completely abstract entity such as Whitehead's eternal "green"—could *have* a mode of location any more than it could have a specific spatial and temporal "ingression."

I shall not elaborate on either of these difficulties except for two remarks. First, just how an *eternal* entity—an absolutely timeless thing—could have a temporal function such as specific ingression or taking on a mode of specific reference is a metaphysical mystery best left to theologians; or else, it is a plain self-contradiction. Second, while I do not naively believe that this view of Whitehead's has any relation to fact whatsoever, I may still hazard, at least by way of analogy with his pure eternal green, a factual statement. This is not unfair, I think, because Whitehead explicitly says that this green may be perceived.[47] When the laboratory psychologist constructs such a special set of conditions for limitation of perception that a subject merely sees green, without seeing any object of any kind (in any other sense) and when care is taken so that even the texture of the green is washed out, the experimental result is that there is no apparent "mode of location" at all, perceptually, at least. As tested within a certain range of distances, the subject cannot tell or distinguish whether the green is ten feet away or fifty feet. Thus green per se has no "mode of location."

I turn to a more general consideration of the theories which have been mentioned. Russell says that his perspectives are "private,"[48] after the manner of his dualism, even though "there may be any number of unperceived perspectives"; still, contrary to his view, I should say that there is no clear sense in which the events in the "biography" of the object are private, for they never belong exclusively or absolutely to any object; for they always are also functions of other things and other conditions.

Russell is stating the object in terms of aspects which have the special bias of occurring in the perspective or frame of reference defined by *another* thing, more specifically a perceiving mind. The result of Russell's view is that he has no unitary object. The thing is blasted into countless aspects which belong to the perspectives of *other* things, and which therefore are aspects *of* nothing; consequently, they are mere apparitions. Thus, he says that "the aspects are real"; and he contrasts the object *in this respect* as being a "mere logical construction."

Whitehead seems to rid himself of Russell's bias, but only in the sense that he generalizes perceptions. Similarly to Russell, Whitehead says, "The shape of a volume is more abstract than its aspects."[49] In some sense, he does not seem to lose the unity of the object; for it also is a prehensive unification of "aspects" of *other* things. Yet he has some of the same difficulties as Russell. The formula, according to Whitehead, is that the "aspect of B from A is of the essence of A. . . . Accordingly, I will say that the aspect of B from A is the *mode* in which B enters into the composition of A."[50] What I wish to *add* is that the "aspect of B" must also enter into the composition of B, or be of the essence of B; for, otherwise, in what sense can it be said to be an "aspect" *of* B? If not, then he has set up a world in which, indeed, everything "mirrors" everything else, but there isn't any mirror and there isn't anything to be mirrored, except mirrorings. And the idea that these mirrorings, if they be such, constitute a "pattern,"[51] is no answer. It is, as Whitehead admitted, a "vicious circle."[52] It must be added, of course, that Whitehead is speaking of volumes that are mirrored. That would seem to be a highly abstract geometry rather than a concrete or existential conception.

Now it might be the case that the phrase, 'the aspect of B from A', is defined in such an abstract and special sense that it could not, without contradiction, be considered as also entering the composition of B. That is to say, the phrase may by definition be stipulated to mean the aspect only as it is strictly and solely with respect to A. Therefore, it is possible that such a contradiction might be urged, or else, at least, it might be said to be a confusion of different analytical ideas, if we say that the aspect of B also enters the composition of B or is of the essence of B. But, then, the aspect has become so private to A that it cannot be stated in any sense as belonging to B. Therefore, we seek a more neutral term, 'transaction'.

One might object that, in substituting 'transaction' for 'aspect', we simply have the same problem all over again. For, of the transaction C, there is an aspect from the standpoint A, etc. However, note first that the idea of simple location is not again involved; for example, the visual transaction of the star is centered at the earth. Second, the transaction indeed "enters" into the composition of A, but also into the composition of the star. If we distinguish the different ways in which it enters into the composition of the one or the other, we may have resolved the contradiction. These different ways would be specified in terms of particular functions.

Whitehead, contrary to the notion of simple location, believes that "in a certain sense everything is everywhere at all times."[53] The difficulty with this view lies in the fact that the "certain sense" is not specified. Perhaps Whitehead saves himself from the implication of an undifferentiated mixture of everything in everything, the "mere fusion of all that is" into the "nonentity

of indefiniteness." Rather, according to him, "The salvation of
reality is in its obstinate, irreducible matter-of-fact entities, which
are limited to be no other than themselves."[54] Again, "An event
is there and not here (or here and not there); it is then and not
now (or now and not then)"; it "is a fundamental property of
events" that they "can only be in one place at a time."[55] All this
still does not specify the sense in which "everything is everywhere," and that vagueness gives Lovejoy the opportunity to
quote Plotinus and Nicholas of Cues, as though relevant, and to
conclude that "the sense in which 'everything' is asserted to be
'everywhere at all times' is no literal sense."[56]

My problem is one that is prior to these ponderous and cosmic
questions. While I should be most doubtful that "everything is
everywhere," still that is not my problem. I am concerned with
the specific sense in which anything may be said to be any particular place at all. And I do mean this in a literal sense, namely
that it must be stated in terms of a specific function and must
specify events, or provide for the specification of these functions
and events.

One difficulty with setting up perception as the metaphysical
foundation of reality is that perception is made to be autonomous. Some think, and I would say, that perception does disclose
an objective world in which the organism is operating; but that
would require that perception be stated in such a way that it is
continuous with other transactions with that world. To do so
requires that perception consist of a good deal more than the
sensations or sense-data of Russell or the ingressing eternal green
of Whitehead, for they are the abstract immediate content of
perception and these immediacies are just what uniquely distinguishes perception from other transactions; they do not connect them in a continuity. It it little wonder that when thus
isolated abstractly they are thought to be subjective, for this isolation is an analytical abstraction of immediacy as such, and the
abstract results are indeed secondary qualities. More strictly,

the abstractions are not qualities at all but are references to the immediacy of qualities. In any case, perception as a genuine function has been lost.

The world, so far as it is disclosed, must answer to the whole act of the organism, even to frustrations of the act, and this is essential if perception is to perform its biological function in the act. Thus perception is shot through with meanings and impulses which arise out of other transactions of the activity. And so the reaction of the organism as a whole can enter into the perceptual act.

In the more reflective and systematic views of men, the so-called secondary or consummatory qualities of the distance receptors have never been essential characteristics of the world from Democritus until today. This may be substantiated if one remembers that, in ordinary or usual activity, perception does not exist for its own sake but to facilitate the larger act of which it is only one phase. For the same reason, perception is not the central thing in the higher epistemological functions. However, traditional epistemology has not only concerned itself more or less exclusively with perception, but worse than that, with the still more narrow sense of abstract immediacies. Obviously, there is such a thing as observation, but it consists of a great deal more than mere presences of sense-data. Yet even so, while observation plays a very important role, experimental, scientific inquiry nevertheless consists of a great deal more than observation. Emphatically, if one indicates something and wants to know "what it is," he is not answered by merely pointing to what is present in its sheer immediacy.

Russell's strange ambivalence is that when he is arguing for his epistemological dualism he treats all appearances as subjective and states his external world in terms of the concepts of abstract physics. The external world is a distribution of energy. But in his attempt to set forth a relativism, he seeks to state everything in terms of appearances. The logical positivist does the same thing, using the equivalent word 'phenomena', although he seeks to do this under the guise that it is just so much talk.

I have sought to return the qualitative and consummatory things to the natural world, for they are just as real if and when they occur and, under certain conditions, just as much characteristics of things, as is anything else. But while they have their continuities and connections with other things—the fact that colors are extended has been noted often enough, and forgotten —nonetheless, like anything else, they are peculiar, and we cannot adequately state the world merely in their terms.

We must, I think, turn to other functions of the object, in addition to appearances, in order to get a more adequate account, even of appearances. If there is any plausibility in Russell's alternative theory, his idea of the star located a thousand light-years away, it does not lie merely in the common notion that a thing is located in terms of its boundaries, but also in the notion that its boundaries are in turn defined in terms of a function, namely resistance. If we approach the thing we bump into it. Even Russell, defining the location of the penny as a point of intersection of lines, somewhat naively remarks that if we are to extend the lines to their intersection we must remove the penny.[57] In the first place, if the penny is nothing but a series of visual aspects, one wonders what it is that has to be removed. Moreover, if the removal is nevertheless required, it would seem that, upon removal, his intersections of lines would only indicate where the penny had been, at most. In any case, I suggest that it is this resistance of the unremoved penny into which we bump that would be much more commonly used to define the location of the penny than would Russell's series of appearances or aspects, and, indeed, this location is too readily assumed to be the only function. Something of that sort is just what Russell does use in respect to his distant star. Moreover, the act of removing the penny can hardly be stated purely in terms of visual

aspects. Suddenly, the penny must answer to the hand that re-
moves it.

It is admitted or, rather, asserted, that the boundaries of a
thing, which is in some cases its hard surface, may be used as one
function with which to define the location of the object in that
respect. But it has previously been noted that this is implicit in
the doctrine of the absolute object. What that doctrine did was
to seize upon one function to make it absolute. I am not setting
up resistance as the ultimate function for defining location. Its
use is an historical fact. My point is not to disparage the use of
one or the other function to define the location of the penny but
merely to point them out as alternative functions among innumerable others in terms of which to define the location of the object. That is to say, more ordinarily, the concept of the location of
the object is given the specific meaning that the thing is in a
boundary defined by the function of a hard and rigid surface so
that we reach the thing only upon contact. If one goes in the
direction of the thing he sees until he bumps into it, then he is at
the thing. We can lay our hand on the hard surface and say,
"This, here, is the thing." Much too unqualifiedly or uncritically,
something of this sort is what is commonly meant by the physical thing of ordinary experience.

I wish to do two things in this connection: to define the thing
in terms that are not necessarily perceptual, much less merely
visual, and in terms of events which belong to the frame of
reference of *that* thing. These events will also belong to the
frames of reference of other things. Obviously, there is no sense
in which the aspects in a variety of perspectives can constitute a
unitary thing, unless they can be identified with the thing itself.
That means the identification of an aspect in one perspective
with an aspect in another as being the same thing. The multipli-
cation of perspectives, frames of reference, or spaces does not
multiply objects, for the object is an organization of perspectives.
If we substitute the term 'transaction' for 'aspect' then we can

say that the transaction is an event in the biography of the thing.
It constitutes a property of the thing and so it constitutes the
thing. Transactions involve other things as well—they are intersections of biographies. When Russell calls them "private," it
seems to me that he is confusing relativity with subjectivism,
which is the traditional view. Russell, enclosed in the private
space of his own mind, seems unable to enter or to conceive of
the perspective of the object. To this extent he is, if not a solipsist,
then a Berkeleian. This is the problem which Mead met and
resolved in his treatment of the physical object; namely, the
sense in which the physical object has a perspective of its own,
or, in his phraseology, the sense in which the object has an inside and not merely surface aspects. It is not a mere phenomenon
or appearance or an aspect in the private perspective of a mind.

Russell tries to save himself from Berkeleian idealism by organizing all these private perspectives into a superperspective
which he turns over to the physicist. But the frame of reference
from the standpoint of the object is not obviously any more a
superperspective than is any other frame of reference. Moreover,
I suggest that the organization of frames of reference is made in
terms of transformation equations and not in terms of a superperspective which, as a perspective, is meaningless. The idealists
called it the Absolute.

Mead, of course, recognized that at simpler levels of ordinary
human activity, we do not get into the perspective of the object,
or bring any other perspectives within our experience, by means
of abstract transformation equations. We do so by means of the
social act, as he defines it. And that is the same means by which
we get the perspectives which Russell takes for granted as the
private perspectives of *other* minds; and, correspondingly, it is
the way in which we come to a recognition of our own perspective *as such*. There is, in principle, no difference.

Russell's analysis of the thing in terms of aspects releases one
from the naive assumption that the hard surface is the only
function for defining the location of the object. And, indeed,

not everything lends itself readily to being defined in terms of hard surface. Numerous examples to the contrary suggest themselves—a cloud with feathery edges on which we cannot lay a hand, or a cyclone. Let us consider, however, only one example, an explosion. In our day of the fission and the fusion bombs, explosions are becoming more important, and perhaps worthier of consideration than tables and pennies.

Where is the explosion located? Hardly at a mere point, for an explosion is not confined within a point. But if not at a point, what are its boundaries? Perhaps the atmospheric shock wave is taken to be the explosion. It does not, however, remain in one place, and whether near at hand it sweeps aside a building or at a greater distance it breaks windows, the explosion is wherever it does anything. However, the ground shock wave, with equal legitimacy, may be called the explosion. Again, the flash of burning light searing things in an expanding area and affecting retinas at a great distance is also the explosion. Perhaps a theoretical physicist would limit the explosion to the region in which atomic changes are going on.

Location is not simple. We are likely to define the extent of the explosion in terms of any of its significant functions. I suggest that the location of a thing within its hard surface, if it has one, is legitimate enough for some questions, but it is not absolute or final. Rather, any direct function or transaction of the thing has equally a legitimate claim to constitute the thing and hence its location.

I believe that the problem of temporal boundaries is just as relevant as that of spatial boundaries, for location is not merely spatial but spatiotemporal. I do not wish to pursue this problem, but it may be noted in passing that temporal boundaries are no simpler than spatial boundaries. For instance, consider a man who has had an ax for twenty years. He has changed the handle four times and the blade twice. Again, consider the meaning of the present suggested by James in his concept of the specious present. We speak of the present hour, the present year, the present century. If we do not agree to an instantaneous present, then we have the problem of its duration. And the notion of an instantaneous present, rather than being possible, is a mathematical abstraction. However, I return to the problem in terms of spatial location.

It has been noted that a penny does not merely appear. It is handled. It works in coin machines and reacts to acids. Thus, in place of Russell's word 'aspect' I would prefer to substitute the word 'transaction' as Dewey suggests. I am defining the thing in terms of transactions of whatever kind. A thing is what it does, and therefore it is wherever it does anything. Anything that it does involves other things. Therefore, when we see the star, there is indeed no such magic by which a mind snaps back like a stretched rope to something a thousand light-years away, for *the star is here*. No paradox is involved, for this does not imply that the whole burning mass that would vaporize us, were we near it, is here.

The idea that the star is here may seem too strange and paradoxical to some, or else, perhaps, plainly false. But possibly the scientist is more imaginative in this respect than the philosopher. A writer of scientific articles remarks that several astronomers now think the sun's corona or outer atmosphere actually reaches to the earth and beyond in tenuous form. Thus the earth and sun really touch one another. I mention this not to accept scientific speculation as final but to support two points: (1) that the idea that the sun is here is not a nonsense notion if taken with explicit definition; and (2) that for the purpose of this remark, the 'sun' is defined in terms of one of its functions, its corona. To this I would add another function, namely the light that it gives off.

When we say that a thing, a building for example, is here as we lay our hand on it, we would not be taken to mean that the whole building is located in the small area of immediate contact. Neither, in saying that the star is here, need we mean that the whole burning mass of the star is here, but only as much of the star as constitutes a photon or so of light. The perceived twinkling light, not to mention other conditions, is a transaction between us and the star, and it is a minute constituent of the star. The fact that the photon of light is only a minute part of the star does not put the twinkling light into one metaphysical realm, mind, and the rest of the star into another, the external world. Hence, it is unnecessary to assume the metaphysical baggage that goes with that arbitrary division. Rather, we identify the distant twinkling light with the star, and the astronomer turns his telescope in the direction of the twinkling light that he sees. He analyzes the spectrum of that same light and identifies the elements of the star exactly as he analyzes something in his laboratory. The result is an analysis of the star.

We may distinguish between the thing in its own perspective and the thing as perceived as distinct perspectives, but perspectives in which things in one perspective are identified with things in another. From the standpoint of the object, the object is here, to the extent of its function. From the standpoint or perspective of the perceiver, the object is there, and the twinkling light is a distant object. Of course, it is not perceived as being many millions of miles or light-years away; that is a calculation of astronomy. To the ancient Greeks, the heavenly lights were as so many campfires, or "bowls of fire," a few miles away. Perceptually, they are merely "out there."

It still may seem that I have merely substituted two perspectives, that of the object and that of the perceiver, for the two worlds of the metaphysical dualist, and with the same results. However, I am not stating the perspective of the perceiver in terms of abstracted immediacies, but rather in terms of transactions. This would be better represented by the intersection of two biographies. A biography of General Grant would not be complete without presentation of his transactions with General Lee; transactions which are, therefore, not merely and solely Grant's, but into which Lee enters from his own standpoint. That is to say, one could not understand the problems that

Grant faced, without understanding Lee and his problems. Stated more generally, no adequate view of a transaction can be given purely in terms of one perspective. Otherwise, there are anomalies. The advancement of the perihelion of Mercury cannot be accounted for purely in terms of a single frame of reference. Therein lies the need for a theory of perspectives.

Lovejoy objects that "if a datum, whatever its supposed situation, is *only* a perspective appearance, if it is what it is solely from the standpoint of the percipient and only for him, and in the last analysis, only by virtue of his individual constitution, then his experiencing of it would not appear to afford what is commonly understood as knowledge." [58] This criticism may have some pertinence to Russell's theory of perspectives, because his aspects are mere immediacies. However that may be, the difficulty which Lovejoy here ascribes to relativism may be applied to his own position, redoubled. "If a datum," that is, all experience, is merely one's own subjective mental states, "then," indeed, "his experiencing of it would not appear to afford what is commonly understood as knowledge" of a metaphysically separated external world. This is so blatant that it has commonly been recognized as the solipsistic implication of that view, as, for instance, in the case of Russell. The realist has attempted to brush it off as merely the inevitable egocentric predicament which must simply be ignored. I do not refer to the difficulties of the dualist in order to make use of a *tu quoque* argument, but to introduce a contrast between the two views by way of method.

Lovejoy says, respecting objective relativism, "It is quietly assumed that the event may be *known* from many standpoints." [59] The point is that this is exactly what is characteristic of *knowing*, especially in its most emphatic sense (Lovejoy emphasized the word), as distinct from mere dumb presence. Mead was a good deal more than quiet,[60] for he gave considerable attention to the question of how the organism may come to adopt the attitudes of a variety of perspectives. I need not review his work. It is striking in that he could construct a genuine theory about it, in contrast to the simple appeal to faith by dualists like Santayana or Russell.

There is no more need to refer the twinkling light to a subjective mental state than there is in the case of the telescope that the astronomer points in the direction of the twinkling light, and the astronomer identifies the telescope that he sees with the telescope that he points, as a matter of course. Similarly, it is the real star that we see, just as much as it is the real telescope or the real building that we touch.

I do not assume that these remarks serve to refute mind-matter dualism, for the dualist may always retranslate the situation into his own terms. I seek only to offer an alternative view. Thus, perhaps, we can state the case with reasonable adequacy without that dualism. It is desirable to do so because the addition of the dualistic assumptions does not make the story any more adequate with respect to admitted facts, yet carries with it some insoluble problems. Not only does the problem of solipsism dog it, but also the connected difficulty of metaphysical dualism presenting the problem of other minds in an insoluble form. It is a pseudo-problem, because it presupposes self-consciousness, while calling into question the conditions required for self-consciousness. That is to say, according to the thought of Mead, in one's early social development one comes to take others into account from their standpoint, not only for the advantage of dealing with others, but as a condition for self-consciousness. It is only as one can adopt the attitude of another that he can become an object to himself and have self-consciousness. Thus other minds appear in the experience of the individual as a part of the process of his having a mind of his own.

The statement that the star is here serves to indicate that location is not simple and is ambiguous unless defined in terms relevant to the specific case. What the realist is doing when he locates the visual world inside the brain is illegitimately shifting from one function to another, or, as we may now say, he is confusing perspectives. This is, indeed, a fallacy of simple location.

The illegitimacy of the shift is exhibited when the dualist labori-
ously traces the wave of energy from the star to the retina and
up the optic nerve to the brain, and then suddenly announces a
"sensation" or "percept," as though that were part of the same
story. Evidently, he merely stops one story and begins another.[61]
The so-called causal theory of perception is a misnomer. No one
ever suggested a theory as to how nerve energy can cause a sensation. There is no such theory either to be asserted or denied.
The reason why no one has or can suggest such a theory is that,
in this case, the so-called cause and effect have nothing in common because they constitute different frames of reference. Thus,
there is no causal relation between them, but there are transformation functions.

   In earlier views, what is relative or what is presented as perspective was taken as a distortion of the "real." And we have
seen that, in terms of one major line of thought, it could be considered to be a distortion because the real or absolute was reduced to contact. That is to say, while—as Democritus and
Berkeley put it—the expression 'were we at the thing' is taken
more nearly to be a criterion of its reality; nevertheless, that is
not absolute but is another perspective. Even were we at or near
the thing, we still do not get something absolute. If we photograph the track from nearby, but from one side, and if we put
a straightedge on our photograph, we find that the track in the
photograph is curved. Thus, in the present sense, any perspective
far or near is a distortion; what is near may in some respects be
taken to be less distorted, but actually, in some respects, it is
more so. At any rate, the ultimate standard is contact.

   The alternative to the contact view is that we state the nature
of things in terms of points of view other than our own. This is
irreducibly a distance function. The older view dealt with the
distant thing, but only in terms of what it would be were we at
it, ultimately in contact. This is a promise, which is temporal;
but if we say the thing now is such a thing, then we are setting
up, or supposing, simultaneity. In this 'reality' the perspective

is eliminated. But if the nature of the thing involves irreducible points of view, then the contact notion is eliminated and distance becomes essential. This is not chaos, for we may translate from one perspective to another, but the formulae of translation do not themselves denote an absolute. They identify a thing in one perspective with a thing in another and are reconciliations of perspectives.

One perspective is a distortion, not in the sense in which an absolute object is implicated but, rather, in the sense in which other perspectives are implicated. Thus the phenomena in our perspective cannot be accounted for except in terms of other perspectives. When Fichte proposed to treat others as merely a creation of his own ego, some wanted to know what Frau Fichte thought about that.

So far as we bring varied perspectives into our own perspective, we have objects. This bringing of perspectives into our own is, perhaps, not literal; it is constituted by the meaning of the thing and it is constituted in a peculiar way. There is, for instance, the sense in which meanings arise from perspectives within the history of the individual. But so far as the object is an *other*, with its own perspective, it does not belong to the history of the individual, except at an intersection. The sense in which it is brought within the individual's experience is a social act in which the individual takes the attitude of the thing. There is also the sense in which the object is there as a common object, belonging to a number of perspectives, and this is also social. So far as the thing has meanings which belong to other perspectives, it is a common object. In that sense the object is an intersection of perspectives. The perceptual object is the result of the conservation of perceptual perspectives within the individual's experience, and conservation is in the form of meanings. The meanings are constituted by the habits or tendencies to act developed in other situations and appearing as inhibited impulses which release or guide action. The conceptual object performs somewhat similar functions.

V

The Metaphysical Status of Qualitative Things

I am concerned with the metaphysical status of qualities and values. If, as has been suggested, we define 'metaphysics' in larger terms—to mean any theory of reality—then we have a more neutral definition. There may be various theories of reality, among which there may be some having as a content a general theory of nature that is quite independent of any question of a transcendent reality. I wish to present such a view in the form of a relativistic view of the status of values. From the standpoint of pragmatism, it will have a factual meaning because it will be stated in empirical terms. However, I refer to an earlier discussion for the sake of saying that I am not implying acceptance of a traditional interpretation of 'empirical' in terms of sensations—an interpretation which plays so prominent a role in the views that the realist and logical positivist have carried over from the seventeenth and eighteenth centuries. My intent, rather, is to present a metaphysical theory of qualities or qualitative things as objective, thus constituting objective grounds for generalization as properties, and to extend this view to include values, for values belong to a qualitative world.

With respect to the use of the word 'property', it may add clarity to note once more that the word is commonly used in different senses. One ambiguity is that it may be used to denote concrete or particular instances, although the word 'instance' implies generalization. Again, it may refer to the generalization and hence it may mean generalized characteristics. Of course, the expression 'generalized characteristics' is a pleonasm, for the word 'characteristic' implies some degree of generality. The concrete and the generalized senses, to which I have referred, seem to me to be confused in the realistic metaphysical doctrine of universals. Thus, Whitehead's eternal green ingresses into and is constitutive of the particular event. On the other hand, Dewey distinguishes between 'green', which refers to the particular quality of direct experience, and 'greenness', which indicates the generalized characteristic. I would prefer to reserve the word 'property' to mean, more strictly, a generalized characteristic; although to express this consistently would seem to result in circumlocutions that would distract attention from the main point of the moment.

The major objection concerning the assignment of objectivity to qualities and values occurs in "epistemological dualism." As that is in direct conflict with what I have to suggest, some attention to it is called for. It should be remarked, however, that my stated aim is to develop a metaphysical view; not to deal with epistemology. Upon considering a genuinely epistemological distinction, I would go so far in agreeing—not in objecting—to the extent of saying that there is indeed a difference between a beefsteak and ideas or knowledge about a beefsteak. Almost any hungry man would vouch for that distinction. However, epistemological dualism, as traditionally developed, includes a metaphysical dualism and, I should say, confuses the two. Locke calls the qualities of experience "ideas," an epistemological term. It is the metaphysical dualism that is relevant to my problem.

One difficulty, to which I shall later refer, is that the injection of the epistemological into the argument leads to a confusion of the treatment of perception as an occurrence—with which I am concerned—with a treatment of the epistemological function of perception—with which I am not concerned. Connected with this is the repeated use of the term 'cognoscendum' by the epistemological dualist, as though it were a necessary concept of perception. As a term, the word seems to be epistemological in meaning, and so it is readily used by the epistemological dualist as a matter of course. The term might be used appropriately to refer to objects of knowledge; for instance, to refer to a "scientific object." However, the term appears to be defined as the object from which the causal chain ending in perception is assumed to have started. It is not at all clear that the starting of causal chains, even those that end in perception, is an epistemic function.

Moreover, when the epistemological dualist is enthusiastically proving that the qualities of experience cannot be ascribed to the physical things of the world, he elaborates on the idea that the mechanism of perception is such a complex matter that an indefinite number of numerically distinct objects are causally involved in the perception. This idea provides some difficulties, I think, for a simple subjective-objective dualism, because, it would seem, each of the indefinite number of numerically distinct objects causally involved in the perception would be starting causal chains that end in the perception and would thereby qualify for the generously defined meaning of 'cognoscendum'. This surely does not lend itself to the simplicity of a dualistic correspondence doctrine.

I am only concerned incidentally with epistemological dualism, and not with a general refutation of it. Its refutation has already been accomplished adequately by Hume, Santayana, and Russell, when they drew its solipsistic implications, from which they escaped by playing backgammon, or by faith, or by dogmatic assertion. If the conclusion is false, then all or some of the premises are in some major way false. Thus, a refutation is hardly a matter of interest, unless to exhibit some novelty of argument. I need not mention attacks which have been leveled at this dualism by pragmatists and analysts. But while it may therefore be the case that one need not take this dualism seriously as an acceptable view, and it does seem to be a dead issue in current philosophy, still there remains something to be learned, I think, in the study of some of the problems and arguments raised by those eminent thinkers.

In the previous chapters, it has seemed most relevant to

discuss this problem in terms of an historical development. This may raise the question whether more nearly contemporary dualists need consider that discussion to be relevant to their views. I think that, in this respect, one may extend the scope of some remarks of William P. Montague:

> When one turns from the original and richly varying metaphysical affiliations of the Critical Realists to the bare nucleus of epistemological doctrine on which they were all agreed and which constitutes the definition of Critical Realism itself, I am myself unable to see anything either rich or original. The theory may be true but it is certainly not new. It is, indeed, nothing but a restatement of the Epistemological Dualism which is explicit in Locke and Descartes and implicit in Hobbes, Spinoza and the other modern Philosophers prior to Berkeley.[1]

The dualistic doctrine that all the things of our experience are merely our own subjective mental states is so strange a doctrine that it would require meticulous proof. It is strange because we cannot and do not act on that doctrine in our normal activities. Yet it may be complained that by that remark I thus pay undue attention to the way the ordinary man treats perceptual qualities. Very well, then, it is so strange that even so ardent a defender of dualism as Lovejoy cannot rest comfortably at home with it:

> ... in the warmth and facility of perceiving it is somewhat difficult even for the convinced dualist to bear in mind that the table that he sees or the pen that he feels between his fingers is merely a private 'idea' (in the Lockian sense), distinct from the independent existent which is once for all 'out there' (as he at least supposes) for his and other men's knowing. To think dualistically all the time puts, at least, a considerable strain upon the human mind; and it was natural to seek relief from that strain.[2]

My only suggested change of this passage would be to enlarge the opening words; for even the dualist, I imagine, is not always engaged in merely perceiving. It is not merely perceiving—on which the dualist focuses in a myopic, hypnotic way—but the conduct of human affairs that puts this strain on belief, for one cannot act upon this hypothesis. Therefore, if the dualist, when his views logically end in solipsism, can forget his logic and say simply that it just isn't so, we may equally take that attitude toward the dualism itself and with better grace, for we are not committed to propositions that imply dualism or solipsism.

Lovejoy begins by simply injecting "subjectivity" into his treatment by definition: "In a sense which we shall call 'causal subjectivity', anything is described as subjective when it is assumed to have as a necessary condition of its existence the occurrence of a percipient event."[3] Just what does this mean respecting what is perceived? Presumably, having "as a necessary condition of its existence the occurrence of a percipient event," means that the "entity" or "character"—the words are his—or what is perceived is in some sense a result "of a percipient event." But just what is meant by a "percipient event" which is distinct from but has, as a result, what we perceive? All that I would mean by 'a percipient event' would be a case of perception, namely, a case in which x perceives y. According to that meaning, perceptual qualities would be constituent in part of the percipient event. But Lovejoy's point appears to be that what we perceive is a *result* of the percipient event. Yet it seems to be nonsense to say that what x perceives is a result of x perceiving y.

Lovejoy is extremely ambiguous and vague as to precisely what he does mean by 'the percipient event' and this ambiguity is a most significant difficulty because it is repeatedly a key term in his argument for subjectivity. As an alternative to the above, perhaps he means by 'the percipient event' not the perception at all, but the conditions for the perception. Certainly, I would not deny that the organism is a condition, among other conditions, for the organism's perceiving y, for that would seem to be a tautology. Yet, that hardly gives Lovejoy what he wants. He says of what is perceived, "such characters form a class of mind-begotten, or at all events of brain-begotten, existents."[4]

For a metaphysical dualist—of all people—this ambivalent

confusion of the all-important metaphysical distinction between brain and mind is amazing, and not a little disconcerting for the purposes of discussion. At any rate, there is no obvious sense in which the results of physical and physiological processes belong to some metaphysical realm differing from that of the physical and physiological processes themselves. On the other hand, his injecting of the mind into the definition is merely begging the question respecting a subjective or mental realm.

Lovejoy seems to go even further than making the percipient event, whatever that may be, "a necessary condition." It is not quite clear, but he seems to mean that it is the sole condition. He says:

It is, of course, not immediately apparent that a character which exists only as a consequence of a percipient event in me, and only while I am perceiving it, *can* legitimately or intelligibly be said to be an attribute of an object or an "event" assumed to exist independently of perception.[5]

If one accepts his hypothesis, his reasoning may be quite correct. However, in referring to what is perceived, I am not referring to what "exists *only* as a consequence" (my italics) of conditions of the organism. That will be developed subsequently.

According to Lovejoy, the argument for metaphysical dualism has two stages. First, there is the claim that the qualities could not be identified with objective things; i.e., that they are numerically distinct from those things. Curiously, Lovejoy labels this numerical distinctness "epistemological dualism," a label that may suggest that he has proved more than he has, even were the argument conclusive. Second, the metaphysical dualist claims that qualities and values belong to a second metaphysical realm, a mental or subjective realm, and therefore could not be properties of things in a different metaphysical realm, the objective world. Lovejoy calls this "psychophysical dualism."[6]

It is essential to distinguish these two arguments, because the argument for numerical distinctness, while it may be a condition for a subjective-objective dualism, does not imply that anything is mental or subjective in the metaphysical sense as Lovejoy emphatically admits. Nonetheless, he reiterates this admittedly inconclusive argument throughout his book. The question of numerical distinctness has been discussed in Chapters III and IV, "The Nature of Things" and "The Location of the Object." So, I turn to the second argument—that qualities and values belong in a subjective rather than the objective world—because it is more relevant to the present chapter.

In his argument for psychophysical dualism, Lovejoy first makes the point that "The world of 'mental' entities served as an isolation-camp for all the 'wild data,' "[7] such as dreams, hallucinations, illusions, errors, and objects of imagination. The required proof of membership in that camp is that *"the experienced properties and relations of the datum are . . . incompatible with the defining properties of the class 'physical objects.' "*[8] However, getting to the crux of the matter, Lovejoy admits that this still leaves the question whether "normal and veridical perception" should equally be assigned to this realm of "wild data."[9] On this all-important point, the central issue, Lovejoy's argument suddenly becomes exceedingly vague and uncharacteristically brief. A search of the pertinent pages in *The Revolt against Dualism*[10] discloses almost no argument whatever directed toward the precise point, the extension of the mental to cover "normal and veridical perception." He assures us that this extension is "intelligible and natural,"[11] although, a few lines before, he admits that it may "seem paradoxical" to lump illusions and hallucinations with "normal and veridical perception."

Apart from a reiteration of the numerical distinctness argument, what he says on this precise point is a summary of what he had said on the previous page—not about "normal and veridical perception," but about "imagination" or "illusion," namely, a case of having "a visual image of your friend sitting in a chair which is in fact empty." The argument is: "if you assume the presence in the space before you of a physical object with the character which the percept is experienced as possessing, *at the time when it is experienced,* you disturb the order of the physicist's world, and even the world of common sense, not less than if you thrust into it the creatures of your imagination or your dream."[12] Almost on this sentence alone rests the whole weight of the metaphysical realm of the mental; I mean, so far as it is to be extended, supposedly, to include "normal and veridical perception." Yet we see that this is merely a repetition of what was to be proved.

In what way does the penny that I observe to fall violate the laws of physics, or act in any way, as observed, "incompatible with the defining properties of the class 'physical objects' "? There is nothing in the "character" of the observed penny to bring it into question as a physical object. The reference in the above argument to the "character" of the observed thing is a red herring which disguises the fact that the argument is merely a repetition of the numerical distinctness argument, as the next lines show:

The astronomer, for example, takes account in his computations of the distant star which *was* in a certain region of the heavens some thousands of years ago; but he does not assume, in addition to this, that there is *now* in that region a second star with precisely the same spectrum and luminosity.[13]

But, once more, how does this prove that the spectrum and luminosity or a photograph of the twinkling light or an observation of it is in any way mental or subjective? Nothing is said in the argument about the "character" of any of them that would make them questionable. Indeed, it is asserted, by the hypothesis, that the two have "precisely the same spectrum and luminosity." Obviously, this is merely a reiteration of the inconclusive numerical distinctness argument, which is the source of his second star.

By the "character" to which reference is made above—as if it were relevant to his psychophysical argument—Lovejoy may have in mind, for instance, the circular and elliptical appearances of the penny, although he neglects specifying what he means at this key point. However, the appearance of the penny would not be precisely pertinent to the present and central issue, for it is a matter of the geometry of optics. Thus, it belongs to his numerical distinctness argument which was considered in Chapters III and IV, and to which further reference will be made, in principle, in this chapter. Once again, that argument is admittedly inconclusive respecting any mental realm of a metaphysical sort.

Lovejoy continues to repeat his point and refer to the above as "sufficiently" establishing it.

The percept . . . fails, in definite ways, to manifest the usually accepted criteria of membership in the material world. Put the percept, *in addition* to the objects which it is taken to reveal, into that world at the actual moment of perception, and you seem to play havoc with the laws of physics—as has been sufficiently pointed out in the first lecture.[14]

When Lovejoy speaks of putting "the percept, *in addition* to the objects which it is taken to reveal," into the material world, he is begging the question of his own dualism. Many things revealed in normal and veridical experience have extension, shape, size, motion, resistance, weight, color, sound, odor, taste, beauty, etc., and do not obviously violate the laws of physics. It is Lovejoy's problem, on his own terms, to show that all of them do. He does not do so.

In speaking of physical objects or of the laws of physics, it may be well to note again that physics selects certain features of things, just as other inquiries and concerns do, like geology, the real estate business, biology, psychology, or jurisprudence. It is a fallacy to treat things as if they have no other features than those that answer the concerns of a particular inquiry—for instance, those that answer to the concepts of physics, although they do not thereby violate the laws of physics.

I have not considered here the legitimacy of Lovejoy's mental realm wherein he would dispose of "wild data." Some questions of illusions will be discussed later by way of illustration. It may be remarked here that the fact that imaginary pennies will not work in ordinary coin machines does not necessarily call for any second mental or subjective metaphysical realm, because alternative views are at least possible. I do not really know very much about hallucinations, but I suggest that the attempt to explain them by the a priori method of metaphysical realms is so "easy" and hasty as to be almost flippant. They require a great deal of study, on the grounds of other presuppositions. Perhaps they are functions of organisms under various conditions. All these are physical, whatever else they also are. As I will discuss later, further dealing with a situation will assign the object or some character of the object to the place that it appears to have or to some peripheral conditions or to the organism, as a matter of the particular case, not by a priori determination.

Now as to qualitative things, perhaps I can make three summary statements which may clarify the point of view that I will take: (1) The first would seem obvious to common sense; namely, that under certain conditions some things are actually and veridically green. Here I refer to actual occurrences or transactions. (2) We may also say of some such things that they have the characteristic or property of being green, or the property greenness, just as we would say significantly of a tool that it is a hammer, although it is not hammering, or of a man that he is a swimmer although he is not swimming. This expresses the nature of the thing. (3) In general form, the two statements above are the kinds of statements that we apply to all transactions and statements of the nature of things, and hence subjectivity is not any more involved in the one case than in the other. Thus, the question of subjectivity is not necessarily raised when the same analysis is applied to perception.

The present aim is not to distinguish values as such, for that will be the subject of the next chapter. Rather, the aim here is to assimilate inquiry respecting the existential status of qualities of experience, by means of a theory of qualities which treats them objectively in a methodological sense; that is to say, as functions of sets of conditions rather than as things located somewhere in a special realm set up by a subjective-objective metaphysical dualism. Thus, without choosing either side of that dualism, the thesis may be stated—in first approximation—that qualities, including values, are just as objective as are any other occurrences.

The use of the word 'quality' does not presuppose a substance-attribute dualism, if one does not interpret 'quality' in terms of such a dualism. In particular, there are some who claim to have given up that dualism, but who nevertheless insist upon an emphatic distinction being made between saying 'Some qualitative things are values' and saying 'Some qualities are values'. It may clarify my intent to recall that this chapter by its title is concerned with qualitative things, assuming at the same time that all existential things are material things; i.e., that they have material properties. And I may inject also, as nominal definition, that by 'values', in the concrete sense, I mean good things. This question leads directly to the very issue to be discussed, but the point of view can be anticipated in a very general way by saying that it will be obvious that some phases of processes are more enduring than others and depend therefore upon somewhat different conditions. The more enduring is sometimes identified with the *thing* which is then said to *have* the less enduring phases. Nevertheless, while such distinctions are often important, they are not final and are not metaphysical distinctions. But before going on to discuss the main problem, I should like first to remark upon what seems to me to be its larger import.

The theory to be set forth has a direct bearing upon certain views mentioned in Chapter I; i.e., that there are no such things as ethical judgments. We have seen that one of the reasons given for this view is more often stated axiomatically than argued. In its slogan form it says one cannot infer the "ought" from the "is." In other language, it is the proposition that no factual statements can be normative. In a previous article,[15] I have given some reason to suppose that this proposition is false and that it does not appear to be made intelligible by those who do argue for it rather than, as is often the case, taking it as a pure dogma.

My suggestion—contrary to the foregoing views—is that, if values may be dealt with in some objective fashion, especially in the methodological sense, then empirically factual statements may be made about them, as values; and that such statements constitute the grounds for normative statements, within any useful sense of that word. In brief, the proposition may be made that if there is anything worthwhile in life, then there is, to a reasonable degree, a factual ground for some sort of ethics, except for those who are still troubled by a need for approval from some "higher" authority. I agree with the logical positivist or the analyst that many other meanings are superstitions or merely express tribal customs or else are emotional ejaculations. I propose to discuss the antecedent of this hypothetical proposition— the objective status of values—but not the consequent, for there is not space to discuss the latter, except for two brief remarks by way of qualification. First, if values are relative, then the "norms" are relative, presumably, in the relevant sense. Second, ethics can be defined with reference to objective values. Conduct which is essential for the security and development of values is right or moral; conduct which renders values impossible is wrong or immoral. Therefore, the question of right and wrong becomes a factual question, however complex it may turn out to be, if values are objective.

In a general way, I mean by a value[16] an object (or function) which can give human beings deep and growing satisfaction. I may here anticipate an argument by noting that the word "give" designates a causal relation and, consequently, a real property of the object, although not an absolute property. The implication is that values are far from being absolute or certain or eternal or self-subsisting or self-guaranteeing; that is, in part, why they require discrimination and the enlistment of our active endeavor.

Values are too numerous to mention except by most general *kinds*: aesthetic objects, homes, friendships, other various forms of human associations, vocations, thought and inquiry, as well as other forms of human endeavor, if and when they give human beings deep and growing satisfaction. However, a value—like any real or existing thing—is particular and unique, although not one of Russell's "ultimate simples," and would have to be indicated by a proper name or by a definite description. Absolute uniqueness is not implied, of course, for things are more or less comparable. But one home is never quite like another.

The view of the objectivity of value which will be stated may be clarified by contrast, at least in summary fashion, with other views. Both history and current discussion impose recognition of the fact that quality and value have been conceived in terms of a subjective-objective metaphysical dualism. According to this conception, objectivity is supposed to be absolute, and whatever is relative is subjective. The purpose of this discussion is to develop an objective theory that is relative.

Extended discussion of the subjective theory can be avoided by noting here that the typical argument for the subjectivity of value is often negative; namely, that objectivity is absolute, while values are not. Consequently, attention may begin with the theory thus denied. Doctrines that values are objective in the sense that they are absolute have been developed along rather different lines, but they may be distinguished as of two kinds: one stated in terms of universals; the other in terms of the absolute object.

The doctrine that values are universals means, I presume, that there exist or subsist—either in value objects or in some eternal realm—fixed universals which somehow or other determine their own value. Such a view has only negative relevance to the use of the term 'value' in this book because I am concerned with a theory that must provide for an empirical or factual approach. Consequently, it is only briefly considered here. It is noted at all because the subjectivist[17] sometimes argues as though he has disposed of objectivity, particularly in reference to values, when he has disposed of the doctrine of universals. Not only does the doctrine of universal values have difficulties on its own account, but it also carries the full weight of objections to the more general metaphysic of universals. I have already given some attention to universals, and I am not concerned with giving any full analysis either of the more special doctrine of universal values or of the more general doctrine of universals, but only to indicate their inadequacy respecting an empirical or factual method.

One objection to the doctrine of universal values is that it implies that, if one learns to appreciate or to know the absolute universal beauty in one thing, then he should appreciate or know it in some or all other things in which it subsists. But it is evident as a matter of fact that this is not the case, for he who appreciates or knows good music does not necessarily appreciate or know good painting.

Another objection to identifying values with universals is that it is misleading. This perhaps may be most succinctly illustrated in respect to aesthetic theory, where it has led to the view that things are beautiful by virtue of embodiment of antecedent form. A corollary is that the matter or medium is indeterminate. In practice, the use of this doctrine, whereby old forms were stamped on new materials like concrete, steel, or aluminum, produced monstrosities. 'Form' in any functional sense means 'design' in the broad and verbal (verb) sense, as Dewey insisted,[18] and any genuine artist is sensitive to the possibilities of the medium. The appropriate forms must be worked out.

The other view of absolutism which was mentioned is the conception of the absolute object, to which attention has already been given. The idea of objectivism which I have to offer requires more careful distinction from this conception; but my interest in this idea in the present connection has to do with the frequent assumption that any assertion of the objectivity of values must imply, in some fashion or other, that value is an absolute property of an object. This assumption is made for the sake of attacking the objectivity of values. Thus, with this assumption, the argument against the objectivity of values merely contents itself with proving that values are relative and not absolute. A not unusual example occurs when one says that, since a painting may have aesthetic value for one person and none for another, then aesthetic value must be subjective. It is for this reason that the epistemological dualist feels untouched by the argument that all qualities, perceptual or other, are relative. It would be a matter of course that he would not consider that an argument for the relativism of perceptual qualities invalidates his idea that they are subjective. On the contrary, the historical argument has been that it is just because perceptual qualities are relative that they are subjective and unreal.

My point is that this historical argument for the subjectivity of experience—qualitative experience—has been that it is relative; but, further, my point is that the argument must rest on the axiom that the relative is subjective and, accordingly, the objective thing is absolute. That axiom is not explicitly stated, it is unproved, it is questionable, it is unacceptable in modern thought, and, so, the supposed argument respecting the subjectivity of the qualitative world of experience is invalid.

As has been previously argued, the view which holds to the doctrine of the absolute object seeks to state the nature of the thing in terms of independent properties. That is to say, what a thing really is, it is regardless of what anything else is. Yet again, what a thing really is, is what it is independently of other things or of what they are. Consequently, any properties naively attributed to it, which can be shown to occur only under particular conditions, are not genuine properties of the thing. Many perceptual properties seem to vary with special conditions. For example, Democritus and Socrates discovered that when one is ill, wine tastes bitter; when one is well, it is sweet. Therefore, they concluded, neither the sweet nor the bitter taste can be a real property of the wine. That which is relative is not a property of the absolute object.

If one purchases a suit of clothes in the back of a poorly lighted store, he may astonish passersby at his choice of color, when he wears it out on the street in the daylight. The latter color is often taken to be the "true" or "real" color; the former is relegated to an "appearance." The medieval painter or the child may paint foliage on the distant mountains the same shade of green or texture as that in the foreground, not because he cannot see the blue of the distant mountains but because the color the distant mountains "really" are is what they would be at closer range. The rationalist philosopher, in his more sharply critical moments, may see that either choice is a choice between perspectives, a choice which involves confusion between reality and what is important to us, the latter also being a relative matter. So, he returns more clearly to the absolute object.

The discovery of the conditions under which a thing occurs is a more advanced development than the mere observation of the occurrence. Thus the recognition that things are related to conditions is an intellectual achievement. Correspondingly, absolutism is, in the first instance, a product of naiveté. If 'natural' is taken in the sense of the primitive, simple, more direct, and uncritical, then absolutism is natural. It is the more direct mode of response, for the reason that it is simpler to accept a thing directly than to search for the conditions to which it is related.

The child, in his experience with things, takes them for what we would call absolute objects. As we would describe the matter, the ball is intrinsically red to the child. That is to say, it is red in and of itself, and the red is the property of the ball regardless of other circumstances. I mean to say that the child does not relate the red to his visual apparatus, nor essentially to the light. The ball is still red in the dark, just as it is round in the dark, only one cannot see that the ball is red, anymore than he can see that the ball is round or can see the ball at all. But the child can feel the round ball, and so his red ball is there.

Naively, the traits which things possess, they possess inherently and independently. Aristotle maintained this primitive attitude as his fundamental view in his concept of inherent "natures." However, this naive view was combined with the rational objective; namely, to state the nature of things in such a way as to imply what they would do. Nevertheless, some consideration of human experience had suggested that not everything was an inherent trait, and accordingly, they had to be relegated to the status of "accidents."

Relativism, which treats things conditionally, is more sophisticated. Scientific prediction is conditional, whereas prophecy is categorical in the sense that it is not arrived at conditionally; it foretells the future as direct revelation.

The customs of one's own tribe were *the* ways of doing things. They were not related to tribal peculiarities, since that would require an attitude in some sense transcending the tribe. Nor do religious sects usually see themselves objectively, each as one among many: the more naive Christian asserts that there is no salvation except through Jesus Christ. It is true that broader experience does tend to produce more intelligence, and that is why some absolutists must exercise censorship and restriction of contact. Similarly, people naively attribute current cultural traits to "human nature," or attribute cultural differences to racial traits. The striking fact about this is both its widespread conviction and its nonfactual character, for the psychologist can find no such "human nature" that is irrespective of conditions.

Conditional or factual relativism is not, however, the only alternative to absolutism of the more positive sort. Cynicism also lays claim to sophistication, for it is far from primitive. Wholesale cynicism is rare, for it is not conducive to dealing effectively with the problems of life, and, when it occurs, it often is merely a pose, although with great and continued frustration it can indeed arise genuinely enough with reference to major phases of life. Often a curious mixture of absolutism and cynicism occurs. What turns out to be unquestionably relative thereby may become the object of cynicism, whereas absolutism is retained in other fields or is grasped all the more desperately when plagued by doubt—as in religion.

Hence, the very recognition of absolutism, as absolutism, represents some degree of advancement in self-consciousness over primitive acceptance, in conception at least, although the resulting attempt at consistency may produce a far more rigid form, ultimately a totalitarian form and the savagery that goes with it.

The ancient philosopher, whether like Democritus or like Socrates, sought to avoid the more naive instances of taking one perspective to be the absolute while taking another to be mere appearance. It may be true that, for Democritus, the white cloud on the distant mountain turned out, upon closer inspection, to be "really" a number of sheep, and that he generalized this principle. Berkeley uses a similar argument in his illustration of the castle. If one could approach closely enough and could see minutely enough, he could observe realities. However, the ultimate in approach is contact. Democritus did not choose between real and apparent colors; rather, he relegated all colors, odors, tastes, etc., to appearance; perhaps it was his view that even weight was excluded from being a real property on the ground that there was no absolute up and down. He retained only some such properties as size, shape, number, hardness, and motion. These were the independent properties of things.

The limit of approach is contact, something which is typically perceived with the hand and not with the eye. So it is that Democritus' independent and real properties turn out to be exactly the properties which one could distinguish in an object held in one's hand behind his back, properties which lend themselves to the manipulatory functions of the hand, as Mead pointed out. This functional concept, however, was not the view of Democritus, for Mead's analysis would not give rise to independent properties of absolute objects.

The concept of the absolute object, basic to ancient and medieval thought, was carried over into modern philosophy.

Aristotle formulated it by defining the absolute object as a "substance." Centuries later, Spinoza expressed the concept most clearly by defining 'substance' as 'that which is in itself conceived through itself', but this clarification led to its breakdown. Locke, for instance, accepted the doctrine of substance, but, with his empirical interest, concluded that substance is unknowable, "a something, I know not what." He thus began the long transition from the earlier doctrine of absolute objects to modern relativism in which "substance," in its absolute sense—the "thing in itself"—is not unknowable but is meaningless. Locke's conclusion was stated in general or philosophical terms; the scientist has had to discover the same point repeatedly in various ways, for example, respecting the absolute mass particle, absolute space and time, or the ether.

There was a corresponding development of view with respect to properties. Locke assimilated Democritus' distinction into his primary and secondary qualities as a subjective-objective dualism. Therefore, the revolutionary feature of Berkeley's analysis lay in its destruction of the main point in the concept of primary qualities—that they were supposed to represent independent properties of absolute objects. Hume drew the skeptical conclusions which were implicit in Locke's theory.

Whatever Hume's merit, the scientist was furthering the development of human knowledge. Perhaps he was doing so, not so much because his formal concepts differed from those of Locke, but because he was developing and using procedures which could not be stated in terms of Lockean sensations and innate propensities of mind, a point which Kant failed to see or saw only in part.

It is notable that nothing in the scientist's procedure answers to the hoary metaphysical yearning for the independent properties of absolute objects. Rather, his procedure answers to exactly the contrary thesis, for what he does may be described in just the opposite way. It is obvious that if a chemist wants to find out what a substance may be, he subjects the substance to tests. He does not conceive of the thing as being "in itself and conceived through itself"; he puts it into *relation* with other things and notes what happens. What anything is comes then to be defined as a function of what it does, and what it does is always a transaction involving other things. Furthermore, it may as well be added here that what some things do upon occasion, in relation to certain other things, is to appear.

The implication is that appearance is no less a genuine and natural transaction of things of certain types, under certain conditions, than is any other function, and that, per se, such transactions no more raise the question of a subjective realm than do any others. By the same token, they do not require a *Ding an sich*. Therefore—with certain qualifications to be stated—appearances, if and when they occur, constitute what those things are, just as do other functions. They do not, however, constitute all that they are, for things have innumerable other functions.

The doctrine of the absolute object carries with it the doctrine of the absolute independence of the "thing in itself." Thus, Khatchadourian asserts, "The crucial point is . . . that so long as metaphysical realism is assumed, the following question is meaningful: 'What is the nature of objects as they are in themselves, independently of their being perceived by a sentient being?' "[19] If we modify that question, the dualist may ask more intelligibly, "What is the nature of objects independently of their being perceived?" This question becomes a riddle, I think, only when, with the epistemological dualist, we confuse metaphysical with epistemological questions. Respecting the epistemological question, "How do we know that something is the case?" the answer surely involves observation either directly or indirectly, from an empirical point of view. Hypotheses to be verified must, together with other propositions, have empirical implications. Apart from that confusion, one may take the position that appearance is only one kind among many functions that things may have. Hence their nature, independently of that function, would be stated in terms of any appropriate functions that do not necessarily involve appearance, a very ordinary matter. We may state the nature of a fire in terms of available oxygen and fuel raised in temperature to the flash point. Thus, it is possible for fires to start in closets while one is asleep.

While we do not get an absolute independence of the object there are two senses in which we do get independence. The first is in the general sense that dependence is not ubiquitous; for, in the absence of evidence, we need not accept the sweeping generalization of the idealist that everything is in every respect dependent upon every other thing. This independence, while it may not be absolute, is sufficient for particular problems. It is, in part, a mark of intelligence to recognize that some things are irrelevant. Therefore, such things do not enter into the statement of the conditions for the occurrence under consideration. A condition for observing something is not necessarily to be stated as a condition for what is observed. However, I am not primarily concerned with the independence of things, or even with the general question of the nature of things independent of perception. Rather, I am here concerned with a more particular question—the sense in which qualities, including the so-called secondary qualities, may be said to be properties of things. That leads me to the next point.

The second meaning which may be given the term 'independence', if one would so use the term, is a relative sense and one which comes to the main thesis of this discussion; I would like to introduce it in brief contrast to the subjective view.

The argument for the subjective view often seems to be limited to some such statement as this: to have a perception, there must be a perceiver (a subject) and something perceived (an object). However, one may at once interpolate a point here, to which further reference will be made. It is that this dual polarity is a marked oversimplification, if not an outright fallacy, for it omits all the other complex conditions essential to a particular perception. But let us ignore its shortcomings for the moment, in order to turn our attention to what the subjectivist goes on to deduce from "the subject."

In this connection, two different meanings of the term 'subjective' become apparent, although they are often confused. One meaning, the one which is of major concern here, refers to the way in which a perception may be analyzed as a function of the perceiver; this is a relative matter in an objective sense. This meaning will be developed subsequently. The other meaning involves the distinction of a metaphysical mental realm, whether of mind or of mental states of a brain, where what is meant is something mental per se and not by virtue of a more or less peculiar function. As Khatchadourian expresses it, "Perceptual qualities are mental . . . by virtue of a function of the mind,"[20] and the mind is, of course, taken to be something mental per se. The questionable character of this mental realm is suggested by Lovejoy's negative criterion for membership in it; namely, that of not obeying the laws of physics. This reminds us that physics is just one inquiry out of many. Its complement is not something called "mental inquiry," but all the other inquiries which have been, or may be, invented on or off college campuses. These do not involve so many distinct metaphysical realms, much less such a mental realm.

If we do not appeal to metaphysical realms, then the term 'mental' may be reserved for certain special forms of behavior of biological organisms that are amenable to experimental investigation. I have no final pronouncement as to the best short way of indicating such special behavior, but one example is James's definition of 'mentality': "The pursuance of future ends and the choice of means for their attainment are thus the mark and criterion of the presence of mentality."[21] This makes the term 'mentality' irrelevant to the qualities of experience, although they may enter into mental functions, as when a chemist notes the change of color in a test tube as a datum in his analysis.

The argument of this discussion is that neither perceptual

qualities nor values are subjective per se, although either may *sometimes* be, in the relative sense of 'subjective' previously distinguished—*as the particular case turns out.* On this view, nothing is subjective in the nonfunctional sense: that meaning is wholly rejected for want of any useful application. There is no general grant of subjectivity, for that is a matter of *particular* determination by empirical methods.

Confusion of the two different senses of subjectivity, previously distinguished, is manifest when a writer argues for subjectivism in the first (relative) sense and then draws conclusions from it in the second (absolute) sense. Another confusion of these two senses is exemplified when one mistakes a denial of the *theory* involved in the second sense, for a denial of the *existence* of feelings, attitudes, etc., such as may be indicated in the first sense. Still a third type of confusion, perhaps the most usual type, occurs when one quite legitimately makes the kind of analysis of a content indicated by the first type, but then assumes that it is final, as though the content could not equally well have been, by another analysis and for another purpose, defined as a function of the object, not to mention other conditions.

The point is that an argument from relativism cannot prove subjectivism in any final sense, because a relation is also analyzable in terms of other relata. Thus, it may be argued that when I am well, the wine tastes sweet; and when I am not well, the wine tastes bitter: hence, the sweet or bitter taste cannot be a real property of the wine, for it depends on me or my condition. However, the conclusion overlooks the fact that if there were no wine, there wouldn't be any taste, sweet or bitter. Varying conditions of taste do not present a contradiction.

An acid etches metal and not wax; still, no one would assume that the etching is subjective.[22] For certain purposes, the etching may be understood to be a property of the acid; we describe that substance by saying it will etch metal. If we mistreat the property as though it were something independent of other relata, we may express this misuse by using words of doubtful meaning; we may say the acid has the "power" of etching metal. Such words as 'power', 'potency', 'capacity', and 'potentiality' are—in philosophy, as distinguished from science—typically used in connection with attempts to maintain the doctrine of the absolute object, by putting future events into the thing antecedently, though not in any intelligible sense. Such misuse occurs in assuming that the embryonic condition bears an imminent future, a condition amenable to observation, but as an antecedently complete, final, or finished form. It is a ghost of the future and belongs to the mythology of spooks.[23]

We can and do speak of things proleptically, which is essential for intelligence. Therefore, these questionable words mean, whatever else they may mean, that we are concerned with things which are significant in terms of possible futures. While we are in some sense assuming that the etching process is an attribute of the acid, nevertheless, the factual basis for this is that acid does etch metal when it has metal to etch. The etching is no less a property of the metal than it is of the acid, although, obviously, not in the identical way, for the etching is a transaction. Consequently, the etching is relative to the acid and to the metal. If, therefore, we say that the etching is an attribute of the one or the other, we imply that the relativity of the transaction does provide us with attributes of things; but it follows that it is a fallacy to ignore the fact that the attributes are relative. Since the relativity of attributes is of major relevance to my thesis, I will give more attention to it, at the risk of belaboring the obvious.

Although I have been most explicit in saying that I am concerned with the *transaction*, nevertheless some may be misled by the ambiguity of the word 'etching'. It may, in one context, refer to a process or transaction; in another context, it may refer to a design left on the metal as a result or effect of the process. However, I am not, in the foregoing illustration, at all concerned with the design left on the metal. Therefore when I say that the etching is no less a property of the acid than of the metal, obviously I do not mean that the design left on the metal is a property of the acid. To shift consideration from the transaction to the resulting design on the metal would merely be an evasion of the argument, a case of *ignoratio elenchi*. I mean rather than the transaction, the process of etching, is a function which defines both the acid and the metal to the relevant extent. The design on the metal is a result of the process. Analogously, perception has results: if one sees a serious automobile wreck he may have memories. But all that has nothing to do with my argument at this point.

There is another possible transformation of the argument that would be equally illegitimate. While I am using the etching process as an analogy with perception—since they are both trans-actions—my doing so is not grounds for injecting "perceptual qualities" into the etching process. In discussing the etching of metal by acid, I am not referring to perceptual qualities as a result of the action of the acid on the metal. Rather, I am refer-ring to the etching process, the removal of a certain amount of metal by the acid, as itself a transaction. The injection of per-ceptual qualities into the process makes it a pseudoepistemologi-cal affair, confusing the matter of etching with what pertains to a logical question. That is to say, if someone asks what *evidence* one has that the metal was etched and wishes to evaluate the evidence as evidence, then one might appropriately describe an *observation*. This sort of confusion, as has previously been noted, creates the illegitimate riddle of the independence of the per-ceived object. Surely, it is by observation that we know that acids etch metal. However, I need not repeat further what has been said.

The main point to which attention is now called is the con-fusion between—and, indeed, the identification by—the episte-mological dualist of perception as an occurrence, which is the sense in which I am concerned with it, with the role of percep-tion in genuinely cognitive functions. The same confusion ap-pears when the dualist appeals, for support, to what he conceives to be "an instrumentalist view" of perception. Compare Dewey, who would surely be presumed to have an instrumentalist view, to the dualist: "It has been implied throughout that the relation to organic apparatus involved in such terms as 'looks', 'sounds', 'feels', 'tastes' is a reference to a causal condition of the production of the particular object which appears, not a reference to a knower, an epistemological reference. . . ."[24]

The major point of my method of analysis may first be exhibited as a characteristic of common scientific procedure, because all occurrences are functions of complexes of conditions. My basic thesis is that the consideration of the way in which *anything is objective* is indicative of the way in which *values are objective*. The procedure involved is one by which the scientist may *discover the nature of certain particular factors, by holding others constant*. There are three ways of holding factors constant: one is by actual exclusion of or isolation from those factors; another is by holding those factors constant and not permitting them to vary; a third is to allow for the variation.

Perhaps the simplest illustration is one involving three variables, that expressed by the gas law. If the question is how the pressure of a gas varies as a function of temperature, then the volume is held constant. It is a constant primarily in the sense that it does not vary, although any container will of course vary more or less with the temperature and therefore allowance is made for the variation. At any rate, one varies the temperature and notes the change in pressure. In this way the scientist finds a way of treating the effects on pressure as a genuine function of the temperature which is an "independent" variable. The "independent" effect of temperature on pressure, evidently, cannot imply an absolute independence, such as the absence of volume, for without volume there could be no temperature, much less pressure. We do get a relative independence; at least we get what we call the causal effect of temperature pressure, independently of the volume. The conclusion is that, though all three variables are inevitably involved with each other, this does not prevent the scientist from determining the effects contributed by each, if he can hold the others constant.

The method of investigation just used is a scientific procedure similar to J. S. Mill's Method of Difference. It involves the assumption that, with certain qualifications, if one thing changes while another does not or vice versa, they are independent, at least to that extent. This assumption is made explicit in Mill's Method of Agreement, in which the conditions which vary while the phenomenon does not are ruled out as causal factors. I am not, however, concerned with this latter question of method except for a brief mention later, and so I return to the former. In making these references to Mill's methods, I am not, of course, overlooking the criticisms of them contained in most texts in logic. I refer to them mainly because they serve the purpose of simple exposition and for what, I suppose, is the reason they are frequently repeated in logic texts: namely, they are schematic, classical statements of method.

My major point with respect to the absolute independence of realistic epistemology and to the absolute dependence, or identity, of idealistic epistemology, is that the question of any particular degree of dependence is settled—so far as I am concerned —in terms of the way in which one variable may or may not be shown empirically to be a function of another variable. If we wish to find the effect that amount of study has on learning, we may decide to correlate the various amounts of time used in study by different students with the grades which the students receive. If we do, we may find a slightly negative correlation. A naive interpretation of this result might be that the less a student studies, the higher grades he will receive. However, it may occur to us to hold "intelligence" constant, for the more intelligent student may study less on a particular subject, but still receive higher grades. If we do this, we find that grades are a positive function of the amount of time put into study.

The relevancy of the foregoing discussion is that these scientific methods are developments and generalizations out of common experience, in which much the same kind of result is often in effect obtained without conscious method. A man who has just been blinded begins to carry a cane. At first, the cane is a foreign object in his hand. He feels the jolts, bumps, and vibrations of the cane and hears its sounds; but he "adapts" to or loses the feel of the cane just as he loses the feel of his clothing, and, in time, the cane itself becomes a constant, just as the volume of a gas may be constant. The jolts, bumps, and vibrations become properties of the objects with which the cane comes in contact, rather than constituting functions of the cane. It is no longer itself so much a perceived object as it is an organ of perception. The blind man perceives *with* his cane, just as one perceives with his eyes. Note that the cane does not become a constant in the situation because of any conscious use of Mill's Method of Difference or of any other method, but because of the phenomenon of perceptual adaptation—among other things. For what is constant tends not to be perceived. Similarly, that scientific methods are developments and generalizations arising from everyday experience may be seen in an illustration quoted by Morris R. Cohen and Ernest Nagel from Pierre Duhem. A scientist does not say, "I am studying the oscillations of an iron bar that carries a mirror." He will say that he is measuring the electric resistance of the spools.[25]

Now I would like to consider ordinary perception in the same manner, in particular, visual perception. The dualist, in arguing for the subjectivity of experience, does so—in his more intelligible statements—by urging its dependence upon the organism because it is a function of the organism. Khatchadourian, going further, says that it is not merely relative to the organism but to his mind. However, I am not called upon to accept the dualist's "mind." I wish to analyze the transactions of experience in terms of the variety of functions involved. As a method of dealing with the objectivity of value, I shall discuss the objectivity of perceptual qualities, including the subject matter often referred to as the "secondary qualities."[26] However, as already stated, the point is not that all supposed values and so-called secondary qualities are necessarily objective in any final sense, but that they are objective as the particular case may be; that is, they are not per se or a priori subjective.

There are three reasons for approaching the problem by way of a discussion of secondary qualities. The first, though not the most important, is that, if it be proved that secondary qualities go with primary, in respect to objectivity, it is quite as likely that the so-called tertiary qualities go with the secondary. Secondly, I wish in a sense to do the opposite of what Berkeley did. He made primary qualities subjective by making them go with secondary qualities. I wish to make secondary qualities objective by making them go with primary qualities, although not exactly so, because any quality must depend upon its own conditions. Thus, some do and some do not. More to the point, I wish to discuss the *manner in which* secondary qualities can be treated as genuine properties of things because such a treatment will at least be helpful in clarifying how values may also be treated as genuine properties. The point is that the sense in which secondary qualities are properties of things is the same general sense in which things have properties of any kind.[27] A third reason I wish to discuss the objectivity of values by means of secondary qualities is that values, as I use the term, belong peculiarly to experience, for they are fulfillments in and of experience, and thus constitute experience at its fullest and richest. Experience is truncated if taken at a moment; it is inherently temporal.

The great variety of variables which exist as conditions for perception suggests such chaos in the face of analysis that some see the only hope of escaping from this apparently chaotic relativism in an appeal to some absolute, as has been shown. Color becomes an eternal object; minds and objects go their separate metaphysical ways; and, in such a world, Santayana's dog must become a professor of metaphysics in order to find his way around.[28] However, these concepts do not lend themselves to a description of anything that observably happens, nor to an empirical method of dealing with them. The case is otherwise. The exigencies of life provide us with "normal" conditions, which in turn provide us with "constants" for the time being. Our eyes and other sensory apparatus are typically a part of us; in that sense, they are constants. So too are the conditions under which things are perceived; which is to say, they are ordinary or usual conditions, even if they are selected or preferred for the sake of reference. Under these circumstances, differences in colors are quite legitimately referred to differences in passing objects; they are, therefore, properties of objects, even though in a relative or conditional sense. The ball does not merely appear red; the ball is red. The common sense man is vindicated, at least under common conditions. Common sense is the basis on which he can deal with his world, and it provides the foundation for science and other inquiry. In general, one approaches any philosophical or scientific or practical question with a background of experience already polarized into common objects of experience by the activities involved in meeting the necessities of life. Willy-nilly, such a background constitutes our presuppositions, although they may not be final. It is against such a background that any particular property comes into question and its status is settled; and this is why the sense-data and phenomena philosophers must always begin by using "object words." To get around this, we would have to speculate about the newborn infant's experience, speculations much more questionable than our knowledge of the active world of ordinary experience.

By way of contrast, I may indicate a question which I am not considering or answering as though it were relevant to the existential status of properties. Especially when faced with the problem of the objectivity of qualities, the dualist asks, in terms of his dualism, "which object?" This means that he has already set up as some kind of "given," an "external" *cognoscendum* over against which there are perceptual qualities in the brain or mind of a percipient organism. He wishes to pose the question of how one can get these subjective internal qualities pasted on his external *cognoscendum*. However, one need not feel called upon to answer questions which presuppose the dualistic point of view; the terms of the question are unnecessary and gratuitous. When the dualist raises his question about "which object," it seems to me that he has overlooked the fact that genuine questions about the existential status of supposed properties are asked in terms of the antecedent polarization which I have already mentioned. In his attempt to state all the affairs of experience at once or in general in epistemological terms, the dualist would appear to wish to bring into question—to say the least—all objects of experience at once. In the more particular case, when one has determined that x is a function of a given y, he has determined the existential status of x in any meaningful sense.

I remarked previously that I wished to make the so-called secondary qualities go with the primary qualities, although anything has its own conditions. This presents no issue to the dualist, for Locke would simply call both these kinds of qualities "ideas," and have no objection to their conjunction. Descartes may seem to have confined extension to his external world, but Locke and the succeeding dualists never denied size, shape, motion, number, weight, or resistance to their subjective worlds, except that they were relative and so could not be real in just that way, in contrast to the external world. That being the case, I take for granted their conjunction and pass on to what is in question, for the dualist is quite ready to admit such conjunctions within his subjective realm. But for the dualist, it is nonetheless a subjective world, although one which in some respects "corresponds" to an external world, especially in respect to the so-called primary qualities.

It is in respect to the so-called primary qualities that the dualist's idea seems most obviously to be gratuitous. At least, this is so much the case that the ancient world did not question the primary qualities as it did the secondary, except for such extremists as the Eleatics and the skeptics. But the dualistic view asserts a duplication of primary qualities, those in the subjective world representing or corresponding to their correlates in an external world; and it is this duplication which seems to be unnecessary, unless based on a dualism which already begs the question. Yet a simple naive realism is not a possible answer, either. It broke down because its absolutism was too obviously inadequate to the relativity of things.

Use of the historic term 'primary qualities' is, of course, dangerous, for it may suggest acceptance of the views in which that term occurred, especially the view that the term denotes and adequately reflects realities; whereas, on the contrary, it indicates abstractions. The preferable expression would be to say that, in the activities of ordinary experience, what is generalized as a physical property has already been given, and we do not need any duplicate. Therefore, since the things of experience have physical properties, they are physical and so do not belong to any nonphysical world. And since these activities do not belong to or constitute an "inner world," and indeed cannot be stated intelligibly in terms of such a metaphysical realm, they do not require duplicates in an "external world." It is a curious fact, for instance, that although Kant assumed a dualism between his phenomenal and noumenal worlds, he nevertheless found it necessary to distinguish also between an "inner" and an "outer" *within* his phenomenal world, and the latter was the significantly useful distinction. Thus, he was sufficiently perceptive to recognize that the metaphysical dualism was inadequate to deal with the needed distinctions.

The dualists claim that if anything is perceived it is subjective. The exigencies of life have taught men (sometimes illegitimately) that if anything is perceived, it is objective. "Seeing is believing." However, with more thought and experience, men have learned that some things are not always objective in the simple way that they may have been taken to be. This, I think, is a major source of the problems with which philosophers have been concerned; more so, I further suggest, than their bad grammar, as the analysts would have it. The distinction between subjective and objective, insofar as it occurs to meet the problems of life, is a distinction *within* the world of experience, whether or not it is also extended beyond that world.

We analyze the transaction with more or less success, attributing different phases or data to different things or objects. Indeed, the point of some recent research is to show that certain characteristics of visual perception must be attributed to cultural conditions.[29] These cultural influences, as influential conditions, do not fit into the simple subject-object polarity, for in the particular case they are neither the subject nor the object of concern. They are in this respect conditions. Furthermore, it is not helpful to attempt to split those cultural influences into an external metaphysical world and into an internal subjective realm. That is to say, the old dualistic view will not fit into modern thought. It is not disproved, for it has no empirical implications. So it is not so much refuted as abandoned because it is irrelevant and useless.

What I am proposing may perhaps be made more pointed by comparison or contrast with yet another view. Thus Winston H. F. Barnes writes,

No one will deny, I think, that a situation may exist in which the following three propositions are true:
    (i)   I see the rose.
    (ii) The rose appears pink to me.
    (iii) The rose is red.[30]

Barnes sets forth these three propositions for the sake of denying that they entail another proposition, "(iv) I see a pink sensum." I have no wish to dispute that point. On the contrary, his strictures on the sense-data theory are in line with the position that had been taken long before by the pragmatist.

I wish to consider the status given to red and pink in this discussion and to question whether it is adequate to the problem that is supposedly raised, the existence of sense-data. What Barnes says with respect to the fact that the rose appears pink to me is merely that it is evidence and that evidence can be misleading: the rose *is* red. I suggest that Barnes is evasive. While the sense-data theory is an attempt to deal with the existential status of what is involved in the empirical report of a fact, Barnes does not meet the issue. In merely stating that the fact that the rose appears pink to me is misleading evidence, he is insofar giving it only a logical status. I am glad to note, as I have argued elsewhere, that Barnes does take the word 'datum' to be a logical term; but his shift from a question of existential status to a question of logical status does not meet the former issue. Since 'the rose appears pink to me' is, presumably, a report of an empirical fact, he cannot legitimately evade its existential status by leaving it in linguistic limbo in competition with the more prestigious remark, 'The rose is red'. Perhaps Barnes feels that he has met the issue by saying that "modes of appearance are not existents." Yet that linguistic exorcism does not cause the empirical fact to evaporate.

One may suppose that, since Barnes has injected the matter of evidence, there would be evidence that the rose is red, namely that the rose appears red to me, but, most likely, under somewhat different conditions. But where does the function of being "misleading" or not come in? Well, not by its nonexistence. Rather, if an appearance under one set of conditions leads one falsely to expect a similar appearance under somewhat different conditions, then it would be misleading evidence, whether red or pink. But that is not grounds for saying that the appearance did not occur, for an actual occurrence is reported; and what occurs, exists. Thus, Barnes leaves the pink appearance of the red rose in an existential void, still crying for the defunct sense-data theory; and that void is not filled by calling the empirical fact "misleading evidence," and in the same breath claiming that it did not exist. That, I think, is an evasion. One must say that the

sense-data philosopher has at least faced up to the problem. But
there is another answer, I think, which neither creates imaginary
entities nor waives empirical facts out of existence.

The facts of the matter would seem to be simply this: as an
actual occurrence, this rose is red under certain conditions and
it is pink under certain other conditions; and, presumably, it is
neither one under still other conditions. Of course, I may be too
hasty in taking certain conditions for granted. There may be
reasons in the particular case for not ascribing the pink character
to the rose; it may be a function of something else, irrespective
of the rose, as might occur if a pink haze settled over everything.
Such exceptions will be further elaborated. But, accepting the
prior assumptions, the fact still remains that some of those conditions are much more usual or more important than others. It
is not normally useful to run around in rose gardens in the dark.
So, like Barnes, I am glad to say, 'The rose is red' and go on from
there to classify separately red roses and pink roses, but not red
roses and pink appearances, much less existential red roses and
nonexistential pink appearances.

If one wishes to change the color of his room, he treats the
color as a function or property of the room. One might, conceivably, perform an operation on his eyes, although I do not
know how this might be brought about. He could change the
light, but that may be inconvenient or disturb other activities.
The housewife simply changes the paint and wallpaper. However
much her philosopher husband may argue that color is merely
subjective or is merely a property of one's visual and mental apparatus, his wife is unimpressed; she finds it easier to treat color
as a property of the object. I am suggesting that she is not wholly
a fool in preventing her husband, by force if necessary, from attempting to change the colors of a room by making rash changes
in his visual organs.

There are questions, however, which do call our attention to
the sensory apparatus. If we are testing for color blindness, our
question is different and so is our procedure. We are now treat-

ing the visual apparatus as a variable. Correspondingly, it is the object which is constant, as well as the surrounding conditions. We standardize the object: an Ishehara color book, or particular skeins of wool. In this case, differences in what is perceived are attributed to differences in the visual apparatus and belong to the observer. It may as well be added, contrary to the dualist's exclusive subject-object polarity, that the other conditions of perception can also be treated as variables and manipulated.

My remark concerning the exclusive subject-object polarity recalls the words of Descartes: "For knowledge of objects, only two things need be considered: we who know, and the objects themselves which are to be known."[31] These words seem clear enough: there are only two pigeonholes. In Khatchadourian's words, "If we hold that perceptual qualities are not in objects, it follows that they are located in the percipient."[32] The dualist's argument is carried on entirely in terms of a *cognoscendum* on the one side and subjective qualities in a brain or mind on the other, reiterated time after time, with never any hint of other conditions entering that relation.[33]

A child knows enough to turn on the light in a dark room. Yet the character of the light is only one of many variables. By suitable manipulation of these conditions, the psychologist may cause the blackest thing he can find to appear to us as white or, rather, gray. Still other variables present other "illusions." It is a curious wonder to note how philosophers have been so greatly bothered by the effects of these other surrounding conditions; their predisposition toward a subject-object dualism of absolute objects does not allow for other conditions; I refer to conditions like colored spectacles, mirrors, or the submerging of sticks half way in water. But the most amazing "illusion" of all is the argument itself for the *subjectivity* of appearance, based on the "bent stick," especially when argued by philosophers to whom the concepts of physics constitute the ultimate metaphysics; a camera is affected in the same way. More consistent, if not more illuminating, is Russell's suggestion that cameras too are subjective. So too, I suppose, is the refraction of light. This is the *reductio ad absurdum*. The only illusion which can legitimately be affirmed is that of taking an appearance under one set of conditions for a necessary guarantee of an appearance or any other reality under another set of conditions.

The convergent rails on a photograph of railway tracks receding into the distance, which is the kind of thing to which Russell refers, cannot be accounted for in terms of metaphysical subjectivity but must be accounted for in terms of optics and the geometry of perspectives. Obviously, these conditions do not make anything subjective. The attempt of the dualist to bring in subjectivity by injecting perceptual qualities is gratuitous. Even in the dualist's own account, there are physical effects evident in the physical photograph. Does he mean that in his external world there is a physical photograph on which the tracks as pictured do not converge? The point is that the relativity to which some refer in respect to "bent sticks" or "convergent tracks," in order to prove subjectivity, infects their objective world just as much; and the obvious relativity agreed to by all sides must in these cases be accounted for in physical terms like optics.

There is a more relevant sense in which the nonmetaphysical or relative subjectivity which I have suggested may be involved in the camera. Some features on photographs may be attributed to cameras or to films, rather than to the objects photographed: the camera that was sent past Mars was an organ of perception. This, however, is a relative matter in the objective sense, for not all features of the photograph are to be attributed to the camera but to the object of concern, not to mention other conditions. Accordingly, subjectivity is not general, for it applies to some features as discriminated from others. Hence, the "causal subjectivity" which Lovejoy presumes to infect all qualities is irrelevant.

As I see it, most of the fallacies of these arguments based on special conditions reduce to one contradiction: they suggest that the special conditions are constants, while actually treating them as variables. For instance, considering the problem of the colored spectacles, we may say that if the spectacles are genuinely a constant, while objects in the passing field are variables, then whatever is perceived through them constitutes real properties of the things. It is what the things are under those conditions. But the difficulty is that we do not, in fact, readily treat the colored spectacles as constants. Rather, we note the differences between the way a thing appears when we have them on and when we have them off. Therefore, these differences are assuredly functions of the spectacles, for then the spectacles are the variables. Yet even this argument does not inject metaphysical subjectivity or subjectivity of any kind, in general. The arguments of this type that I have read do not seem to keep these points straight; they are fallacies of equivocation. Most of the riddles arise out of just such a tangle of confused ideas, where it is not clear, and is never clarified, which conditions are being held constant and which are taken to be the variables; and, further, where the author does not appear to be aware that his conclusions seem to him to be finalities only because they are the results of his antecedently fixed custom (I do not mean conscious decision) of taking some things rather than others as constants or as variables.

This chaos is compounded when connected with a highly ambiguous use of the word 'appearance'. One use refers to what is directly and immediately presented in the content of a perception on a particular occasion—that is to say, direct, bare presence, now. Another use refers to all or to a number of appearances of a particular thing on any number of occasions, but lumped together as the appearance of the thing. Still a third use is quite different and refers to a suggestion or promise of what the thing present on one occasion may turn out to be under *further* conditions, as when one says that this appears to be a such-and-such.[34]

In either of the first two senses—what is directly and immediately present or what is in reference to a number of occasions—

we may say, with James, that things are what they appear to be, whatever else they may also be; although this will mean quite different things in the two different senses. In the first sense, it means that an appearance *may* be just as much the reality of the thing as is any other function of it, although, obviously, no particular phase of a thing constitutes its full reality; nor does the existence of other functions necessarily depend on the one function. In the second sense, the proposition would mean that what the thing turns out to be may be given in further appearances, insofar as it is given at all. One does not eventually reach a reality which is behind all appearances; he compares promises to further appearances. What the proposition does *not* mean is the third sense, that what the appearance promises can never be misleading. When the term 'appearance' is intended to mean a promise, as is often intended in the sentence, 'This appears to be an *x*'; then, surely, the appearance at the moment is not itself the reality which is promised, although it is itself a reality. To solve riddles which have been propounded respecting appearance and reality we need, it seems, some attention to the meaning of terms used, rather than a metaphysical distinction between appearance and reality. Ptolemy may have laughed at the astonished Stoic attempting to eat the waxen pomegranate, for the Stoic had said that perception is infallible. Perception is not infallible, no matter how *real* it is, for the terms 'fallible' and 'infallible' are relevant to a suggestion of something beyond what is directly given in the promise; but the question still remains, how did Ptolemy know that it was really waxen, save by other appearances? Perhaps the Stoic had the last laugh, even if a wry one.

The distinctions which have been stated on more general grounds apply to values; and, in this respect, there is no difference between values and other qualities given in experience. The distinctions provide clear senses in which we can say that one thing seems to be a value but is not or that another does not seem to be a value but is, without involving ulterior realities or antecedent authoritative prescriptions or any absolute status. In the same senses, just distinguished, we can hold that values are given in experience without treating them as subjective mental states. However much pleasure, interest, or emotion may be involved, still, insofar as they are involved, they cannot be subjectively interpreted in the metaphysical sense. Nevertheless, values are not to be identified with pleasure, interest, or emotion. Neither need values be strictly identified with "objects of desire" or "objects of concern," for values are not merely things desired— when they are—but are desirable, as Dewey has insisted; they are not merely objects of concern—when they are—but are worthy of being so.[35]

The argument for the subjectivity of value has often taken some such form as this: the beautiful is too clearly beautiful *for me* for it to be considered as inhering in the object itself.[36] Yet this assumed universal dualism of the subjective and an objective *thing-in-itself* is precisely what this book has called into question, although some evaluations are indeed subjective. The subjectivist asks, "If one person finds beauty in an object and another person does not, can this be due to real differences in the same object?" This, I take it, is the same point made by Democritus and Socrates respecting the bitterness or sweetness of the wine, a point already discussed. I submit that this suggestion of contradiction is answered adequately by pointing out that there is no contradiction whatever between saying that a thing exhibits one property under one set of circumstances, and another under a different set, however much it may be the case that a good deal more needs to be said. The crucial point of the subjectivist position, as stated in terms of the view that I am suggesting, is this: *if we were to hold constant the observers and the conditions of observation, then there would be no difference whatever corresponding to objects in respect to values.* That is to say, there would be no aesthetic difference whatever between the casual daubings of first-grade children and the paintings of masters.

Of course, an alternative view must be more positive than merely pointing out the outrageous implications of subjectivism. If there is a causal relation, it should be stated. Now the particular way, relevant to values, in which different objects affect a particular observer differently, I shall attempt to set forth in the following chapter. I believe that this method is quite adequate, although it permits the possibility that a particular object may be good in relation to a particular person under certain conditions, even though it is not actually good in relation to anyone else in the world. This is not contradictory to an objective approach, although it is surely contradictory to the traditional dogmatic view of the Good as absolute. The case may be illustrated by food, which is also relative. Some persons may require a relatively rare diet. Let us note both that the question as to how many others require such a diet is entirely irrelevant; nevertheless, there are reasonably good scientific methods—medical or dietary —for dealing with such problems. The virtue of science, as set against prescientific dogmatism, is that it can deal with individual differences.

What the subjectivist wishes to do is to hold the objects constant and to vary the observers. This method, I have suggested, is quite legitimate exactly insofar as it is or is not appropriate to some questions. The subjectivist insists that the same object may be beautiful to one and not beautiful to another. Here the object is constant while observers are variables. (It would be wiser, too, if the subjectivist also held other conditions constant.) But note that this method is designed to give information about observers and not about objects, so that the subjectivist has merely deluded himself as to the finality of his results when he discovers that his information about values is a function of person. Of course, holding the object constant and varying the observer without variations in effects would indicate that the effects were independent of observers. It has not been my intention to go so far as to establish any such conclusion, since it goes much further than my thesis does. The subjectivist often seems to demand this more extreme view as the only alternative to his position, but to accept such a view is a fallacy.

However, we can defeat the subjectivist on his own ground: fortunately, there is experimental evidence of a sufficient degree of agreement—for our purpose—among independent judges respecting particular objects, even though it is difficult to control all the variables. It is the correlation of independent judgments which constitute the logic of the evidence in this case, as, for example, in methods commonly used to develop art judgment tests like the Seashore or literary judgment tests or composition rating scales. Since such agreement is treated on a statistical or probability basis, the fact that there are a few exceptions is not fatal, as is the case when a philosopher's assertions about these matters are universal generalizations. One may conclude, then, that whether or not there may be differences in value effects is a matter which can be settled empirically and, therefore, objectively, if they are adequately defined. If there should be any differences, they would, under the specified conditions, be functions of the objects and therefore would be properties of those objects.

It is possible that some subjectivist might hold that if we were to keep observers and conditions constant and were to vary objects placed before the observers, then there would—and could—be no corresponding differences in respect to color. Under some conditions, however, that would merely define total color blindness, which in itself may be an objective condition.

VI

Empiricism and Objective Relativism in Value Theory

I

It is only as some things are found to be good and identified as values—independently of any value theory—that theories of values can be developed with any probability of verification. In turn, theories may be used, provisionally at least, to determine values. Whitehead asserts, "There cannot be value without antecedent standards of value. . . ."[1] This has been said often enough. Perhaps at more sophisticated or higher levels it may be true. However, the word 'standards' can be used in such a vague sense that it is difficult to determine what is meant. When a young child says, "This candy is good," he is not, I think, referring to any standards so much as he is noting a direct experience, just as he might say, "This is yellow." See, for example, G. E. Moore's argument, later discussed. But it would seem that the child might experience these things denoted without making any statement about them at all, and he must experience these things or else he would not have anything to talk about in that respect. So that, at simpler levels anyway, men may find things that are good without anything that may significantly be called "standards."

If the child does say, "This is good" or "This is yellow" those expressions may be said to be comparative. But I do not see that the comparison need be with something called a standard so much as it is a comparison with other things in that respect. Of course, presumably, one could not say that this is good or this is yellow unless the words 'good' and 'yellow' had some meaning. And the dialectician may insist that the meaning, whatever it is, be called a "standard." At any rate—to note something rather different—later, more sophisticated meanings and definitions may be proposed; a random illustration may include Aristotle, Spinoza, R. B. Perry, etc. And I intend subsequently to propose a definition of values.

The point is that such standards do not antecedently fix in a final way, on some mysterious authoritarian or arbitrary ground, what is good, but, rather, they are proposals which are more or less verified as they seem to lead men more effectively to find good things in life. They may be dogmatically asserted, but in practice they are tentative, for men may abandon them if they apparently fail to serve as effective guides. But that tentative standards may grow up in this process of finding more or less good things and may be used as tentative guides need not be doubted. The growth of standards by this means is a matter of growing sophistication, and it makes available to the new generation the experience of previous generations, for whatever it may be worth. It may set a desideratum to be reached, but that desideratum is not antecedent to the process; it is not the origin. The formalized aesthetic standards of the seventeenth and eighteenth centuries are now thought ridiculous, but they were steps toward setting today's standards and, as such, they have not been futile.

The attempt to shift the good or values away from the basic experience of men into mere linguistic gymnastics is, I think, an exercise in futility. Equally futile, though in the opposite direction, is the view that the idea of the good must first rest on certain antecedent metaphysical postulates. Only an undue emphasis on the formalities of pedagogy would suggest that men must first have standards before they can find anything good; however it may be that without standards finding that which is good is all the more accidental and uncertain.

I do not wish to carry on a "hen-egg" argument. A dialectical game may seek to prove that there cannot be any such things as tools because one requires tools in order to make tools. One need not take space to resolve that old tangle: we alternate between proposed theories and practical findings. In any case, some such theories will likely be more general and some less general, and some more or less specialized theories may be developed in specific fields. One may study paintings or poetry which are accepted as good to develop some theory as to why they are good. This, however, presupposes that he has already identified some painting or poetry as good, or as likely to be good, as many people have, of course. I presume that a large collection of paintings that men pretty generally agree are good paintings will probably contain a significantly higher percentage of paintings of worth than will a large collection of paintings which men agree are worthless.

To be sure, the identification of some things as good need not be absolute and final. There is some shift both in the course of individual development and of cultural history. This shift can be a matter of growth, and not necessarily of caprice. A thing may be good under one set of circumstances and not good under another.

At any rate, I am not concerned with such theories as have been mentioned above. Rather, I am concerned with the antecedent identification of some things as values, or as being good, in the nonethical sense of that word. I mean "nonethical" in the sense that, although ethics is concerned with values as the presupposed condition for its validity, nonetheless, the subject matter of ethics is not values, and values are not in the first instance defined in ethical terms.

The alternative to the view that I am proposing, expressed in older language, is that values are subjective. The word 'subjective' does not seem to be much used in the most recent philosophy, perhaps because of its association with metaphysics; that is to say, with the old subjective-objective dualism. But it makes sense, I think, to say that, in the literature of the positivists and of the analysts, values are treated as subjective.

The answer to an assertion of subjectivity is to produce objectivity. But first perhaps an assumption should be made explicit: the theories that I have to suggest are only intended to refer to realities which are actual occurrences; they are specific individual happenings in particular situations. As such they are things noted, but theory is concerned with what to make of them—their meanings. Hence, we use generalized conceptions of things.

The objective fact to which we would point as a beginning is the emergence in nature of the means-end relation in the biological act. When and as this relation emerges in nature, it is as much a real and objective fact as any other occurrence. Accordingly, I shall refer to means and ends as matters of fact. But means and ends are not external to one another: one may say that they are merely different functions of the same act. Nevertheless, their discrimination is not to be ignored, and the one is not reducible to the other. Further, there is the evolutionary development of the effective or means function of the act from the level of biological activity to that of the simple, and then to the more complex, arts, including the arts of social conduct, and eventually to the sciences. Correspondingly, and in an interrelated way, there is the evolutionary development of simple biological ends into long-range ends and into the great ends of human life. The study of values is the study of human ends; philosophically, it is a study of the critical grounds for being more intelligent about ends or objectives.

I cannot assume that this reference to the means-end relation will be taken for granted. Superficial criticism of the description of conduct in terms of the means-end relation has identified it as a type of utilitarianism, although not necessarily a hedonistic form. It may be truly avowed that deeper moral consideration is something more than mere prudence or cold-blooded calculation of how to achieve ends, but such an avowal is pointless in the present case. The essence of such criticism is that utilitarianism is concerned merely with the means and not with an evaluation of ends. But since the present discussion is primarily concerned with values and not with ethics in the more restricted sense of right and wrong, I shall indicate, in summary fashion, that some principles of ethics which are rather hastily assumed to be contradictory to utilitarianism are not at all exclusive of a means-end analysis of conduct. They are, on the contrary, an elaboration of that view. In this connection I shall make three points.

First, moral consideration implies consideration of all values or ends that seem to be involved, and not merely "the end." This is both a social doctrine—as the traditional utilitarian axiom, the greatest good for the greatest number, would indicate—and, furthermore, it implies concern for long-range and more remote ends as they may be evaluated.

Second, moral consideration involves the use of principles, because generalization is essential to intelligence. Principles may appear as proposed modes of social conduct, whether proposed by moral teachers or gradually worked out by a culture. That they do so neither implies crass expediency nor blesses inexpediency as a virtue.

Third, moral consideration involves conscience which, in the way Mead elaborated, arises in self-consciousness and is variously indicated by such expressions as self-approval or self-disapproval, self-esteem, or self-respect. Of course, self-esteem may be maintained by all manner of "observances" or standards of conduct, but there is no obvious reason why some such standards of conduct may not be intelligent. Self-consciousness, in Mead's view, is a social product.

The skeptic insists upon the variety of value differences. This is reminiscent of the argument which attributes multiplicity of properties or qualities to the object and which rests on the supposed difficulties. We have considered extensively, in the present work, arguments of this type. Both arguments operate on the "either-or" assumption that we must choose either absolutes or nothing.

I might remark parenthetically, since it does not—even if true—provide a final answer to the skeptic, that value differences are not quite as important as skeptical arguments would make them. That is to say, even very heated social or political arguments are basically concerned with much the same sort of thing. The real difference may be how best to achieve such an end. Two persons may agree that a particular outcome would be bad, yet differ in judging the probability of such an outcome. Often it seems that if a proponent would interpret the outcomes of a proposal in the way that the opponent interprets them, he might also be against it. I trust that it is not altogether too naive to say that the Russian people want about the same basic things as the American people. However that may be, there certainly are value differences. The anthropologists have industriously taught us that fact. One person may look forward to marriage with a home and children, while another may want a markedly different kind of life.

A writer may seek amid all the differences among cultures some "universal values," and he may find them in leadership and power. However, I am not at all sure, even if there are some universal values, that they are the ones just mentioned. Some cultures do not seem to emphasize those things. Moreover, leadership and power may often and to an important extent be means rather than ends. But what needs to be clarified, and this is the point that I want to make, is not whether they should be classified as primarily instrumental rather than as ends or values, but rather what the implications are of doing so. Doubtless, in some sense, leadership and power are often values; that is, they are admired or desired for their own sake: some people may love to be leaders or love to display power. But an *evaluation* of leadership or of power is often directed not toward leadership or power as values but as means. What is important is that—for the sake of appropriate analysis—the two, means and ends, should not be confused. Yet sometimes what presumes to be a discussion of the one turns out to be a discussion of the other. The idea that means and ends cannot be separated may be true enough, and some of the same facts may enter into the consideration of both; but if this obscures the different ways in which those facts are relevant, then the analysis is much too vague.

There are countless ends, desires, or interests; and such ends have all manner of causes, some more or less known and some unknown. Some arise from the unconscious influence or from the deliberate propaganda of a particular culture. Some arise out of bitterness and hatred, and such causes may be thought of as pathological conditions of life. There are so many ends that they may frustrate each other in a number of ways. All this chaos cries out for a "moral economy," as R. B. Perry says, or a value economy: it is just this fact of life which requires a theory of values. Each preference or interest is a matter of fact to be taken into account; and for that reason, while any one of them may represent what we would like to do, no one of them can be taken automatically as ultimately determining what we really want to do, except at peril.

One method of attacking moral judgments—one not often taken very seriously in recent literature—is to consider causation and the assumptions which have gone with the notions of cause, especially where those notions have not profited from a study of Hume. I refer to determinism, but only for the sake of introducing another point. This problem may be quickly clarified in connection with the idea of punishment. Actually, I would not be seriously concerned with an ethical view that gives a major consideration to punishment, except critically. But the idea of punishment seems to play a central role in ethical treatments by analysts, to a surprisingly frequent degree—all of which is irrelevant here. The point of the matter is this: the dilemma—or trilemma—may be, first, that no one should be punished for what he cannot avoid doing; while, second, it may be held that everything has a cause and so is necessarily determined; and yet, third, some people should be punished sometimes. Hobbes' solution to the problem is to accept the determinism but to deny the first premise. One is not punished because he could have done differently but because what he did was noxious.

Hobbes' solution may be seen to be more rational by making a distinction. In some cases it is effective to hold people responsible for some of their acts and in some cases it is not: it may be futile to hold an insane person or an idiot responsible, or to hold anyone responsible for consequences which he could not have foreseen even as a reasonable possibility. But in other cases holding people responsible may cause them to mend their ways or, better, to come to have a sense of responsibility and to act generally in a responsible way.

I do not intend this brief mention to constitute adequate analysis of the problem nor am I even concerned with whether the solution given is adequate. Rather, I am concerned with the method which the answer illustrates in its more rational development; namely, the attempt to transform the question from one of moralistic and metaphysical riddles into a problem of dealing in an effective way with human problems and difficulties. It is this sort of attempt which is the rational method in ethics, or which leads in that direction. I do not mean that the abstract ideas which lie behind the riddles of ethics should be as abruptly brushed aside from consideration as my brief account may suggest. But I do believe that they must be restated in the light of the attempt to deal rationally with difficulties, including, indeed, the intellectual difficulty of formulating adequate systems of ideas. Failure to meet such difficulties will be the reason why men will not be satisfied to remain caught by the riddles. The result will be that they will treat them as trivialities or, at the most, interesting puzzles, puzzles whose only serious aspect lies in the fact that attempts to resolve puzzles and paradoxes may sometimes lead one to hit upon important ideas. Often, for instance, men arrive at important ideas only by recognizing that some of the assumptions of the dilemma or paradox are false and must be discarded. My insistence, therefore, that ideas must come to grips with realities and human problems does not deny an interest in ideas; for actions without ideas are stupid, unnecessarily frustrating to human ends. That is why a more adequate ethics and theory of values is essential.

I am concerned with the intelligence that is implicit in the biological or human act, both with respect to means and to ends, and with the elaboration of conditions under which that intelligence may be recognized and further developed. However, the traditional slogan, supposedly stemming from Hume, is that one cannot infer the "ought" from the "is." Actually, a more accurate statement of Hume's position would be that the "ought" cannot arise solely from the "is." As much may be said of any idea, if we do not accept the view that ideas are mere copies of things. But as for the slogan, one may note that, like most slogans, it has a number of meanings. In one sense, it expresses a great moral truth. The fact that something *is* the case is no proof that it *ought* to be the case. But in another meaning, this slogan is the grounds for the attack upon any naturalism in ethics and upon any attempt to present an ethics upon a rational and factual foundation. That attack has been carried on by Moore and later by R. M. Hare on the general grounds that no description can entail or give rise to prescription. Because I do not believe that these arguments are relevant to both means and ends in the same way, if to either at all, I shall consider them separately.

Hare injects prescription into the question of ends or values by insisting that "the primary use of the word 'good' is to commend."[2] In turn, Hare uses the word 'commendatory' in the prescriptive sense. He says that "what is wrong with naturalistic theories is that they leave out the prescriptive or commendatory element in value-judgments, by seeking to make them derivable from statements of fact."[3] He then summarizes his view as follows: "The argument of the preceding chapter establishes that 'good', being a word used for commending, is not to be defined in terms of a set of characteristics whose names are not used for commending."[4]

I would not deny that in ordinary language usage, 'commend' may and often does connote 'recommend', which may be a euphemism that can descend into, 'You're a dirty dog if you don't'. However, Hare's argument that 'good' is used to commend is not as compelling as it might be, simply because he also denies it or denies that it is always so used. Thus, contrary to the foregoing statement, we discover that "there are cases, however, in which we use the word 'good' with no commendatory meaning at all,"[5] and, furthermore, "It is worth noticing here that the functions of the word 'good' which are concerned with information could be performed equally well if 'good' had no commendatory function at all."[6]

With due gratitude for the umbrella that Hare provides, I shall not use the term 'good' in any sense of prescription. We can note, not merely as a matter of fact, that not only are there ends in biological acts, but also men may sometimes find very great goods in life. In no sense, however, is their doing so a prescription for others, since it is a question of empirical fact whether something similar will prove to be very good for another. And I shall come eventually to define what the latter concept might well mean.

We have not found prescriptions to be essentially entailed by values as such. But prescription would be injected into the problem by any attempt to impose values on others. In that case prescription may be as arbitrary and irrational as the positivists and analysts suggest. The alternative to this is that we have to find out empirically what may come to be of value to men.

However, the problem may not be brushed aside so easily. Can we avoid forcing our values on others or having values forced upon us? A frequent argument is to construct or imagine situations in which values are thrown into inescapable conflict. It is, of course, a matter of ordinary experience that the individual must choose between values, as actual achievements, for one cannot have everything. And it may well be that people are sometimes so bound together in their common activity that a choice for some is a choice for all. But the problem involves how, most nearly, the major interests of all involved may be conserved.

While it is true that there is no antecedent guarantee that any problem will be solved; nevertheless, situations are never immediately found to be insoluble. Human invention and ingenuity are always possible means of solution and the struggle to establish values is still going on. The important point, however, is that the problem becomes one of means, so that we pass to the ethical or moral side of the question. According to James, the conflict of ends is the condition under which the moral question arises.[7]

Yet I think that it is false or misleading to present the problem of values as though it were merely one of conflict between ends. And it is just this falsehood which sometimes makes the conflict seem insoluble. Rather, conflicts are often resolved by the institution of larger and more inclusive ends. It is this inventive and creative process which needs to be brought forward and, more hopefully, made the center of attention. By the same token, it is a task that is more nearly akin to that of the artist and prophet —a sufficiently practical prophet—than it is to that of the moralist, especially of the more traditional variety.

In this chapter, I am not concerned with the moral or the ethical, but with values. The ethical problem has intruded only because of the uncritical confusion of ethics and values, under the general term 'value judgments', the grounds of that confusion presumably being that they certainly are related. On the face of it, it would seem that there is a good deal more excuse for the injection of the notion of prescription into ethics and morals than into values. But this, I think, requires more analysis than the analyst gives it. It is an historical fact that moral rules have been, by long tradition, stated as commandments, issuing either from a theological source or from a mythological lawgiver or from both. And thus they are expressed as imperatives. However,

the grammatical use of the term 'imperative' covers a number of
rather different expressions, such as commands, requests, and
entreaties. Yet, in practice, commands are quite different from
requests, unless the latter is a mere euphemism for the former;
and this difference is more, I think, than one of polite manners.
One's reaction to a command might be to demand some cre-
dential of authority if it is not already obvious—a policeman not
in uniform must show some token. In essence, Hare is demanding
the credentials of moral commandments, and he doesn't find
any. However, all that is irrelevant to an ordinary request, and
we do not make any such demand of a beggar. Rather, we may
wish to be shown some need that makes the request reasonable.

It is difficult and uncertain to trace causes and influences, but
the cause of our response to human need cannot with confidence
be traced wholly to moralistic preachments and theological beliefs. There would also be a question of the source of the moralistic preachments themselves, if one does not resort to theological
origins. Their sources are not always as accidental, I think, as
Hare's arbitrary decisions would make them. One source may lie
in sympathetic responses which are outgrowths of man's social
nature, in the sense that Mead elaborates. We identify ourselves
with others and respond to their needs, and, if so, we tend to
respond more readily to those with whom we can more readily
identify ourselves. However, I am not concerned with sympathetic sentiments, but rather with the needs and values thus
recognized.

The concept of need is, of course, brushed aside by Hare as
being "evaluative," but I suggest that some evaluations may be
based on fact and reason. The significance of the fact that there
is need is that some great value is in fact at stake, or else some
major condition for values. Thus it is in terms of the actual
threat to major values that some action becomes imperative. Now
it may very well be that men vaguely recognize these things and
formulate them as general principles of conduct in the form of
commandments, and seek to give them weight by attributing

them to theological sources. What I am suggesting is that it is an error to model ethics on commandments, incapable of any authority; rather, ethics should look to the imperative of need, which in turn is defined by the ends of major value that are at stake.

Plato destroyed the subjective relativism which he attributed somewhat hesitantly to Protagoras, the view that truth is merely a matter of opinion, by an appeal which has become the essence of modern science and pragmatism. That appeal was to anticipation and to the observed outcome.

The followers of Protagoras will not deny that in determining what is or is not expedient for the community one state is wiser and one counsellor is better than another—they will scarcely venture to maintain, that what a city enacts in the belief that it is expedient will always be really expedient. But in the other case, I mean when they speak of justice and injustice, piety and impiety, they are confident that in nature these have no existence or essence of their own.[8]

Granted that it is meaningful to speak of worthy ends or values, the problem may be stated as: How may men achieve social forms of conduct, including economic, political, and other forms, which will produce "the greatest good for the greatest number"? This formulation may, of course, be turned into a commandment, and its authority brought into question. While criticism of a principle is valuable because a principle is not self-interpreting, nevertheless, beyond that, challenging it on authoritarian grounds is irrelevant to anything more than authoritarian claims. I have a different claim to present—that claim based on the definition of the ethical as means in terms of ends, all ends involved.

It is a matter of fact that some methods, including conduct, are apparently more fruitful in enabling all men involved in the case to achieve worthy ends, than are some other methods. This defines the "ought" so far as it is rational, and it does not appeal to the arbitrary. But it does push the question over into one of values, for we are required to define 'worthy ends' in empirical terms. The temporary separation of fact and value is itself a fact of life, leading to human frustration. Consequently, the distinction of fact and value is a necessity of intellectual consideration, for they are often not the same; but a logical distinction is no proof either of logical irrelevancy or of factual separation; and the ultimate separation of fact and value leads to a perversion of life—a perversion in the sense that value possibilities are not realized in fact. But the distinction between value and fact is violated when a logical distinction is misinterpreted to be an existential separation. Descartes exhibited this fallacy when he based a metaphysical or existential separation of mind and body on a logical or definitional distinction.

The normative presupposes ends. In general terms this may be expressed by the hypothetical: If certain ends, then certain means. But the actual case is expressed in categorical terms. The only place for the hypothetical in the actual case occurs to the extent that the actual case is problematic or indeterminate. But when the basic security of great and actual values is at stake, then there are urgencies as matters of the specific situation. These urgencies are then categorical and they are imperative. The absurdity in Kant's argument for the categorical imperative is that, to make morals both absolute and rational, he attempts to deduce directions for human conduct from logical consistency. This I take to be another instance of the "ontological fallacy."

The disjunction between value and fact causes artificial difficulties. It is created, I think, by the attempt to put into sharp contrast highly formalized systems of thought, such as the well-developed sciences, with what, on the other hand, Hare calls "judgments" "which are not informative in the least,"[9] but which he considers to have the nature of value judgments—as though those were our only alternatives. But Dewey has pointed to something else as "qualitative thought."[10] Qualitative thought is the first type of thought to emerge because it can and does operate when we have no well-clarified ideas, but merely a sense of things. Men sensed that some arguments were better than others long before Aristotle organized logic. Qualitative thought has its advantages and its limitations. It lacks clarity and thus is more or less confused, as the early modern rationalists insisted. Hence, it is readily influenced by adventitious things, and being more or less vague, is not so explicitly verifiable as are more clarified ideas. In addition, it may be infected by the more superstitious notion of luck. But, of course, scientific hypotheses are not always so conclusively confirmed or disconfirmed as the oversimplified versions of that process seem to lead many to assume.

Moreover, hypothetical generalized principles, whether in science or other areas of inquiry, emerge at first as qualitative intuitive ideas, some to be discarded, some to become dogmatic, while others are to be further clarified, developed, and more rigorously tested. Attempts at clarification are themselves proposals, and this chapter is only one among countless other attempts. Those proposals must, to a significant extent, fit our antecedent qualitative sense; and they must facilitate and increase rationality as it is validated by effectiveness in dealing with relevant human problems. Some of their effectiveness might be little more than eliminating false or misleading starts. Even clarified, precise, and formalized systematic thought does not so much abandon the qualitative as it selects and builds on and beyond it in more dependable ways, thereby opening up new and more powerful means. And yet, ultimately, science remains an art. A good research man "knows" or senses what questions to ask. That is a qualitative, intuitive judgment as to which line of investigation will prove to be more fruitful.

For centuries, men knew very well that an argument in the following form is valid: New York is larger than Chicago. Chicago is larger than Philadelphia. Therefore, New York is larger than Philadelphia. It is valid even though it could not be put in the syllogistic form of three terms connected with the copula.

It is also true today that there is no sense in which we can use a computer to discriminate between a great painting and trash; and yet directors of art museums must make such judgments all the time. Of course, as we have seen, the objective validity of such judgments is denied by many analysts.

Qualitative judgments are, indeed, not too dependable. The qualitative judgments of essay examinations or of English compositions lack reliability to a notorious degree and are easily influenced by the adventitious. Nevertheless, it is still a fact that they are not futile; they have some objectivity. And by greater care in method, one can eliminate or reduce some of the adventitious influences which are more pernicious. And so the fact remains that, by qualitative judgment, we manage to deal more or less effectively with most of the common problems of ordinary life.

II

Like other words in the dictionary, the words 'good' and 'value' have a variety of meanings, and I am not selecting one meaning for the sake of saying that this is the true meaning. But I am concerned with rational consideration of human ends and appropriate human conduct. Or rather, I am more directly concerned with the grounds on which rational consideration of these things may be possible. The felicity of human life is to secure and love some things that prove worthy of being loved. This is the occasion for questions of value and value judgments, in any sense that I am concerned with them. But if this is to be the foundation of a treatment of values, then values are matters of human ends.

Yet further dialectical analysis may require clarification of a number of distinctions, although they are distinctions between things which are so closely connected as to be all matters of values in one way or another. For instance, some things may be worthy of being human ends, although no one may actually take them as his ends. At least we must provide for the expression of such a distinction, because what is worthy of being an end and what is an actual end are not precisely the same thing. Some ends are not worthy; and, of course, worthy things may be possible ends, but the fact that they are possible ends does not imply that a particular individual may make them all his ends. For instance, worthy possibilities may conflict. No individual can do everything. He cannot make every worthy possibility his actual end. Hence, to say that the good is what we ought to do is nonsense in more ways than one. The point here is that we could not possibly do or have every *kind* of good thing, much less *every* good thing. Therefore it is not true that we ought to do or have every good thing, for 'ought' does imply 'can'. But, rather, what is appropriately judged to be good is what is worthy of being done or worthy of being had.

There is also a host of ambiguities in the common use of such words as 'ends' which it would seem tedious to make explicit each time such a word is used, and perhaps even tedious to mention. The word 'end' is used in two different senses. There is the "end-in-view" which guides the act before the "end" is reached, and both are called "ends." The latter of the two will not, of course, be reached or achieved in the frustrated act. Again, we speak of things as actual occurrences and also as possibilities, and apply this distinction to values. Thus we may judge that some actual achievement—for instance, a work of art—is worthy; or again we may judge that something merely considered is or would be worthy. Both of these may be called "values," but only the former is real, at least as I shall use the word. Doubtless it would be better to speak of the latter as a "possible value." But I shall trust that the context will clarify what is meant, although this may sometimes prove to be too trusting.

While actual ends and what are worthy of being ends are not the same thing, for a number of reasons, they are nonetheless closely related. And the particular kind of relation they have is most important. Possible ends are ends in a proleptic sense. It is the fact of having ends in actual conduct (not as merely contemplated or dreamed of) that constitutes the empirical conditions under which worthy ends are developed, and, in the final analysis, the confirmation or disconfirmation of what is judged to be worthy.

Kinds of judgments may be distinguished. Some are inventions; some are primarily inferences from other similar or supposedly related cases, while other judgments may not only include inferences but depend also on more direct experimental investigation. Common knowledge of murder is adequate for inference. One does not need to commit murder to know that it is evil. But not all cases of inferences respecting human conduct or human possibilities, good or bad, are this much settled; and many inferences are most doubtful, being infected with prejudice, social approval either by fad or custom, and various extrinsic and irrelevant matters.

Values are things properly valued: they are things properly judged to be values. Proper judgment, including experimental judgment, is based on properties that things have as experimentally determined. I wish to consider the properties with which judgment of things as values might well be primarily concerned. In this connection, I wish to propose grounds on which some ethical and value judgments can be rational. This requires an appropriate definition of values or the good. Doubtless, attention has already alighted on my use of the word 'worthy'. My intent is to define values or higher values in a sufficiently empirical manner that they may be located and used in testing ideas about them. There are those who identify ideals with values, but I am not concerned with the term as thus defined. Ideals, I take to be, not values in the first instance, but *ideas* of what are values or possible values. This would be the most direct relation of ideals to values. But words, of course, have a variety of meanings, and another use of the word 'ideal' is to refer to basic standards of conduct, sometimes called "principles."

I wish to define values in objective terms. However, Moore says that 'good' is indefinable. Thus some consideration of his view would seem to be called for. If we accept the traditional distinction between real and nominal definition, what Moore may be saying is that we cannot give a real definition. In discussing his view, I pass over Moore's distinction between 'good', which he says is indefinable and 'the good', which he says is definable. I do this because his definition of 'the good' is somewhat vacuous. That is to say, his definition is the whole of that to which the adjective 'good' is applicable. Moore himself indicates that he must depend on his own intuition to know when 'good' is applicable, which would surely be the case if he cannot define it.

Moore says, "My point is that 'good' is a simple notion, just as 'yellow' is a simple notion; that just as you cannot by any manner of means explain to anyone who does not already know it, what yellow is, so you cannot explain what good is."[11] Now I have the greatest difficulty with this key passage. The point that one cannot in the relevant sense explain what yellow is does not clearly have anything to do with whether the *notion* of "yellow" is simple, much less with the question whether the notion of "good" is simple. Moore's remark is ambiguous since it seems explicitly to be about "notions"; whereas I believe that it gets its plausibility respecting simplicity by reference to the color yellow as it appears in experience. It is possible that this equivocation occurs because of the correspondence theory of truth which realists usually hold. However that may be, I do not follow the logic of it.

It may be true that, in the evolutionary process of developing the great values of mature life, we do begin with the simple little goods of earliest childhood: "This candy is good." Perhaps the growth of love and affection begins with the simple bodily comforts that a mother administers in infancy. Perhaps, too, the child learns to say 'this is good' in much the same way that he learns to say 'this is yellow' or 'this is an automobile'. Yet all this, so far as I can see, has nothing to do with what Moore is saying.

The simple goods, such as I have mentioned, are not the simple "good" that Moore is discussing, whatever else it may be.

Rather, Moore connects his view with the atomistic analysis peculiar to the philosophy of realism, not to mention later philosophies, wherein wholes are to be broken down into parts, and into ultimately simple parts which are not further analyzable —a view which was considered and rejected by Plato in the *Theaetetus*. Thus yellow is indefinable, Moore says, because "a definition states what are the parts which invariably compose a certain whole,"[12] and neither yellow nor good has parts. I would say that whether or not 'yellow' is definable, yellow is certainly not definable in the same sense of definition, for it is not a term. I do not demand that he put the word in quotes necessarily, but I do think that he should clarify the confusion already mentioned. It may be noted, however, that in saying that good is not analyzable, Moore is not denying that things that are good are analyzable. However, I wish to analyze them in respect to being good.

This definition of definition which Moore insists upon is peculiar, to say the least. First, one will hardly find this view of definition in any book on logic; and, second, he will probably find a variety of methods of definition. Hence, it does not follow that 'good' is indefinable. If Moore means only to say that yellow is simple and unanalyzable, he should say just that. But his error, as I view the matter, is that he takes the fact that yellow is unanalyzable to be proof that the *notion* of yellow is unanalyzable; and, what is worse, he extends this by analogy to good and to the notion of good. I suggest an alternative view; namely, that it is yellow, taken—as he seems to take it—as an *immediate quality* that is unanalyzable. But an immediate quality is not a notion of any kind, if one does not adopt Locke's assumption that qualities are ideas.[13] Moore's analogy, so far as it is relevant to what I have to say, would lead to the conclusion that all values are simple. But I suggest that the great values of mature human life, including some that Moore mentions, are anything but simple, even *qua* values.

There is, however, a tendency among realists to treat values in simple ways, and this is equally evident among realists who, unlike Moore, do manage to give definitions. "A value is any object of desire." "A value is the object of any interest." Perhaps this bias toward simplicity arises from the realists' bias towards analysis and its attendant atomistic philosophy. In contrast, the view which I have to offer may be a kind of naturalism. But, "Naturalism offers no reason at all for any ethical principle whatever," according to Moore.[14] Hare says, quaintly, "It is best to confine it [the term 'naturalism'] to those theories against which Moore's refutation (or a recognizable version of it) is valid."[15] This use of 'naturalism' does not obviously appear to be "ordinary linguistic usage."

At any rate, one cannot get an ethics out of such a conception of good as Moore offers, for the great objects of human devotion are far from simple. Their greatness requires richness. Their roots or the materials upon which they feed are, indeed, the elemental things of life. These latter become life's very substance when transformed and incorporated by the metabolic processes of life, which give rise to new objects with new qualities and which serve more significantly as new ends of human aspiration. The poet, perhaps, is more likely to be aware of this fact:

One day in 1938 a man climbed out on a window ledge
Twenty-three stories or so above the street and he wouldn't come
    back.
Come back, come back, they cried, please come back,
And they offered him a Hershey bar.
But he shook his head no.
They offered him a nickel-plated cocktail shaker and a subscrip-
    tion to *Life* and a scholarship to Yale and a round trip to both
    Fairs.
No, no, no, he said, no, no, no.
They offered him love, beauty, goodness, and truth and the nif-
    tiest chorus girl in all New York.

So finally he jumped, and people spoke with a strange light in
their eyes,
Saying, He was mad, I tell you, mad, mad.[16]

If 'good' were truly indefinable, one would not know how to
use it and it would not be a word. However, Moore does claim
to tell us "what 'good' means."[17] Certainly, when he comes to
point to some good things of life, he is not misled by his theory;
and I think this is so because, as he says, he does so by intuition
and not by theory. His theory would be quite useless.

The greatest goods, Moore says, are "personal affections and
aesthetic enjoyments."[18] I am not at all sure that it is true that
these are the greatest goods. For instance, there are the assertions
of Aristotle and of Spinoza as to what is the greatest good, and
I do not know how Aristotle's contemplation or Spinoza's ambiguous God or love of God,[19] not to mention other possibilities,
would fit Moore's claim. Moore himself has other values or
concerns. Thus he writes, "What I am concerned with is knowledge only—that we should think correctly and so far arrive at
some truth, however unimportant: I do not say that such knowledge will make us more useful members of society. If anyone
does not care for knowledge for its own sake then I have nothing
to say to him: only it should not be thought that a lack of
interest in what I have to say is any ground for holding it un-
true."[20] It does not seem wholly obvious that knowledge for its
own sake would be identified as either personal affection or
aesthetic enjoyment, although the term, 'aesthetic enjoyment',
might be made vague enough to cover anything and everything.
But if knowledge for its own sake is not to be identified with
either, then, since they are "by far the greatest goods," it would
follow that knowledge for its own sake would be "by far" secondary to them.

Nevertheless, it still may be the case that the goods to which
Moore points are very great goods. Yet the way in which he
points to them leads to difficulties, for he says explicitly that

the goods to which he refers are "certain states of consciousness." The nature of his discussion indicates that Moore is led into this by his realistic assumption of a subjective-objective dualism. But the difficulty that is immediately to the point is that, when he identifies these goods with subjective states of consciousness, he does not make a place for or invite analysis which is most relevant to actual problems that men face in respect to what is good. Possibly he would conceive that states of consciousness are analyzable, but to do so is not adequate. The most obvious fact of common observation is that human infatuation notoriously dogs personal affection and aesthetic enjoyment. And it is strange that, even though Moore has reached the height that would "include *all* the greatest, and *by far* the greatest, goods we can imagine," he never mentions that notorious fact.

Perhaps Moore would pass off infatuation as another state of consciousness, but this subjectivism has the difficulty of precluding analysis of the objective situation, namely, to discriminate between the genuine and the spurious. That is to say, it is analysis of an objective situation which may show that the affection or enjoyment is based on adventitious elements. Later, anyway, one may ruefully ponder the question, "What did I ever see in that?" or in him or in her? This cannot be accounted for nor be reasonably dealt with merely in terms of states of consciousness, except as being totally capricious.

Moore's view that naturalism offers no reason at all for any ethical principle whatever would seem to constitute a breakdown of his analogy between good and yellow, for percipient organisms seem to arise in nature and so do their functions, such as color vision. Yet his view is consistent enough with the view which he also states, "That which is meant by 'good' is, in fact, except for its converse, 'bad', the *only* simple object of thought which is peculiar to ethics."[21] This last view, that "good" is *peculiar* to ethics, would, I agree, not only make naturalistic ethics impossible and incapable of any validation, it would also make that particular ethics, together with its "peculiar" conception of good, to be of no importance whatever. Any ethics in which its concept of good is peculiar to itself could only be eccentric and dogmatic. These characteristics are common enough in ethics, but they are certainly not naturalistic.

Of course the words 'natural' and 'naturalistic' have a number of different meanings as signified by their various opposites: natural versus supernatural, natural versus matters of art, and so on. Furthermore, their opposites may have different meanings which in turn give further different meanings to 'natural'; 'artificial' may signify 'made by art', or it may connote some "make do" that is inappropriate. But when, for instance, C. D. Broad merely uses 'non-natural', that is not helpful in clarifying what he does mean positively. I shall not use the word 'natural', although I welcome it in the same sense in which one may say that the sciences (all sciences) are concerned with the natural. But, as we have seen, they are not mere descriptions.

Also, the word 'good' is used in a variety of senses. For instance, there is the ethical sense. Often when one is told to be good, what is meant is to be virtuous or to do what is right. (Of course, popularly, the word 'virtue' has come primarily to signify conformity to sex conventions, but I am ignoring that.) I mention the use of 'good' in the ethical sense for the sake of making it clear that this is not the sense in which I use the word. I shall not use it in that sense because it easily leads to and lends apparent support to the common confusion of ethics or morals—in the sense of right and wrong—with values in the sense of ends.

Ethics is concerned with values because values or ends are matters of concern other than merely ethical. Values of some level emerge in life antecedently to ethics, and more or less independently of ethics; and more so, so far as the ethics is inadequate. Good is what men find to be good. It is just because of this that good things may and should become objects of ethical concern, and this affords the ground on which the validity of ethical views may be questioned and confirmed.

The restriction and subordination of value theory to ethics

may be an inheritance from traditional moralistic dogmatism, which has its roots in sources which have no logical bearing on the issue. Moreover, it has other difficulties that find expression in the assertion which we have noticed before; namely, "the good is what one ought to do." But if we define 'the good' in terms of 'ought' in any final sense, then we, in turn, have no way to derive the "ought" except from dogmatic authoritarianism or else intuition. Therefore, doing so subordinates things found good to unbridled moralism. This moralism is unbridled because it is not grounded in fact and reason and so it is not restricted by them. Thus it is that the subordination of values to ethics puts both into question and clouds both value theory and ethical theory.

The pearl of great price which one can extract from the analysts is that to subordinate values to moral and ethical commitments (as they would) is to destroy the moral and ethical (as they would), in any rational sense. It is this presupposed subordination, I think, which is the source of pseudoquestions. Discussions of values often seem to be carried on with the presupposition that the value must have some kind of authorization or antecedent grounds of approval to make it legitimate. Or, for Hare, it "is almost entirely prescriptive." I suggest that historically this doctrine has been vicious, and that the intelligent and humane alternative to it is the experimental method. At any rate, finding no such rational grounds for prescriptions, some conclude that values are subjective or arbitrary.

I submit, however, that approval or disapproval of values, as distinct from morals, is impertinent and irrational. To put this point in different words, one may say that the only rational grounds for any approval of values is just that they are values. Of course, some ends may have a causal bearing on other ends, and in that way become legitimately subject to moral considerations. Moreover, ends may be evaluated in respect to whether they are worthy. The value words—'worthy', 'satisfactory', 'admirable'—are judgmental or evaluative words. They pertain to possibilities respecting ends, and while they may in some sense commend, they do not recommend. Respecting ends, as Kant said, love cannot be commanded. Pressure may cause people to give the appearance of adopting certain ends, but the actual end will often be merely to avoid the pressure.

A connected idea which is sometimes posed is the pseudo-problem of the verification of a value. No fact is verified, except as it is an elliptical expression of the verification of the proposition that such and such is a fact; but it is the *proposition* that is verified. Facts, including values, are neither true nor false, although there may be a question as to what kinds of facts they may be. And in a particular case, there may indeed be a question as to whether a thing is a value. The idea of verification of a value is sometimes interpreted in further irrelevant ways. If *A* says that *x* is a value, then *B*, upon questioning that statement, may seek to verify it by determining whether it is a value to *B*, as though that had any bearing on the issue. The relevant point would be for *B* to verify that *x* is a value for *A*.

When ends are already taken for granted, then there is no genuine problem or question of value. But when ends are not antecedently given and are to be formulated, then there is occasion for intelligent evaluation. The professional counselor in the public school, who deals with the formulation of ends, is trained to avoid letting his own preferences enter the situation. His training has used slogans to this purpose such as 'child-centered' or 'client-centered' counseling. He studies the pupil and helps the pupil study himself. In some cases of counseling, the end has already been established. The child has a love for science or he wants to go to college. The question is then one of means, such as what to do in meeting certain requirements. In other cases, such as vocational counseling, the problem may be one of formulating an end. In this case, not only the aptitudes, but also the many interests or preferences of the pupil or client must be studied and taken into account, as well as the possibilities open to him.

I have taken the view that, in the first instance, the means, including ethics, is to be defined and evaluated in terms of ends. Ends or values are not to be defined in terms of ethics. But this view, while it expresses the basic means-ends relation, is an over-simplification of the complexities. For instance, we adopt some ends for the sake of other ends. In that case, an end is a means to other ends, an obvious point. There is a more important sense in which ends must be defined or analyzed in terms of means, if the supposed means is to be genuinely a means to that end. Our ends or values, if they are not to be mere ideals or dreams, must be stated in terms of materials. If we consider a vacation, we must, for instance, state it in terms of dollars and cents, or else it is not likely to get beyond the stage of mere contemplation. The fallacy would be to take the dollars and cents statement as a statement of the value of the vacation.

Even more important, the means enters into the end value in a still more significant sense; namely, to give it richness of meaning and significance. This fact is recognized, although in-adequately, in the common observation that we appreciate more what we work for. A more significant illustration is the way in which the medium enters into the aesthetic function of a work of art; as stone, in contrast to other materials, contributes a par-ticular aesthetic quality, and the particular kind of stone, wheth-er a coarse-grained stone or a fine-grained stone such as marble. Both the stone and the scaffolding are means, but the one enters into the end result in a way that the other does not. The artist works out and develops his ideas in the medium, just as a scientist works out and develops his ideas in the laboratory. Thus the material is something other than a merely unfortunate condition of limitation: it is the very substance of the achieved end value. At any rate, the fusion of means and ends is a characteristic of the unity of the act.

Any rational approval or disapproval of an end on grounds extrinsic to its status as a value will always presuppose other ends or probable ends of major value in some definite way. But then, the subjection of values to moral judgment must be in that way explicitly justifiable in the particular case. Yet if rational approval and disapproval presuppose ends; then, apart from an infinite regress or a circle, approval and disapproval of ends will in some cases be irrational or nonrational, which is to say, nonpertinent.

III

It is often the case that even when ends are admitted, the logical treatment of them is singularly inept. Thus when Hare uses learning to drive a car, as an illustration of moral instruction, he says, "We establish at the beginning certain ends, for example the avoidance of collisions."[22] Now, while in the practicalities of driving instruction, we may readily pass over things that may be taken for granted, Hare wishes to generalize this illustration, as a philosophical view, and that requires a greater care and exactness. Hare uses this inexact analysis of ends for the sake of subordinating ends to the moralistic. Hence he goes on to say, "The ends of good driving (safety, the avoidance of inconvenience to others, the preservation of property, and so on) are justified ultimately, if justification is sought, by appeal to moral considerations."[23] But I should have thought that the end of driving is usually to get to some specific place where one wants to go, and justification of that would rarely be concerned with "appeal to moral considerations." The ends which Hare mentions are important in two ways; namely, that they are more or less incidental or essential to getting to where one is going; and, secondly, that they signify the relation or infringement of that activity upon other ends, including the ends of other individuals. This infringement does introduce moral considerations. To carry out an act in view of an end in a way that ignores this relation to other ends is to be fanatical and ruthless. That does indeed introduce moral considerations, but it does not constitute the end of driving or justify such an end, nor do moral considerations justify the other ends involved. Rather the considerations are moral, and so are justified morally, just because they are considerate of the other ends.

When it is not accepted—or not clearly accepted—that the question of values is the question of human ends, the results are sometimes so strange that there would not seem to be any unifying concept at all. For the sake of clarifying this point, I refer to a treatment of the "concept of value"[24] which is both general and systematic. The fact that this treatment is in an introductory textbook does not, I think, affect my point, which is that the examples of values given are, generally speaking, not anything that would constitute a human end or an object of appreciation in any sense. "To a man in the forest on a cold night, flint takes on a greater value than diamond."[25] Evidently, the author means that the flint would be more useful. Again, "Why do we regard milk as having greater 'value' for health than gasoline?"[26] "The taking of medicine is good."[27] In these two examples, 'value' and 'good' are again used strictly in a utilitarian sense; namely, as a means toward health. "We say that a real estate lot has economic value—it has a good economically if not otherwise. . . . Nor do we necessarily mean that the lot is valuable because it can be used pleasurably; for it may have value as a garbage dump."[28] The philosopher has descended so far, in his search for values, into these utilitarian trivialities, that he winds up— rather appropriately, I think—in a garbage dump. When I call them "trivialities," I mean as ends, though not necessarily as means. Surely there are human ends that reach higher than garbage dumps.

I hasten to add that the authors do mention in passing, without elaboration or emphasis, paintings and musical compositions.[29] Are they, as values, on a level with garbage dumps? I hope that I may be excused one value judgment; namely, that garbage dumps are hardly among the values of men at their finest. They may be, as Heraclitus suggested, the appropriate endings of men, but they are not thereby the appropriate ends. If these remarks are truisms (one cannot be sure what will be taken for granted), they are not said in any lack of respect for these excellent and distinguished authors, but to emphasize the distinction, not separation or irrelevancy, between values as ends and the instrumental or material functions of things which are not intrinsic to values.

One of the above quotations mentions the possibility of a city lot being "used pleasurably," as though that were the only alternative. There is such a theory of values which has been criticized so frequently that some excuse would seem to be called for to introduce it; namely, the identification of the good with pleasure.[30] In criticizing that view, I do not wish to give aid and comfort to the opposite view of aesceticism, that pleasure is evil or bad. Neither do I wish to amass all the arguments of the past against the pleasure theory of values, but rather I would like to state some arguments that are of particular relevance to the view I am presenting, that is to say, the treatment of values in terms of ends. If values are at least possible ends, then a value can be an end, and what cannot be an end or satisfy the conditions for being an end cannot be a value.

First, the actual occurrence of pleasure, I presume, is the case in which x pleases y. That is to say, pleasure is an interrelation, under specific conditions, between an object being what it is and an organism being what it is, including its state and condition. For instance, the organism may change, over a shorter or longer period of time, and what at first gave it pleasure may no longer do so, or what did not give it pleasure may come to do so. The eating of food which gave pleasure to the hungry man may no longer give him pleasure after a heavy meal. A person may come to appreciate some form of art, and what once gave him little or no pleasure may now give great pleasure. Since pleasure is an interrelation between the object and the person, then the fact that one finds pleasure in a particular object is indicative of the kind of person that he is. This point would also, of course, be the direct implication of the views that have been advanced in the previous chapter. The person who finds pleasure in the suffering of others is a sadist. The conclusion that follows is that when one begins to find pleasure in sarcasm or in the misfortunes of others, the pleasure, far from being an inevitable mark of the good, is on the contrary a warning of the kind of person that one is becoming. Moreover, it may be added that, if pleasure is an interrelation between an organism and an object, then, if in the attempt to state values purely in terms of pleasure the object is cut off, the relation is truncated. Rather, it is the object which is the end or goal; or, more strictly, the end is some transaction with the object.

Second, is it true that there are no qualitative differences between pleasures? For instance, is there no qualitative difference whatever between, let us say, the pleasure or enjoyment we may have in reading a novel, in eating when we are hungry, in finding that our child who was in great danger is saved, in taking great amusement at a comic situation or joke, or in watching a tragic play? Are all these pleasures exactly the same in quality? They do not seem to me to be so. Indeed, it would seem that not only in reading different novels, but in reading one novel, our pleasure or enjoyment would differ markedly in quality with the varied and different situations that the novel would present.[31]

Yet we are faced with the startling fact that there is no way to so much as intimate the quality of the pleasure except by mentioning the object in which pleasure is found.[32] Thus the random illustrations of the foregoing paragraph, which indicate qualitative differences between pleasures, had in every case to mention such an object. The point is that the quality of the pleasure cannot be indicated purely in terms of the pleasure itself. An apparent exception might seem to be indicated when one says that a certain pleasure is "the pleasure of a sadist." However, a kind of person, the sadist, is defined in terms of the object, and so is "sadistic pleasure." To say that the expressions 'sadistic pleasure' and 'sexual pleasure' indicate the qualitative differences of pleasures without mentioning the objects in which they are found is implausible. A sadist is one who finds pleasure in the suffering of others. Similarly, 'sexual pleasure' is defined in terms of the object: that is, the act in which the pleasure is found.

Bentham, therefore, had a fine logical sense when he recognized the implication of his pleasure doctrine; namely, that if pleasure is the good, then there are no differences whatever between pleasures except quantitative differences. To be sure, he wanted to make pleasure quantitative for the sake of his calculus, but that of itself would not deny qualitative differences. Rather, it was his elimination of the object that made one pleasure the same as any other. The significance of this general point is that in any particular instance we are likely to get further intellectually by considering the objects in which we may find pleasure, assuming for the moment that something of the sort is what we are concerned with, rather than attempting to consider pleasure per se on the assumption that it is our goal. This point is so closely related to the next that I go on to it without further development.

Third, a major point of the view of values presented here is that values are defined in terms of ends. Hence, it must be that anything with which values are identified must satisfy the conditions for being an end or goal. Consider, then, one condition which they must meet; namely, that an end or goal operates to direct conduct or to define, regulate, or delimit a line of conduct in specific ways. But pleasure fails to meet this criterion. Thus if someone were to propose, "Let us have pleasure," we would not know what was meant or what specifically to do, or to consider. While, negatively, it may eliminate doing anything presumably unpleasant, it obviously does not propose anything specific, and so it is not a specific goal; hence, pleasure is just as obviously not an end or goal. If, on the other hand, someone says, "Let us go see a (certain) play this evening," then we know what to do or can find out what to do in these specific terms. That would organize our conduct along specific lines.

It has previously been suggested that it is the function of theory, including ethical and value theories, to provide presuppositions on the grounds of which judgment may be made more intelligent. Thus, in presupposing that it is seeing the play which is the objective or goal, we then have the conditions for rational consideration. We have an object to consider, and its implications: What would be involved? Can I spare the time or the money? What is the play about? Where is it being given? Only upon some such grounds can there be a rational evaluation of the proposal. Now someone may argue that some of the same questions could be raised meaningfully about the proposal to have pleasure, at least the question, "What would be involved?" But the meaning of such a general question would be quite different. Indeed, the meaning of the question in respect to the mere proposal to have pleasure is that it calls for a specification of the objective or goal.

The implication of this view is that pleasure is not and cannot be an end or goal. For that reason there is no such thing as "pleasure seeking" in any literal sense. The idiomatic expression, 'pleasure seeking', may indeed denote things that actually occur, just as does the expression, 'sunrise', but it does not indicate a truth about them. Rather, what is called "pleasure seeking" is the seeking of goals, but goals which are too trivial to be considered seriously as goals. In any case, the pleasure itself is not the specific goal actually sought.

Fourth, the pleasure doctrine of the good contributes to an extremely misleading, and, I think, immature conception of the things that come to have the deepest significance in life, and of the conditions that attend them, although I do not suggest that having pleasure is immature. It is like a teenage conception of marriage, "and they lived happily ever after"—but teenagers grow up. It may very well be the case that anything worthwhile will give some pleasure and satisfaction, but it will provide plenty of heartache as well, and call for a good deal of drudgery in the bargain. Moreover, it has been noted often enough that pleasure, in the ordinary sense of the term, is evanescent; the great values of life are enduring. "Pleasure" is not an adequate concept even with which to describe the satisfaction of the deepest human emotions, nor is it an adequate description of values or of value situations. A parent sitting up all night with a child whose life is in the balance is not likely to find much in the situation to denote as pleasure, though, often enough, he may turn his anxious eyes upon the beloved child.

While aesceticism may be a perversion, still there is a partial truth in it. The things for which we have made the greatest sacrifice, and of which the costs go down to the very depths of our being, cannot be reached by mere pleasure. One may well doubt that Socrates found his execution pleasurable. Some, of course, may argue plausibly that, by the same token, his execution was not a value but an evil. However, while value situations may be analyzed, values do not occur in a vacuum, but in concrete situations. It is an essential characteristic of great values that they may be lost or destroyed, and so may require great sacrifice to be secured. Hence it was that Socrates himself was convinced that, under the circumstances, being executed was an essential phase of the particular value situation which he faced, the salvation of his beloved city. According to the story, he could have run away to Megara.

With these arguments I now conclude consideration of the good as pleasure. There are more elegant arguments than those I have used, but it is not my main point to refute the notion that pleasure is involved in ends. I do not take it that seriously. Rather, I merely wanted to elaborate on the idea of values as ends.

IV

The basic hypothesis of this theory of values as ends, by way of method, is the extension of ideas which have been experimentally developed in more narrow fields of values to the generalized field of values. The problem of values has come to us entangled with the subjective-objective dualism which much of contemporary philosophy is struggling to abandon. However, that dualism is still so much taken for granted by many, especially in value theory, that their approach is to begin by asking, without more ado, whether values are subjective or objective, this question being intended in a metaphysical rather than a methodological sense. Since nothing can be both subjective and objective in the metaphysical sense, the only possibility left is that they are neither. Although I shall use the word, 'objective', I shall not use it in any way as a choice of either of these metaphysical alternatives, but in the sense that follows.

There is, as Dewey has noted repeatedly,[33] a subjective-objective *distinction*, but it is methodological; it is not a metaphysical distinction and it is not necessarily a dualism. Subjectivity, in this sense, refers to the influence of such attitudes as prejudice and bias upon thinking, in ways that are not evidential. That is to say, it is a particular class of sources of error among others. In that sense, it cannot be one side of a dualism. The conclusion follows that we will think objectively about values or we will probably not think about them at all in any valid sense.

The further supposition is that we can think about values objectively insofar as we have some empirical method of testing our ideas. Accordingly, I will adopt the view of pragmatism, that the relevant concepts should be defined in experimental terms. Valid judgments about values are possible, I assume, if values are of the nature of fact;[34] accordingly, the problem of defining values, so as to permit verification, is a species of the problem of fact, namely, by what empirical criteria or marks are they observed or noted.

The traditional metaphysical dualism provides no basis for stating concepts in experimental terms, not necessarily because it is metaphysical, but because of the kind of metaphysics which it is; that is, a dualism of ontological realms which cannot be brought to terms with each other. Modern dualism carries over the medieval separation of the value or spiritual world from the material world. From the empirical point of view, this represents the erection of the frustrated act—where, to an important extent, a dualism of the ideal and the real does occur—into a metaphysical finality said to characterize the universe. The dualism which we have been considering was in early modern times combined with another distinction to form a view which, however unstated, underlies much of the argument of the time very like an axiom: that what is objective is absolute and what is relative is subjective. As was argued in chapter III, such an axiom is required, for example, in the arguments of Descartes and of Berkeley, if either is to be rendered logical. That is to say, for either, if a quality can be shown to be relative, that is a sufficient condition for its subjectivity, for then it is not absolute and so it is not objective. I reemphasize this axiom because, although it is now discredited in a number of fields of thought, it is still most often presupposed without question in many arguments respecting ethics and values, particularly in the assumption that all forms of relativism can be disposed of as forms of subjectivism. In this assumption, relativism is often equated with the idea that values, morals, and truth are relative to the opinion of the individual or of the group, as though there were no other forms.

Such views, of course, have been held often enough. The idea that morals are relative to the opinion of the individual or are merely a matter of individual opinion is illustrated by the remark that anything is good if one thinks it is good, and bad if one thinks it is bad. Again, one hears it said, 'It is true for you if you think it is true'. Whistler is said to have remarked, "Don't say that it is good art or poor art. Say that you like it or that you don't like it." Art museums, of course, could not adopt these views as methods of procedure, for they could not proceed on the idea that objects are indifferent.

Another variant of this subjective view is that morals are merely a matter of group or society opinion. This was accepted, although not invented, by some anthropologists or sociologists, such as Edward Westermarck, upon finding that morals of all kinds vary more or less greatly from one society to another. However, the very definition of mores—as forms of conduct which a society believes essential to its welfare—would seem to open an avenue for criticism calling for more than mere opinion. Two questions arise: "What is the society's welfare?" and "Is a particular form of conduct really essential to that welfare?" But such criticism would raise the question of validity of opinion and therefore could not accept subjective relativism. That this form of subjectivism is still much in evidence may be indicated by the position advocated by Hare: "The standard became established by . . . making commendatory judgments which are not statements of fact or informative in the least. . . ."[35] One wonders in what conceivable sense such things that "are not statements of fact or informative in the least" could possibly be called "judgments." Yet I do not deny the truth of Hare's statement concerning the origin of many traditional views as itself a historical fact, but recognition of such facts may form the basis of critical evaluation rather than acceptance.

The modern acceptance of subjective relativism in morals and values may be treated most sympathetically as a reaction against the ancient and medieval conception of values as absolute. According to the latter view, values are inherent in the nature of things and as such are antecedent to and independent of men, if not of Man. Each *kind* of thing has its fixed end or purpose to which each *particular* thing of the kind must conform upon pain of being an accident or a monster. Such absolute values could always be used as a weapon to discredit the values of men. Thus, in Greek thought, the philosopher set himself the task of selecting values for other men and censoring art; and, in the medieval world, the church fell heir to these prerogatives by the same arguments.

The absolute or universal values were always higher than the values of men, because they stemmed from Socrates' "easy method" of explanation. According to this familiar method, things are what they are by virtue of partaking of absolute and universal "Ideas,"[36] which are, curiously enough, only substantive forms of adjectives. It is by Beauty that things are beautiful. Accordingly, the naive argument throughout history, reappearing as the fourth Thomistic argument for the existence of God, is that one cannot say that one thing is better than another without admitting an absolute good. In this respect, the "special agents" of the Absolute occupied a strategic position. And so it came about that the purposes of men fared badly indeed when contrasted with the alleged purpose of Man. Inquiry after truths was forbidden for the sake of the worship of Truth; beautiful things were decried in the name of Beauty; and the Good served to rationalize some of the most vicious practices known to history.

The attack upon final causes, with which early modern thought began, not only freed science from Aristotelian medievalism, it freed the purposes of men from purposes antecedently fixed for them, presumably by nature or by God, but, in practice, by institutions and their traditions. The appeal of the subjectivist's position is that, if he can transform purposes and values into subjective states of consciousness, he can deny the authority of institutional imposition and can find freedom. That these subjectivists are not wholly deluded in being wary of institutionalized values is substantiated in our own day and country and, even in the profession, by the Harvard Report,[37] which *turns to tradition as the source of values and ideals rather than to the needs of the individual.* Yet the extreme and cynical solution of subjectivism is not the only way of escape.

If science[38] cannot accept traditionalism, as the Harvard Report admits, neither can it accept subjective relativism with its implication that truth is merely a matter of opinion. If one opinion is just as good as another, whether in science, morals, or art, all are equally worthless. The scientist is concerned with how opinions align with facts. He defines the objective validity of his ideas in empirical terms, i.e., the experimental test of ideas. Yet it is equally true that he does not find any absolute

truth; he never has "all the facts." He is continually discovering
new facts and revising or developing his ideas. Indeed, this
process is science in the modern sense, research science. If we
ask for a physics textbook, we want the latest edition. The
principles contained in it are relative to the experimental evidence available to the scientist when he wrote the book. Thus,
in our statement of science and of scientific method, we find no
place for the old axiom which equates the objective with the
absolute, for the scientist arrives at an objectivity which is relative. Here, then, is *a second form of relativism, one which is
not subjective.*

Similarly, with respect to values, the difficulty of the subjectivistic theory is that a fortiori it provides no basis for discrimination of validity. Once, while watching an artist at work, I noted
that he was studying his work intently, looking at it from different angles and distances; he even turned it upside down. Turning
to me, he remarked, "It is sometimes difficult to be sure whether
what one sees in the picture is really there or not."[39] But what
appeared as a problem to this artist would be antecedently
ruled out by the subjectivist. My point is made clearer, I think,
by reference to those subjectivistic forms called "projection
theories." DeWitt H. Parker believes that "values belong wholly
to the inner world, to the world of mind."[40] Accordingly, he
goes on to say, "We project value into the external world, attributing it to the things that serve desire."[41] Similarly, Santayana says, concerning the value, beauty: "Beauty is pleasure
regarded as the quality of a thing."[42] I agree with these gentle-
men that quite often we do just as they say we do, but it is of
equal or, even, of greater significance to note that their views
define the very condition which the artist took to mean failure
of observation.[43]

The objective status of values consists in the fact that they
arise in the lives of men; and life, as any biographer knows, is not
something confined within the skin, much less is it confined to
Parker's "inner world." The values which existed in the planta-

tion life of the antebellum South, so many people insist, are not identical with the values of life in a twentieth-century industrial society. The things which made life worthwhile to the nineteenth-century cattlemen are not those of the hunter who preceded him, nor those of the farmer who broke up his prairie. One would find it difficult indeed to transport the values portrayed by Whittier's *Snowbound* to a New York apartment, but no more so than the reverse. I do not wish to exaggerate the differences, for that is not my point. The point is that values are functions of the kind of life which one leads and which that life makes possible; and life is made up of objective occurrences, conditions, and situations.

By way of summary of what has been said in previous chapters as well as of introducing the idea which I have to present, I wish to state briefly the basic philosophic assumptions here adopted in contrast to some of those previously mentioned—assumptions which are, I think, required for experimental work. They are, stated flatly, that a thing is what it does; that what it does, it does in relation with other things; and that one property which some things may have is that they appear. Thus, a chemist decides what a substance is by testing it, that is, by noting what it does under certain conditions. The older conception of substance, for instance, Spinoza's definition, is irrelevant to this approach and is no proof of the inadequacy of the latter.[44]

In referring to the fact that things appear, I wish to eliminate from this consideration of values some of the so-called instrumental values, examples of which have previously been mentioned. I refer to those of the type whose only ends—the ends which they are "good for" or "valuable for"—are *extrinsic* to themselves. Such expressions as 'economic values' have no relevance to values as the term is here used. The wisdom, in any particular case, of considering *all* foreseeable results that are important is not denied, of course.

Yet, two things more need to be said. The first is to note the fact that instruments do come themselves to be valued. A good workman loves good tools. Instruments of torture come themselves to be hated; no less do those things which seem essential in standing guard for whatever appears most worthwhile; for example, freedom and property come themselves to be loved. Thus do the cardinal virtues—temperance, justice, moral courage, and wisdom—become themselves values, or moral values, although I prefer to call these things *secondary values*. They are not secondary in importance in every instance; they are secondary in the sense that, especially in their more specific formulations, they must be judged ultimately in terms of their facilitation or frustration of other ends.

That instruments themselves should be valued is in a certain degree a good thing. The workman who loves his tools will give them more than minimum care. The fact that universities or states or ships are loved results in the security and development of these great instruments. Moral principles are far less likely to have weight in the crises of life if they are not deeply valued. Moral principles should become moral values. But all this sets the condition for possible perversion. When the instruments as ends become superior to the ends which they rationally serve, they are perverted bcause they serve to discredit greater ends of life. The worship of instruments to this degree is materialism in the sense of that word which makes it a moral epithet. The churchman who makes man to exist for the Sabbath rather than the Sabbath for man is as much a materialist as any worshiper of mammon. Moreover, the raison d'être of the instrument as an instrument has vanished, and moral principles become the object of cynical questioning.

The second point to be made is this: all values, even as values, are nevertheless instrumental, for the affective phases of things are inseparable from the efficaciousness of things. The affective depends on efficacy in relevant ways. Discrimination of the two is an abstraction, vicious when it results in a metaphysical separation.[45] Thus, in eliminating the merely extrinsically instrumental, we are not eliminating all efficacy. The efficacy of things is, moreover, the required condition for the objective approach to anything. In respect to our problem, the objective question is *what the thing does to the individual* upon, and in terms of, his direct experience with it. The characteristics by which this is noted no more involve a question of subjectivity than does a test for color blindness.

By way of contrast to this point, it may be relevant to note how discussions of values are easily vitiated in favor of cynicism by taking absolutism for granted. Thus, Russell says, "Questions as to 'values'—that is to say, as to what is good or bad on its own account, independently of its effects—lie outside the domain of science, as the defenders of religion emphatically assert."[46] I suggest that this truism is irrelevant. It is truism, for we could not consider anything "independently of its effects." For instance, we could not observe anything if it did not affect us or our instruments in some way, such as reflected light upon the human eye. Regarding anything "independently of its effects" would not only lie outside of science but also outside of all consideration, except in such negative propositions as Russell's. It would indeed "lie wholly outside the domain of knowledge," as Russell goes on to say. Thus I have argued that the conception of a thing "independently of its effects" is the conception of an absolute object and must be discarded.

V

I come now to state, by means of three points, how the thing, *as a value*, affects the individual. The first is this: the fundamental test of a value is, that upon further experience with it under reasonably favorable conditions, it will "grow on us" in meaning and appreciative significance; *it will increase our capacity to cherish and appreciate it*. The empirical objectivity of this test is demonstrable. I have used it experimentally, following the work of others, in helping children to come to appreciate literature.[47] Basically, this method centers upon the individual and the observable effects of the materials upon him.

It should be remarked that the word 'appreciate' is used here in the relevant sense as given in the dictionary; it means 'to esteem, cherish, prize, hold dear, or value'. It does not mean *primarily*, to acquire information, to analyze, or to treat a work of literature as one would an arithmetic textbook, helpful as some of those procedures often are. There can be no intelligent objection to such excellent procedures as the acquiring of information or analysis; nothing important should escape them. But it is objectionable to confuse those things with love and appreciation, although they are not necessarily unconnected. It is characteristic of the materialism of our society and of its educational system to regard only *means*, such as information and analysis, as important and to find no place, except in graduation orations, for learning to love and cherish things. So much is this the case that even the few courses devoted to appreciation of literature or of art often constitute marked examples of this materialism.

One further qualification I want to make is that, while values are not identical merely with the external conditioning of emotion, and neither are values to be identified with pleasure, nevertheless some degree of pleasurable experience with a thing is required in order for direct appreciation of it to develop. A special case involves adjusting literature to what a child can find interesting; for the ability to appreciate, like the ability to understand, is relative to the individual, to his maturity and his background.[48] This is true because appreciation is a matter of growth, if for no other reason. These remarks illustrate the necessary qualifications.[49] The main point is concretely illustrated; good literature is that which causes growth in appreciation; poor literature is that which does not. Short-lived excitement is, of course, not to be confused with dependable, long-term growth of appreciation.

Again, consider two pieces of music, both of which may delight or amuse us the first time we hear them. Yet, in one of them our interest wanes upon further experience. This is not merely a matter of sophistication. Any band leader knows that it happens to everyone, almost; so that after a time people are bored with the superficialities of a tune and it is heard no more. Another piece of music may have the opposite effect; one returns to it with renewed and increased delight. The point is that whether or not one chooses to flit from one excitement to another,[50] some kinds of music do not increase in richness upon experience with them, while others do. In speaking of further experience, I do not suggest that any single value is adequate for human life. There can be too much repetition of anything. Even loving mothers sometimes find that their children are too much with them. Nevertheless, the difference in effect of the two pieces of music remains an empirical fact, and this fact is the required condition for saying that one is poor music and that the other is good music. Now the view which I am suggesting is that the *question* of why one piece is good and another poor is one which must be raised subsequently to the discovery, in some cases at least, that one is in fact good and another poor; and that any theory in answer to such a question must be tested in terms of further similar factual discoveries.

The criterion or test of value is stated as one which must appear in further experience. In other language, the test of a value is to live with it. Nevertheless, this more ultimate test is not always required. I do not mean, merely, that we can note how things have affected others, although those effects do indeed represent more or less similar possibilities for us; I mean something else. After we have had considerable experience with good things of a certain type, we develop a more ready sensitivity which is sometimes called "good taste," a term often degraded to the merely conventional. I mean, rather, an ability to decide more or less immediately how a thing would affect us upon further experience. This ability can be measured, in some cases at least. At any rate, the ability will not be absolute; it will be relative to the types of things with which we have had experience. For anything quite different, we must resort to further experience to note how it affects us. The art critic is no less in this predicament than anyone else.

Having noted the effect of a value upon our capacity to appreciate it, I would like now to add that this increased ability is not limited to the thing itself. It will tend to carry over to other things, at least to those which are similar. The very idea of "good taste" just mentioned implies this, for it involves types of things rather than merely one single thing. My second point, then, is this: *values tend to sensitize us to other values.* We recognize this mutual enhancement clearly enough in respect to things which are quite similar: indeed, we would assume it to be rather improbable that one would learn to appreciate music, if one were strictly limited to hearing only one piece. Thus, there must be some mutual enhancement. This fact of mutual enhancement is, moreover, doubly significant: on the one hand, a value tends to sensitize one to other values; while, on the other, some degree of variety of experience is required for fuller appreciation of any one of these values.

I have used the word 'tend'; for, insofar as things differ, we may find less carry-over from the one to the other, although development of breadth of appreciation will facilitate further transfer. The word represents a probability function which may be measured, in some cases, at least, as a degree of correlation.[51] In a particular case, however, one may indeed appreciate novels without appreciating poetry. Yet weak and uncertain as the word 'tend' may seem to be, it indicates the contrast, which, in the extreme case, involves the openness of attitude of those who have found some things deeply and vitally worthwhile in their lives, and the callousness of those who have been frustrated and desensitized by a sordid and ugly existence.

VI

Inasmuch as the first two points—the effect of a value upon one's capacity to appreciate it and the tendency of values to sensitize one to other values—have been stated as generalizations respecting human beings, they suggest a third point which is, I think, in common with many others, one of major and fruitful significance. Values appear as something worthy of being recognized by others as values in the sense that they would be so if the conditions required in my first two points obtained. *Values are sharable.* A value stimulates one toward sharing it; and conversely, values sensitize one to the values of others; thus values are social objects. The intrinsic[52] value of anything, as a value and not as a mere occasion of animal emotion, resides in its shared qualities. Nothing is intrinsically worthwhile if it cannot be shared. The test of a good life, Socrates said, is that it enables one to have communion. Consequently, values, like the processes of reflective thought, as Mead pointed out, can appear only in the life of social beings, beings capable of taking a community attitude toward things.[53]

The use of the word 'social' may suggest the word 'antisocial' as its opposite. Possibly the latter is a word which may more wisely be avoided, for it is often used merely as a substitute for the older word 'heresy', against which Sebastian Castellio so manfully inveighed by defending the right to believe heresy. Thus, the word 'antisocial' is often used to attack any views that propose marked changes in the social order. But in a strict sense, such views may not be antisocial at all, for they may and often do propose a new or different society, whether or not the proposal may seem wise. However, there is another meaning that may be given the word 'antisocial', a meaning which would be more relevant here, and that meaning is 'parasitical'. Parasitism is not a basis on which a society can be founded; it requires a society on which to feed and to which it contributes nothing, but against which it is inherently destructive. In some cases these conditions will be fairly obvious, as in the case of a gang of thieves. But even to maintain itself, such a society must have rules for itself, the "in" group, which it does not extend to the "out" group. The point is that the rules which govern its relations to the "out" group and constitute its basis of existence cannot be generalized to form a society. In this sense, its ends are inherently unsharable with any who are not members of the gang. Other cases, however, are not so obvious, or, at least, they are debated and judgment on the matter may become a social issue. Thus capitalists, somewhat more respectable members of society, are sometimes referred to as "bloated plutocrats" and "parasites." In the complexities of debate, some distinctions may be drawn respecting the variety of ways in which the capitalist may function. At any rate, what is in question is the service or disservice of the capitalist in his various possible forms.

The idea, that values are in some sense social in nature, is no novelty. It has been a traditional view that values are to be socially imposed, and society—for instance, the church—has traditionally been accepted as the authority on values. It is their sharable feature which, I think, in part, leads men to desire to impose or to recommend similar values for all men, forgetful of the fact that, as Kant noted, love cannot be commanded. Doubtless, the fact that mutual values do organize forms of social cooperation has also led to the imposing of values. However, I am not basing a theory of values upon social approval, for the approval of what is evil is a perversion. Moreover, imposition even of what is worthy is also evil. Anyone with experience in the educational world knows of fathers who have attempted to impose careers of their choice on their sons, even to the latter's ruin.

Kant observed that "The empirical interest in the beautiful exists only in *society*." Doubtless, the more or less isolated individual may have some interest in the beauty which he comes upon, but the fact of social conditions which give rise to objects of great aesthetic value—for example, a Greek temple, or French Impressionist or Italian Renaissance painting—is wholly obvious, and expresses itself in the types and styles of art products. That the peculiar nature of things like homes or careers is a social product is too obvious to belabor. None of these facts, however, reduces the importance of the individual; for only the human individual can achieve the capacity to love and cherish things and to provide the individual contribution to invent, create, or develop things worthy of that love, though he is a socialized individual. Society or institutions do not love or cherish.

I am stating the nature of values in terms of the effects of things on individuals. This would imply evaluation of a thing as a value in terms of its effects on all individuals involved. The utilitarian slogan, the greatest good for the greatest number, points to some great goods, but yet it may overlook others. There may be times when only a few may find something to be good, but nonetheless, those few find it to be a very great good. Some few men like Aristotle or Santayana may find a life of contemplation to be a great good while vast numbers do not.

A distinction, however, must be drawn in speaking of the few and the many. Consider the rajah who lives in lavish luxury at the expense of many thousands who are without necessities of life. The objection of the utilitarian is not to the fact that the rajah may find something good, if he does, but to the fact that countless others are prevented from also finding good. Against this, the utilitarian slogan must logically prevail. One might, however, also cite another culture where great rewards act as an incentive to build industry that will enhance the lives of all. However, I abandon these digressions in order to mention a second distinction.

That values are sharable does not mean that they are universally shared, and there is very large although not universal agreement on that point. Thus Kant treats values, at least aesthetic values, as pseudogeneralizations. The idea that values are, or should be, universally shared in a direct sense is not merely idealistic optimism; it has another face, namely, the loss of integrity by which the individual gives up values or is pressured to do so because they are not directly shared by his fellows. I have suggested the statement of values in objective terms, what the thing does to the individual. That a thing does affect an individual may then be the case regardless of what the thing would do to some other individual so long as its availability to the one is not a cause of injury to the second. The fact that something is a good food for one individual is not erased by the injury it might do another who ate it.

It is the social nature of values which I am emphasizing. A point which many discussions overlook is that there can be a social sharing, which is the important thing, without a direct sharing, although direct sharing facilitates social sharing. The child may find delight in watching his pet eat lustily. The child is a social self and can share without partaking of the pet's food. The pet is not a social being and finds no delight in watching the child eat. I may find nothing of direct value to me in the life of an ascetic mystic like St. Francis and much that to me would be objectionable. The later Franciscan order took very much this view. But my objections need not prevent me from recognizing that he found vastly more in his chosen life than he probably would have as a tradesman in his father's warehouse, a life against which he rebelled. My objections need not prevent me from feeling sympathetic appreciation for St. Francis in his poetic odyssey. The point is that, as social beings, we can enjoy the pleasure of others in things in which directly we would find no enjoyment, and we are the richer for it. However, on the other hand, we most often do not enjoy or share the pleasure of the sadist or of the ruthless individual, and at a more social level we cannot. Such empathy is self-defeating. Our very social nature, by which we might share, is flagrantly violated and revolted by consideration of innocent victims.

The "universal" character of art and of other values has been emphasized throughout history, although in an absolute fashion which ignored the uniqueness of particular works of art and of their relations to other unique things, human beings. Although anything, except an idea in its referential character, exists as a particular, nonetheless some things may be social objects. This does not mean, merely, that a thing is an object in the experience of a number of individuals, but that when the group experience of the object appears to some extent within the individual's experience, the object appears to the individual as a social object, and the individual is a social being. Now it is a characteristic finding of behavior problem clinics that when—along with achieving relief from sources of insecurity, frustration, and anxiety—an individual finds something which seems to him eminently worthwhile, social and personality problems, in the pernicious sense, disappear. The relevant sense in which anything is shared, therefore, is not that it is parceled out, but that one takes a community or group attitude toward it. What is required for the social or shared act, as Mead elaborately sets forth, is that the individual is capable of responding to the object in the role of another as well as in his own role. One can share his marriage, not as a case of polyandry, but as a public event—however modest the number of individuals immediately present—in which the marriage receives the blessing of the community. This, I take to be the significance of ceremony; as a public manifestation, it deepens and confirms the realization of value that was already social so far as it was a value.

The assumption then is that while an individual requires a society—a public situation—in which to become social, he may thereafter remain a social being in his attitudes and actions even in private. Nevertheless, those social attitudes may be reinforced and developed by his further relations in society. How these social attitudes may also actually lead one into conflict with the group, as in the case of Socrates or Jesus, was pointed out by James.[54]

There was common enough recognition of the fact that the intensity and richness of the quality of experiences, especially those that are more complex, are increased when it is shared. In another dimension, the social nature of art has been so well recognized that a number of theories go to the extreme of treating art as communication, reducing it to a kind of language, even though it is not the essence of aesthetic art to be symbolic in the sense of being explicitly representative or a combinatory idea, and it is not symbolic in the linguistic sense, i.e., that of prosaic language as distinguished from poetic language. I would like, therefore, to distinguish the idea that values are sharable from these views, as well as from such views as, let us say, Tolstoy's "communication of emotion." The emotions of anger, fear, joy, and sadness are doubtless more or less contagious, but I am not referring to values as emotional states, even though emotion is always involved. For the desired distinction, I would like to extend to a general theory of value Dewey's view that a work of art is an expression of the value of an emotion. As an *expression* it involves two factors, among others: a social relation and a medium in which it is expressed. The former has been discussed, and I wish now to consider the medium both as a condition for the social factor which has already been mentioned and as a condition for the existence of a value.

The essential importance of the medium is signified in the very idea of a *work* of art, for, as Dewey says, the idea of "work" has its basic meaning in terms of the resistance of the medium. The value, therefore, is not merely a subjective emotional state of the author, it is an objective achievement; it is something worked out. Real values, as distinct from possible values, are actually achieved in a medium, and, more to the point, as they are worked out and as they are shared, the emotions become disciplined, transformed, and enriched. Moore says that the addition of material qualities enhances a purely spiritual good. I am suggesting much more than that. I suggest that without a medium, the "spiritual" is pure dream and illusion. And, what is still more significant, without a medium in which it may be worked out, the dream is not even a *good* dream, but a creature of impulse, fantasy, whim, and caprice. Those "spiritual" things which are not materialized may perhaps be characterized as ideals. The word 'ideal' is an adjectival form of the word 'idea'. When, in turn, it is used as a noun, the word 'ideal' distinguishes certain particular kinds of ideas, namely, value ideas. But, like any other ideas, they are not self-validating. They require a medium.

Even in its more specialized sense, the medium of art is, of course, not restricted to stone or to paint. It may be language, as in literature or song; sound, as in music; or action, as in the dance. But in the more general sense of the art of life to which I refer, the media will be the great variety of forms of conduct, interaction, and events which make up the bulk of human life. In any case, a condition for the public and social nature of values is that they are expressed in an objective medium. That his hypothetical minds or spirits could not have communion, Bishop Berkeley very well knew in respect to his church service. Thus, he acted as if there were material things such as bread and wine, whatever his heretical analysis of them. Berkeley would have to presuppose a Leibnizian preestablished harmony to avoid a solipsism. Contrariwise, one might opine that if the bread and wine were offered in more liberal quantities, as was doubtless the case in the original supper, there might be even more communion than is usually the case. Putting aside Bishop Berkeley, the fact remains that one cannot communicate even with himself but by a medium. Values are qualities of the developed medium and are, therefore, public in the sense that the scientist's facts are public.

My third point respecting values, therefore, approaches the way in which the scientist finds assurance of objectivity in his procedures: the public verifiability of his ideas. Either in the case of scientific method or in that of values, one adopts, as Mead said, a public or community attitude, for both represent the evolutionary outcome, in the social act, of the manipulatory and consummatory phases of the primitive biological act.

However, some care in discriminating is required in order not to fall into a rather common error. As has been said before, verification of a value as a value does not consist, as seems often to be supposed, in others finding that it is a direct value for them, for its objectivity or relativity is not of that sort, as may be illustrated by factual matters which are not matters of value. The establishment of the fact that something is good food for an animal or for a human being does not depend on what happens to other animals or other human beings when they eat it, but on what happens to that animal or to that human being when he eats it, and that is the verification. What happens to other animals of the same species may establish some probability respecting the individual in question, but a probability is a prediction, and not all predictions turn out to be the case. The significant point is that whether it is good food for other animals is irrelevant, except in the probability it creates respecting the individual case. What doctor would say, "It is good food for me, so it must be good food for you"? But that same doctor, in respect to his values, may not be so intelligent.

Similarly, whether a career of a particular kind may be of very great immediate value to many others when they adopt it as their career or only to few, is irrelevant to the question whether a particular individual should adopt such a career. The latter question is settled not on subjective grounds but on objective facts as to how that career affects the individual. These facts are public and, as such, are shared, but that is not all. As a value it is shared by a wife, a parent, friends, or others, not because they engage in the career in the same way as does the individual in question, or find such a career to be good as their own occupation, but in the social sense of sharing. This social or community attitude is not in all cases a mere projection by the individual nor a matter of group hysteria. The decisive factor is if or how the thing permits the carrying out of the attitude.

The reference to attitudes will make it clear that I do not exclude the presence of meanings from "direct experience." Values are meaningful. In terms of Dewey's distinction, they answer to the imaginative but are not merely imaginary. The idea of a value, a home, is imaginative to an extent that the idea of a house is not, but its meanings are carried out in the eventualities which constitute it a home. Anything which continues to act like a value is a value.

The social nature of ends is such that man may have ends that are achievements not only in the present but which extend into the future, a future to which there is no certain limit. Thus he may identify himself with ends that go beyond his lifetime. In some cases this is true by explicit specification, as in the case of the man who carries life insurance on his own life to protect his family. All such values are in essence social values, for in the nature of the case they are shared by others. So too, in a larger way, one may work for a better world. Death, then, is not final, for it does not end everything with which one identifies himself; neither does it prove that all is vanity, for one's acts are not in vain. I do not mean to suggest any mysterious continuance of the self, but rather of those values or ends which one has made his own.

The ancient world looked back to a Golden Age or Garden of Eden that lay in the past and was already gone. The mystery religions and, later, Christianity transformed this into a future, but a future "life," making it the answer to dreams; thus it would be perfect. Apart from any question of validity, the difficulty arises that all accounts of its perfection suggest ennui and boredom. Moreover, the attainment of this future life, in the official doctrine, was seen to be primarily by miracle and theological will and contrivance, rather than by work and art. On the contrary, the better world for which modern man may work is something larger than himself. It does not pander to his gratifications by offering golden streets or pearly gates, nor will he be there to enjoy it. Thus the end is not confined within the limits of the antecedent self, but rather, it enlarges the self. It is the act of a larger social self, for one both puts himself in a future situation and adopts the attitudes of others in that situation. In his "mind's eye" he looks upon his widow and his orphan children, or upon the future service of the institution which he supports and which is devoted to ends that are shared through its service. This may give him gratification in the present, for it gives the present meaning and significance.

Values have now been defined in terms of three criteria[55] which are empirically objective: (1) their effect of enriching our appreciation of them; (2) their tendency to sensitize us to other values; (3) their sharable nature.[56] To say that values are defined in these terms means that whatever fulfills these conditions is a value; it does not mean that whatever is antecedently or traditionally decided upon as a value will fulfill these conditions. The hypothesis is that such things are adequate for a good life. This view would deny that what momentarily satisfies is necessarily satisfactory, but it is not meant to deny quite a different thing: namely, that a life that is fully satisfying is satisfactory. I have no concern for the nonsense question whether it is better to be a pig satisfied or a Socrates dissatisfied. Better for whom? The question of what is better for pigs or for Socrates or for the common man is something to be determined experimentally in the particular case.

APPENDIX

A Note by John Dewey

The following was written by Dewey, at the request of Percy Hughes, then head of the Department of Philosophy, Lehigh University, Bethlehem, Pennsylvania, as an introduction to the republication of some articles of mine. (Lehigh University Publications, VI [1932], No. 7.) The main article, "Some Metaphysical Implications of the Pragmatic Theory of Knowledge," is expanded as chapter II of this book. Other materials are used elsewhere in the book.

I believe that this note deserves some attention because of its comment on the problem of Mead, one with which I am also concerned.

I had occasion recently in writing a few words about Mr. Mead's forthcoming volume of Carus Lectures to speak of a certain trait of his mind—or rather of his personality, which in his case was identified in an unusual way with mind. The characteristic in question was a union of remarkable originality with deference to the position of others—a deference which apparently obscured his consciousness of his own originality. I cited in this connection the fact that he regarded his own work mainly as an extension of pragmatism. While Mr. Mead was in sympathy with the pragmatic position, at least in one of its many forms, his essential contribution goes far beyond anything found in any pragmatic writing before his own thought received expression. Even the problem with which he was most deeply and uniquely concerned was not one which had found any especial recognition among the pragmatist writers, any more than it had among thinkers of other groups. It was, if I may state it too briefly for adequate expression, the problem of the place of consciousness, that is, of the *objects* of consciousness, in the total frame of things. The problem came home to Mr. Mead from many sides and in many ways. The way which is grasped most readily (because of its connection with the historic tradition of modern philosophy) is well indicated in Dr. Lafferty's article. Physical science had excluded from the realm of its objects all purposes and values, the things which are precious and prized in life experience. Hence, following Descartes, philosophy had created a realm of consciousness which these values and purposes might inhabit—a realm, in Mr. Mead's striking phrase, of the "rejects" of physical science. This consideration, in connection with the allied fact (which Mr. Mead felt more deeply, I think, than any other contemporary philosopher) that the world of objects of physical science is general and public, while the objects of "consciousness," in the modern tradition constituted the personal individual mind as such, determined the general course of Mr. Mead's thought. His attitude toward it, the objective and metaphysical solution he had to offer, was one with his conception of the significance of the *social*. It was worked out in main outline before the change took place from Newtonian physics to those of relativity and related themes. But Mr. Mead, with originality equal to that of his earlier thought, saw that the change could and must be interpreted in a way which gave the social interpretation of consciousness—of mind as individual—a place in the new and enlarged universe which physical science itself was compelled to set up. In his later writings he used largely the terminology of Mr. Whitehead's interpretation of the new physics as a medium for expressing the conception which he had earlier arrived at. The papers of Mr. Lafferty's are a true and yet fresh and independent version of the problem which occupied Mr. Mead's and are faithful to the spirit of his solution. Consequently, while I do not feel that his papers are in need of any introduction from any outside source, my constantly growing sense of the importance of Mead's philosophical contribution has caused me gladly to accede to the request for a few words by way of an introduction.

JOHN DEWEY

NOTES

PREFACE

1 "Some Metaphysical Implications of the Pragmatic Theory of Knowledge," pp. 197–207; "Empiricism and Objective Relativism in Value Theory," pp. 141–55; "The Metaphysical Status of Qualities," pp. 313–28.

CHAPTER I

1 J. O. Urmson, *Philosophical Analysis;* see also Maxwell J. Charlesworth, *Philosophy and Linguistic Analysis.*
2 A[lfred] J[ules] Ayer et al., *The Revolution in Philosophy,* p. 124.
3 Ibid., p. 86.
4 Bertrand Russell, *Wisdom of the West,* p. 309, and "The Cult of Common Usage." For other critical treatments, see also H. D. Lewis, *Clarity Is Not Enough.*
5 Stephen Edelston Toulmin, *An Examination of the Place of Reason in Ethics,* p. 83.
6 Bertrand Russell, *The Problems of Philosophy,* p. 91.
7 Bertrand Russell, *Our Knowledge of the External World,* p. 243.
8 Urmson, *Philosophical Analysis,* p. 199.
9 Alfred Jules Ayer, *Language, Truth and Logic,* p. 13.
10 Ibid., p. 14.
11 Ibid., p. 13.
12 John Hospers, "What Is Explanation?" See also Morris R. Cohen and Ernest Nagel, *An Introduction to Logic and Scientific Method,* ch. 11.
13 Ayer, *Language, Truth and Logic,* p. 13.
14 S[tephen] E[delston] Toulmin and K[urt] Baier, "On Describing."
15 Ayer et al., *Revolution in Philosophy,* p. 113.
16 Urmson, *Philosophical Analysis,* p. 174.
17 Ayer, *Language, Truth and Logic,* p. 41.
18 Ibid., p. 45.

19 Ludwig Wittgenstein, *Philosophical Investigations*, pt. I, sect. 90. (Italics mine.)
20 Urmson, *Philosophical Analysis*, p. 168.
21 Ayer et al., *Revolution in Philosophy*, p. 75.
22 Ayer, *Language, Truth and Logic*, p. 26.
23 Immanuel Kant, *Prolegomena to Any Future Metaphysics*, p. 13.
24 Urmson, *Philosophical Analysis*, p. 47.
25 Moritz Schlick, *Philosophy of Nature*, p. 11.
26 Wittgenstein, *Philosophical Investigations*, sects. 250–70.
27 C. D. Rollins, ed., *Knowledge and Experience*, pp. 88–132.
28 John Dewey, *Reconstruction in Philosophy*, pp. 124, 126.
29 John Dewey, "An Empirical Account of Appearance," p. 463.
30 *The Journal of Philosophy*, XII (1915), 337–45.
31 *Time and Its Mysteries*, pp. 85–109. Reprinted in his *On Experience, Nature and Freedom*, pp. 224–43.
32 John Dewey, *Experience and Nature*, p. 54.
33 Ibid., p. 56.
34 John Dewey, "Discussion. Experience and Existence: A Comment," pp. 712–13.
35 John Dewey, "The Development of American Pragmatism," p. 25.
36 Ayer, *Language, Truth and Logic*, p. 112.
37 Ibid., p. 107.
38 Ibid., p. 109.
39 Ibid., p. 107.
40 Ibid., pp. 112–13.
41 Ibid., p. 111.
42 R. M. Hare, *The Language of Morals*, p. 77.
43 Ibid., pp. 68–69.
44 Ibid., p. 69.
45 Ibid., p. 70.
46 Ibid.
47 Ibid., p. 147.
48 Ibid., p. 77.
49 Ibid., p. 73.
50 Ibid.
51 "Valuation as Cognition."
52 Hare, *Language of Morals*, p. 102.
53 Rollins, ed., *Knowledge and Experience*, p. 42 and passim.
54 Hare, *Language of Morals*, p. 126.
55 Ibid., pp. 117, 124.

56 Ibid., p. 98 ff.
57 Ibid., p. 103.
58 Margaret Macdonald, "Natural Rights." This article is all the more significant, I think, because she is attempting to apply her views on ethics to another problem.
59 Bertrand Russell, "Reply to Criticisms," p. 722.
60 Hare, Language of Morals, p. 155.
61 Ibid., p. 134.
62 Ayer, Language, Truth and Logic, p. 111.
63 Bertrand Russell, Human Society in Ethics and Politics, p. 116.
64 John Dewey, "Qualitative Thought."
65 William James, Pragmatism, p. 68.
66 George Santayana, Scepticism and Animal Faith, p. 191.
67 Alfred North Whitehead, Modes of Thought, p. 144.
68 Bertrand Russell, Human Knowledge, p. 180.
69 Ibid., p. 200.
70 Ibid., p. 239.
71 Ibid., p. 507.
72 Stuart Hampshire, "Are Philosophical Questions Questions of Language?," p. 44.
73 Stuart Hampshire, "Changing Methods in Philosophy," p. 144.
74 Since I have made reference to the philosophy of pragmatism, it may be wise to clarify what is intended, not only by the positive exposition made in the body of the text, but also by indicating what I do not mean. Critics have sought to evade the pragmatic argument by attributing their own invention to it. For the sake of brevity, I shall refer only to two.

　　1.　One invention is that the pragmatist defines truth as any idea that works. For this purpose William James was taken to be representative of pragmatism, and this definition is attributed to him. In turn, some not very compelling refutations were constructed. One was that pragmatism whitewashes lies. Thus, if one tells a lie to achieve some end and "it works," behold it is transformed into truth and so is blessed. I pass over the incidental suggestion that what truths state must always be something good. It is too obvious to require elaboration that there is some confusion in antecedents of the word 'it'. What "worked" was the plan, expressed not by the lie but by the proposition: if one tells the lie then he will achieve the end.

　　There is some point in insisting that, when one is giving a brief exposition of what an author intends to say, some attention be given to what he puts in italics. James, of course, did not define truth as any idea that works. The central idea or definition that he wished to emphasize he put into italics, although that proved to be a futile gesture for critics. Thus in his *Pragmatism* he writes in the chapter entitled "Pragmatism's Conception of Truth," "*True ideas are those that we can assimilate, validate, corroborate and verify. False ideas are those that we can not*" (p. 201). It was equally futile for him to give this view renewed emphasis by republishing it in the Preface to a later book, *The Meaning of Truth.*

I would not defend James against the charge that he was sometimes ambiguous. Dewey made a point of that. But when James cleared up the ambiguity by choosing one meaning rather than another, his critics preferred to ignore it.

I shall add merely that I use the term "pragmatism" as it was subsequently developed by Dewey and George Herbert Mead.

2. Another caricature is the idea that pragmatism identifies experience and reality. This view respecting James was given some prominence by F. H. Bradley, whose metaphysics did just that. He was welcoming James into the fold, a matter to which James immediately objected. Subsequently this myth, together with others, became fossilized in textbooks for the edification of the young.

I am compelled, therefore, to turn to a few samples. B. A. G. Fuller says that, according to Dewey, "Things . . . exist only *as* they are experienced. . . . Reality is for him [Dewey] experience and nothing else" (*A History of Philosophy*, II, 470, 472).

According to H. H. Titus, "Experience is [for pragmatism] the all-inclusive reality outside of which there is and can be nothing" (*Living Issues in Philosophy*, p. 253).

W. T. Jones, in his exposition of Dewey, entitles a section, "Reality Defined as 'Experience'," but neglects to quote anything whatever relevant to this title, even though the book prides itself, with some justification, on its extensive quotations (*A History of Western Philosophy*, p. 955).

Of course, none of the above-mentioned texts quotes anything from Dewey to support their attribution of this idea to him. It would be difficult to do so, because Dewey never said any such thing. Quite the contrary, such views are inexcusable because Dewey was repeatedly explicit on the subject. Compare the following statement by Dewey with the foregoing pretended statements of his view:

No one with an honest respect for scientific conclusions can deny that experience as an existence is something that occurs only under highly specialized conditions, such as are found in a highly organized creature which in turn requires a specialized environment. There is no evidence that experience occurs everywhere and everywhen. But candid regard for scientific inquiry also compels the recognition that when experience does occur, no matter at what limited portion of time and space, it enters into possession of *some portion of nature* and in such a manner as to render other of its precincts accessible.

(*Experience and Nature*, p. 3a)

I put the words 'some portion of nature' into italics to aid the reading of those who, like William Kelley Wright, assert that Dewey uses the word 'experience' in an "all-inclusive sense" (A *History of Modern Philosophy*, p. 557).

Neither can misrepresentation in this respect be excused on the ground that the above quotation was an afterthought or different from what Dewey had already said or that its substance had not been explicitly stated before. Long before, respecting an article which he published in 1905, Dewey pointed out the rather obvious fact that "there is nothing in the text that denies the existence of things temporally prior to human experiencing of them" (*The Influence of Darwin on Philosophy*, p. 240n; see also p. 238).

Wright ponders the question, for the befuddlement of students, whether Dewey has "absent-mindedly retained the word 'experience' in his vocabulary subsequent to his repudiation of the absolute," and advises that "it would have made his thought clearer if he had abandoned the use of the word in an all-inclusive sense, and instead have substituted 'reality' or 'the universe' " (*History of Modern Philosophy*, p. 557). The idea that any philosopher of note, much less Dewey, whose writing is very deliberate, as some who engaged in controversy with him discovered, should have "absentmindedly" adopted a major concept does not merit comment. But it might be noted that some people read absentmindedly.

In reply to these statements, three rather brief remarks must suffice. First, it may be observed that of course Dewey did explain why he emphasized the word 'experience': "If the empirical method were universally or even generally adopted in philosophizing, there would be no need of referring to experience" (*Experience and Nature*, p. 2; see also *Essays in Experimental Logic*, p. 8 n, for much the same point, and pp. 61 ff.). In order to make that remark more pointed, one example of that need may be quoted. "Any philosophy which takes science to be not an *account* of the world (which it is), but a literal and exhaustive apprehension of it in its full reality, a philosophy which therefore *has no place for poetry or possibilities*, still needs a theory of experience" (ibid., p. 63; italics mine).

Second, Dewey did not use the term 'experience' "in an all-inclusive sense," a fact already shown above.

Third, as to Wright's suggestion that Dewey use a more inclusive term such as 'reality' or 'the universe' in place of the word 'experience', it would seem that, if Wright had done little more than examine the title of the very book he was supposedly discussing, he would have come upon a more inclusive word, the word 'nature', in the title *Experience and Nature*.

Having attributed the view to Dewey in the manner quoted in the foregoing, it is an easy matter to call such nonsensical views into question, as Wright does, by rather obvious truisms: "Now from a naturalistic point of view, the earth, and probably the universe as a whole, certainly must have existed long ages previous to the presence of any organism, and during these ages there could have been no such thing as experience" (*History of Modern Philosophy*, p. 557). To these truisms the appropriate remark is that in this case they are pointless.

Several decades before Wright made these remarks, Dewey apparently did suspect that "science makes known a chronological period in which the world managed to lead a respectable existence in spite of not including conscious organisms. Under such conditions there was no experience, yet there was reality" ("Reality as Experience," p. 253). Dewey, however, was interested to go on to show the continuity of realities outside of or prior to experience with the realities of experience. This would be in sharp contrast to the traditional dualism, which had relegated the two to entirely separate metaphysical realms, making experience into mere appearance as distinguished from

an external "reality" from which it was forever barred. His view was that things are what they are experienced as, whatever else they may be. That does indeed identify experience with reality when and insofar as the reality is a matter of experience.
75 Dewey, *Essays in Experimental Logic*, p. 63.
76 George Herbert Mead, *Movements of Thought in the Nineteenth Century*, ch. 13.
77 Robert Andrews Millikan, *The Electron*, p. 214.
78 Ibid., p. 228. (Italics mine.)
79 Russell, *Human Knowledge*, p. 196.
80 Ibid., p. 181.
81 Bertrand Russell, *An Inquiry into Meaning and Truth*, p. 207.
82 Russell, "Reply to Criticisms," p. 683.
83 Russell, *Human Knowledge*, p. 179.
84 Ibid., p. 396.
85 Ibid., p. 174.
86 Russell, *Inquiry into Meaning and Truth*, p. 408.
87 Ibid., p. 387.
88 Russell, *Problems of Philosophy*, p. 103.
89 Ibid., p. 106.

CHAPTER II

1 Josiah Royce, *The Spirit of Modern Philosophy*, p. 168.
2 G. H. Mead, *Mind, Self and Society*.
3 G. H. Mead, *The Philosophy of the Present*, Supplementary Essay II.
4 Ibid., Supplementary Essays IV and V.
5 G. H. Mead, "The Genesis of the Self and Social Control."
6 "Subsistence and Existence in Neo-Realism," p. 279. Helen Keller's reconstruction of her prelingual existence as a "phantom," "before the soul dawn," is highly pertinent to Mead's views (Helen Keller, *The World I Live In*, ch. 11).
7 Arthur O. Lovejoy, *The Revolt against Dualism*, pp. 131–32.
8 G. H. Mead, "A Pragmatic Theory of Truth," p. 70.
9 Ibid., p. 85.
10 Herbert W. Schneider remarks, in his review of Paul E. Pfuetze's *The Social Self*, "This behavioristic theory of universals was really worked out better by John M. Brewster, 'A Behavioristic Account of the Logical Function of Universals' (*Journal of Philosophy*, 1936), on the basis of Mead."
11 P. W. Bridgman, "Statistical Mechanics and the Second Law of

Thermodynamics," p. 236. The whole discussion of models is
highly significant and to the point of this paper.

CHAPTER III

1 George Berkeley, A *Treatise concerning the Principles of Human
Knowledge*, pt. I, sect. 3.
2 Ibid., pt. I, sect. 10.
3 George Santayana, *Scepticism and Animal Faith*, p. 102.
4 Ibid., p. 274. According to Santayana, an essence is "a universal
of any degree of complexity and definition which may be given
immediately, whether to sense or to thought." (Durant Drake
et al., *Essays in Critical Realism*, p. 168 n.)
5 J. O. Urmson, *Philosophical Analysis*, p. 20.
6 John Dewey and A. F. Bentley, *Knowing and the Known*.
7 Aristotle, *Physica*, 185a9.
8 Aristotle, *De Generatione et Corruptione*, 325a19.
9 Aristotle, *De Caelo*, 298b17.
10 Emile Meyerson, *Identity and Reality*.
11 John Locke, *An Essay concerning Human Understanding*, ed.
A. C. Fraser, Book II, ch. 8, sect. 17.
12 Berkeley, *Principles of Human Knowledge*, pt. I, sects. 24, 3.
13 Arthur O. Lovejoy, *The Revolt against Dualism*, p. 133.
14 Ibid., p. 145.
15 Berkeley, *Principles of Human Knowledge*, pt. I, sect. 11.
16 René Descartes, *The Meditations and Selections from the Principles*, p. 89.
17 George Berkeley, selection from *Alciphron* in *Works on Vision*,
pp. 104–8.
18 Locke, *Essay concerning Human Understanding*, book II, ch.
8, sect. 21.
19 George Berkeley, *Three Dialogues between Hylas and Philonous*,
p. 18.
20 David Hume, *A Treatise of Human Nature*, pp. 226–27.
21 Arthur Danto and Sidney Morgenbesser, *Philosophy of Science*,
p. 23.
22 Aristotle, *Metaphysica*, 1005b18.
23 Lovejoy, *Revolt against Dualism*, p. 141n.
24 There may be some disagreement as to just what Democritus
held in this respect. It is not my intent to express certainty on
the historical matter, for I am more concerned with the ideas.

25 Alfred North Whitehead, *Science and the Modern World*, p. 95.
26 Ibid., p. 65.
27 Principle LI, *Meditations and Selections from the Principles*, p. 156.
28 René Descartes, *Rules for the Direction of the Mind*, pp. 20–21.
29 Aristotle, *Metaphysica*, 1003b18.
30 If it is objected that the injection here of the concept of "substance" from the standpoint of the chemist is an irrelevancy respecting Spinoza's thought, it may be retorted that the difference between the two is just my point. Spinoza thought that his ideas were sufficiently relevant to those of the chemist to admit of controversy.
31 Bertrand Russell, *Human Knowledge*, p. 117.
32 They may even go on to say that I am merely repeating in an unusually insistent manner the old wail of philosophers from Parmenides on that "the senses are deceivers." But I could not accept that wholesale view of rationalists, for it does not give adequate consideration to the objectivity that we find when attention is given to conditions.
33 Ludwig Wittgenstein, *Philosophical Investigations*, pt. I, sect. 79.
34 William James, *A Pluralistic Universe*, pp. 212–13.
35 Whitehead, *Science and the Modern World*, pp. 230–32.
36 Ibid., pp. 257–58.
37 Ibid., p. 157.
38 Russell, *Human Knowledge*, pp. 458, 467.
39 F. P. Kilpatrick, "Statement of Theory," p. 88.

CHAPTER IV

1 Alfred North Whitehead, *Science and the Modern World*, pp. 71–72 and passim.
2 Ibid., p. 84.
3 Arthur O. Lovejoy, *The Revolt against Dualism*, p. 98.
4 Haig Khatchadourian, "On Professor Lafferty's 'The Metaphysical Status of Qualities'," p. 400.
5 Ibid., p. 407.
6 Ibid., p. 409.
7 Alfred Jules Ayer, *Language, Truth and Logic*, p. 69.
8 Bertrand Russell, *Our Knowledge of the External World*, p. 94.
9 Ibid., p. 112.

10 Ibid., p. 114.
11 Ibid., p. xi. "The only philosophical change in the present [1929] edition is the abandonment of the distinction between sensations and sense-data. . . ."
12 Ibid., p. 96.
13 Ibid., p. 95.
14 Ibid., p. 93.
15 Ibid., p. 131.
16 Ibid., p. 93.
17 Ibid., p. 95.
18 Ibid., p. 97.
19 Ibid., p. 131.
20 Bertrand Russell, "Reply to Criticisms," pp. 705–6.
21 Russell, *Our Knowledge of the External World*, p. 81.
22 George Berkeley, *Three Dialogues between Hylas and Philonous*, p. 11.
23 Khatchadourian, "On Professor Lafferty's 'The Metaphysical Status of Qualities'."
24 Ibid., p. 410; also, p. 407.
25 Ibid., p. 411.
26 Ibid., p. 406.
27 Ibid., pp. 405–7.
28 Ibid., p. 406.
29 P. 155, below. I speak of Khatchadourian's argument as a priori in order to contrast it with the empirical reference that I shall make.
30 Khatchadourian, "On Professor Lafferty's 'The Metaphysical Status of Qualities'," p. 407.
31 Ibid., p. 406.
32 See Chapter V, below.
33 *The State* (Columbia, S.C.) July 19, 1965.
34 Whitehead, *Science and the Modern World*, p. 151.
35 Russell, *Our Knowledge of the External World*, p. 93.
36 Ibid., p. 95.
37 Ibid., p. 112.
38 Bertrand Russell, *Mysticism and Logic*, p. 121.
39 Russell, *Our Knowledge of the External World*, p. xi.
40 Russell, *Human Knowledge*, p. 47.
41 Richard Held, "Plasticity in Sensory-Motor Systems," p. 84.
42 Whitehead, *Science and the Modern World*, pp. 60–61.

43 Ibid., p. 101.
44 Ibid., p. 104.
45 Ibid., p. 106.
46 Ibid., p. 103.
47 Ibid., p. 104.
48 Russell, *Our Knowledge of the External World,* p. 93 and passim.
49 Whitehead, *Science and the Modern World,* p. 95.
50 Ibid., p. 95; cf. p. 103.
51 Ibid., p. 158.
52 Ibid., p. 96.
53 Ibid., p. 128.
54 Ibid., p. 132.
55 Idem., *The Principles of Natural Knowledge,* pp. 62, 65.
56 Lovejoy, *Revolt against Dualism,* p. 168.
57 Russell, *Our Knowledge of the External World,* p. 96.
58 Lovejoy, *Revolt against Dualism,* p. 121.
59 Ibid., p. 128.
60 George Herbert Mead, "The Objective Reality of Perspectives."
61 Gilbert Ryle, from a different approach, reaches much the same point of view. *Dilemmas,* pp. 72 ff.

CHAPTER V

1 William P. Montague, "The Story of American Realism."
2 Arthur O. Lovejoy, *The Revolt against Dualism,* p. 35.
3 Ibid., p. 95.
4 Ibid., pp. 95–96.
5 Ibid., p. 97.
6 Ibid., pp. 11–33. Russell summarizes his arguments that all experience is "in my mind" or is mental or subjective, and I may give what seems to be the main principle of each of these five arguments (*Human Knowledge,* pp. 171–73). Of course, these arguments merely take for granted that there is a "mind" for experience to be "in."
   1. There are dreams, therefore all experience is in my mind.
   2. If an effect does not resemble the cause, then the effect is in my mind.
   3. If an effect differs from the cause in time, then the effect is in my mind.

4. If some appearances are mistaken, then all appearances are in my mind.

5. If it is doubtful whether something is in my mind or is physical, then it is in my mind.

I shall make no attempt to refute these principles, although I need not conceal my doubt that they are compelling.

7 Lovejoy, *Revolt against Dualism*, p. 29.

8 Ibid., p. 47. (Italics mine.)

9 Ibid., p. 31.

10 Ibid., pp. 26–33. I may have overlooked something in the rest of the book, but since Lovejoy later refers to those pages with the claim that they "sufficiently" establish the point, one may expect them to do so.

11 Ibid., p. 31.

12 Ibid.

13 Ibid.

14 Ibid., p. 41.

15 "Valuation as Cognition."

16 For the more specific definition of 'value' which I would suggest, attention is invited to the following chapter.

17 In this discussion, I will use the term 'subjectivist' to refer to anyone who holds that values are subjective, since that is relevant to the point. He may not be a subjectivist otherwise. In this connection, it may be noted that many subjectivists often mistake Dewey's denial of subjectivism or mentalism to be a denial of the *existence* or of the *relevance* of certain processes such as feelings, whereas it is a denial of a *theory* about them. As to the question of relevance, one point is that feelings can no more be treated in general as final *evidence* of values than other feelings can be treated as final evidence as to which horse will win a race.

18 John Dewey, *Art as Experience*, p. 116.

19 Haig Khatchadourian, "On Professor Lafferty's 'The Metaphysical Status of Qualities'," p. 401.

20 Ibid., p. 399, n. 10. The complete wording presents us with a shower of negatives which, with some trepidation, I have attempted to brave through: "But not 'mental' *per se*. However, no dualist so far as I know holds that perceptual qualities are mental *per se*, in the sense that they are mental *not* by virtue of a function *of the mind*."

21 William James, *The Principles of Psychology*, I, 8.

22 The apology for introducing so simple an illustration is both that it is, I hope, a simple and therefore clear illustration, and also that it emphasizes the fact that such transactions are the common and general characteristic of things. I am more concerned in this chapter to exhibit the general, i.e., metaphysical, characteristics of values in order to present their continuity with nature, than I am concerned with the more particular conditions of values. Concern for the latter would require extensive discussion of their sociocultural conditions.

23 This was expressed by Aristotle as a nature or inherent tendency, antecedently possessed, although some futures were ruled out as 'accidents'. Leibniz was more thoroughgoing. The whole future of the monad was already there within it to be unrolled. These pseudoexplanations bear the common fallacy of hypostatization. That is to say, eventualities are "explained" by the verbalistic method of creating names or categories for them, and then using the categories as though to indicate antecedent metaphysical entities which are said to cause the eventualities. The eternal objects or universals of the realist are further examples. Genuine explanation looks for antecedent conditions which are subject to observation, or even control, involving, of course, the use of abstractions which are required for calculation. Explanation by verbalism, i.e., by hypostatization, has been traditional, but has been more rapidly eliminated from science as science has become more experimental. Philosophy, as it has remained traditional, has not had that impetus.

Traditional psychology, still admired by many philosophers, explained things in such terms as 'mind', 'memory', 'will', 'instinct', etc. If we find that one person persists extraordinarily against difficulties, we often "explain" it by saying that he does so because of a strong will. But upon seeking any meaning for the term 'strong will', we find that it means little else than that he persists extraordinarily against difficulties, or this same thing expressed in more general terms. The psychologist wants to find the conditions under which one has lived which correlate with the tendency to persist extraordinarily against difficulties.

If we find organisms, such as wasps building nests, performing complex, unlearned activities common to a species, we "explain" it by saying they do so by "instinct." Yet 'instinct' means little other than its *definition*, which refers to the *fact* that some organisms perform complex unlearned activities common to their species, and that is the very fact which remains to be explained. In chapter III, on "The Nature of Things," I suggested that such concepts are legitimate as logical conceptions or statements of the natures of things, having a logical status rather than a causal or metaphysical status. The abstract formulations of the modern physicist are not competing entities, but are developed as methods of calculation in relation to processes or changes going on. In that sense, the object, in the sense of the static object, disappears, except as a limit defined by the process. The older view, on the contrary, sought to assimilate all processes to the absolute object as described above.

24 John Dewey, "Appearing and Appearance," p. 74.
25 Morris R. Cohen and Ernest Nagel, *An Introduction to Logic and Scientific Method*, p. 217.
26 I retain this questionable and misleading term to indicate a subject matter, not to accept the theories associated with the term. My purpose is both to emphasize the reference of the argument to the qualities of experience, and to relate the argument to other *opposed* views. The conception of atomized experience, found in earlier empiricism and in modern realism, is explicitly rejected. So also is the Kantian "phenomenology," which was carried over into positivism and into phenomenology. I have suggested that this conception is a residuum of the Lockean triad—mind, experience and matter—after Hume and Kant crossed off the noumenal mind and matter; it is therefore the result of a mutilated analysis.
27 It will doubtless be clear enough by now that the intended sense in which things have such properties is not the traditional sense in which absolute things had such independent properties as size and shape, but the sense in which a particular thing has a particular weight, for example, under a particular set of conditions. The former are abstract properties in the sense of categories, not properties in the concrete sense.
28 George Santayana, *Scepticism and Animal Faith*, p. 233. Santayana's works are replete with illuminating insights, although the foregoing reference is not one of them, I think. As examples, two of his remarks which are particularly relevant to this discussion are: "To me, experience has not a string of sensations for its objects" (ibid., p. 188). "Experience at its very inception is a revelation of *things*" (ibid., p. 189). Yet these are isolated

sentences which must be snatched from their context, lest they be destroyed by the very next remark.

29 Melville J. Herskovits, *The Influence of Culture on Visual Perception.*

30 Winston H. F. Barnes, "The Myth of Sense-Data," p. 103.

31 René Descartes, *Rules for the Direction of the Mind*, p. 44.

32 Khatchadourian, "On Professor Lafferty's 'The Metaphysical Status of Qualities'," p. 400.

33 Some paragraphs in chapter IV, "The Location of the Object," have such a direct bearing on this discussion that it would be well to consider them as incorporated here. The analysis of the transaction, in which there is a problem of where to ascribe the datum, does indeed raise the question, "Which object?" that the dualist asks. But the conditions of the scientific question admit of evidential methods of answering the question; and the scientific question is not confined to the simple subject-object polarity which the dualist presupposes in his question. In the scientific problem, there is a datum given in the photograph. The question is, is it to be ascribed to Mars or to the camera or to the transmission of signals? There are any number of objects involved, including the organism. It is not a mere dualism. But as an organ of perception of the features of Mars, the focus of attention is on the camera. There is no sense in which the metaphysical subjective-objective dualism enters these scientific considerations or could helpfully do so. It could only confuse matters.

34 I wish specifically to reject one meaning commonly given the term 'appearance', namely, that of being a merely inert content, much like the sense-datum of the realist, which is a bare, abstracted presence without imminence. The term 'transaction' excludes such an interpretation.

35 Recently, philosophers such as the analysts and logical positivists point out that the ease of creating nouns seduces the semantically unsophisticated into saying, 'This is a value', instead of 'I value this'. I think that this is an important and wholesome truth as far as it goes, although not a novel one. I do not mean to disparage but to note that recognition of such truths does not necessarily require the presuppositions of the linguistic analyst. Indeed, what might be called the "semantic illusion" is the assumption that this attention to words serves

merely to end the matter, rather than serving as a warning to beware whether the thing genuinely is a value. The semantic illusion has close kinship, in method, to the "idealist illusion" that ideas are sufficient unto themselves; Hegel was a philologist.

We may note a relevant example of the semantic method. Thus Searle criticizes Hare's remark that "the primary function of the word 'good' is to commend." Automatically and without raising any question, Searle assumes that, therefore, 'good' is identified with 'I commend'. So he proposes the sentence 'Let us hope that it is a good blanket'. He then takes it for granted that it should be translated as 'Let us hope that I commend this blanket'. He does not consider the possibility that the sentence might be translated as 'Let us hope that this blanket is commendable', or, 'Let us hope that this blanket is to be commended' (John R. Searle, "Meaning and Speech Acts," pp. 30–31).

36   In discussing values, I shall use aesthetic values for the sake of factual illustration. I believe that they have been better studied than have others, so that we have more objective data on them; also, our attitudes toward them may be somewhat more objective. I do not assert that what is true of aesthetic values, as this argument is concerned with them, is true of all so-called values; rather, the implication is that if what is true of aesthetic values is not true of something alleged to be a value, then it is not a value. For I am attempting to state the conditions for the objective status of values.

CHAPTER VI

1   Alfred North Whitehead, *Science and the Modern World*, p. 256.
2   R. M. Hare, *The Language of Morals*, p. 127.
3   Ibid., p. 82.
4   Ibid., p. 94.
5   Ibid., p. 124.
6   Ibid., p. 116.
7   William James, "The Moral Philosopher and the Moral Life," p. 205.
8   Plato, *Theaetetus*, 172A.
9   Hare, *Language of Morals*, p. 147.
10   John Dewey, "Qualitative Thought."
11   G. E. Moore, *Principia Ethica*, p. 7.

12 Ibid., pp. 9–10 and passim.
13 Of course, that is not Locke's language. Qualities are powers in the object to produce ideas in the mind.
14 Moore, *Principia Ethica*, p. 20.
15 Hare, *Language of Morals*, p. 82.
16 Walker Gibson, "Gotham." It is perhaps unnecessary to add that it is the poet's recognition of value that I am illustrating, not that of the man mentioned in the poem.
17 Moore, *Principia Ethica*, p. 143.
18 Ibid., p. 189.
19 In different places Spinoza says that God is the greatest good, and, again, that the love of God is the greatest good. But God and the love of God are surely not identical.
20 Moore, *Principia Ethica*, p. 63.
21 Ibid., p. 5; cf. p. 142.
22 Hare, *Language of Morals*, p. 66.
23 Ibid., pp. 67–68.
24 John Herman Randall, Jr., and Justus Buchler, *Philosophy: An Introduction*, Chapter XII.
25 Ibid., p. 144.
26 Ibid.
27 Ibid., p. 146.
28 Ibid., p. 147.
29 Ibid., pp. 144, 146.
30 The above-mentioned text criticizes the hedonistic theory effectively, but does not make use of that critical view at this point.
31 Hume gave better illustrations of the qualitative differences between pleasures than I have, although to his own purpose (David Hume, *A Treatise of Human Nature*, bk. III, pt. I, sec. II, p. 472). It may be noted also that John Stuart Mill distinguished the quality of pleasures, but he was concerned with whether one pleasure was better, more desirable, or higher than another (*Utilitarianism*, ch. 2, p. 16). That is not my point. I am only concerned with whether pleasures are qualitatively *different*.
32 While I am now pointing to an empirical fact, this point would also be an inference from point one above.
33 John Dewey, *Problems of Men*, p. 251 and elsewhere. These views owe so much to Dewey that I am fearful lest many of the statements, where no acknowledgment is made, should have been placed in quotes. Nevertheless, I cannot claim that the views expressed here represent Dewey's position in every way.

34   By 'fact' I do not mean 'true proposition' however particular, nor do I mean strange entities that are not occurrences in the world, but things observed that are relevant to the proposition.

35   Hare, *Language of Morals*, p. 147.

36   These "ghosts of defunct bodies" are continued, of course, in the realist's "universals," "essences," "subsistences," and "eternal objects," which, together with the name of that philosophy, indicate its medieval origin.

37   Harvard University, Committee on the Objectives of a General Education in a Free Society, *General Education in a Free Society*, p. 51 and passim. I give more extended attention to this report in an article, "Empiricism and Objective Relativism in Value Theory."

38   Some react against science when the only validity of their position is in such arguments as those against the "fallacy of reduction" of the possibilities of men to the properties of physics or of biology, or else against the idea that science, as already developed, is adequate to problems of men. With respect to the first idea, while it may be true that man and all his functions are physical and biological, they are not merely so. That is to say, some of his functions cannot be stated in those terms without losing their distinctive character, and, therefore, some of his most important problems cannot be stated in their terms. With respect to the second point, the characteristic attitude of science is that it seeks problems on the very asumption that its views may be antecedently inadequate; rather, it was the characteristic of the prescientific institution that its ideas were assumed to be already fully adequate for the needs of men.

39   My suspicion, to which I will return at the end of this chapter, is that in wanting to assure himself that something was "really there," he wanted to make more sure that others would see it—at least, other sensitive observers.

40   DeWitt H. Parker, *Human Values*, p. 20.

41   Ibid., p. 21.

42   George Santayana, *The Sense of Beauty*, p. 39.

43   It will be noted, of course, that since both the light and the artist's eyes were good, his problem in studying the picture was not to see lines and colors, merely, but to see whether they actually presented the aesthetic quality which they seemed to.

44   Although it is tempting to describe the view here stated as "objective relativism"—which is what it is if the word 'objective'

is used in the methodological sense—nevertheless, it would be better to contrast it with the previous so-called "objective relativism," for the latter never succeeded in divesting itself of the subjective-objective dualism, as Lovejoy showed in his *Revolt against Dualism.* However, he assumed that his conclusions held for some rather diverse views, which he lumped together.

45 Values, no more than the objectivity of the experiment, can be stated in terms of the realist's sense-data, for the latter constitute an atomization of experience by hypostatizing the abstraction of bare and unvaried presences. This view was further confirmed when sense-data later turned out to be "point events."

I might also make another point. While my remarks have been careful in this respect, it might be well to say that since any existent thing has extrinsic consequences, that fact per se does not prove that a given thing is *not* a value.

46 Bertrand Russell, *Religion and Science,* p. 230.

47 This is not the place, I assume, to cite extensively the experimental literature, although it would be somewhat instructive respecting values; neither may I report more circumstantially my own work except for a remark. This work was done in graduate courses which I gave for teachers. The pupils used as subjects were ninth-grade children from the city schools in Bethlehem, Pennsylvania. As to procedure, *Silas Marner* was not antecedently "prescribed because it is good"; rather, a classroom library was provided for the sake of variability of approach.

From the standpoint of technology, the problem which we are considering in general would include the problem of measurement. This is not the concern here, except illustratively. The measurement of appreciation is not nearly as well developed as that of achievement of simpler forms of learning, partly, I think, because we have not long been interested in it. Yet many nodal points of various kinds can be used, just as a physicist may use the freezing and boiling points of water to establish a thermometer. For a simple example, as an indicator of an early stage in the process, we waited, without notice, for the children, who had been selected as having read nothing voluntarily in their lives, to ask permission to take books home.

48 The arguments which one hears in respect to the subjectivity of values seem to require rehearsal of the obvious. The etching of metal by acid is not proved to be solely a property of the metal, by the fact that the acid does not etch wax; much less

does it prove that the property is subjective, nor does it prove that the property is projected into the acid by the metal.

The fact that human beings are vastly more variable than pieces of metal adds to the difficulty of particular determination, but it does not make the problem different in kind so far as objectivity of procedure is concerned. The procedure is a matter of probability in both cases. On the one side, this is obvious enough. On the other, too, those who have worked extensively with steel tend to limit their more specific assertions to probability statements.

49 Value situations are too complex for simple and unqualified statements. So, a further remark may help in clarifying my meaning. Children, as well as others, love excitement and, between a more exciting story and one that is less so, will usually choose the former regardless of literary merit, especially before they have had much relevant experience. I am not, therefore, suggesting that children, or anyone else, will always choose the better. I am raising the question, What is better? It may be said that upon further growth anyone finds, as a matter of fact, that, on the one hand, the *merely* exciting does not have the richness to satisfy, while on the other, things which previously did not excite, now do. But all that is not the main point. The point, rather, is that if we hold other factors constant, there emerges another variable, the eventual effect of the thing upon the individual, in terms of growth of appreciation, and this is the criterion of value.

50 The development of values ordinarily requires work, as will be mentioned later, and, while work may be pleasant, it is not always as pleasant as whimsy, especially before one sees its results, before disciplined attitudes are developed, and before more ideal conditions are instituted.

51 Actually, the degree of correlation is often used, conversely, as the measure of the degree to which things are similar or different in respect to transfer.

52 I have avoided earlier use of this word, because of its connotation of absolute independence. It will be obvious by now, however, that I do not mean to exclude *all* effects and relations, but only those irrelevant to the thing considered as an end.

53 G. H. Mead, *Mind, Self and Society*, p. 385.

54 William James, *The Principles of Psychology*, I, 315.

55 Despite the questions which a plural *differentia* raises, I have

not attempted the formal neatness of a single formulation, and, in this respect, there are precedents enough. However, the three points do seem to hang together. In a field so utterly confused, the primary question is not neatness, but whether we are really talking about anything.

56 "Can there be found ends of action . . . which reënforce and expand not only the motives from which they directly spring, but also the other tendencies and attitudes which are sources of happiness?" (John Dewey and James H. Tufts, *Ethics*, p. 284). "All things that are worthwhile are shared experiences" (Mead, *Mind, Self and Society*, p. 385).

BIBLIOGRAPHY

Aristotle. *De Caelo.* Trans. J. L. Stocks. *The Works of Aristotle Translated into English.* Ed. W. D. Ross. Vol. II. Oxford: Clarendon Press, 1930.

―――. *De Generatione et Corruptione.* Trans. H. H. Joachim. *The Works of Aristotle Translated into English.* Ed. W. D. Ross. Vol. II. Oxford: Clarendon Press, 1930.

―――. *Metaphysica.* Trans. W. D. Ross. 2d ed. *The Works of Aristotle Translated into English.* Ed. W. D. Ross. Vol. VIII. Oxford: Clarendon Press, 1928.

―――. *Physica.* Trans. R. P. Hardie and R. K. Gaye. *The Works of Aristotle Translated into English.* Ed. W. D. Ross. Vol. II. Oxford: Clarendon Press, 1930.

Ayer, Alfred Jules. *Language, Truth and Logic.* New York: Dover, 1946.

Ayer, A[lfred] J[ules], et al. *The Revolution in Philosophy.* London: Macmillan, 1956.

Barnes, Winston H. F. "The Myth of Sense-Data." *Proceedings of the Aristotelian Society,* XLV (1944–45), 89–117.

Berkeley, George. Selection from *Alciphron.* In his *Works on Vision.* Indianapolis: Bobbs-Merrill Company, Inc., 1963.

―――. *Three Dialogues between Hylas and Philonous.* Chicago: Open Court, 1925.

―――. *A Treatise concerning the Principles of Human Knowledge.* Indianapolis: Bobbs-Merrill Company, Inc., 1957.

Bridgman, P. W. "Statistical Mechanics and the Second Law of Thermodynamics." *Bulletin of the American Mathematical Society,* XXXVIII (1932), 225–45.

Charlesworth, Maxwell J. *Philosophy and Linguistic Analysis*. Pittsburgh: Duquesne University, 1959.

Cohen, Morris R., and Ernest Nagel. *An Introduction to Logic and Scientific Method*. New York: Harcourt, Brace and Company, 1934.

Danto, Arthur, and Sidney Morgenbesser. *Philosophy of Science*. New York: Meridian Books, 1960.

Descartes, René. *The Meditations and Selections from the Principles*. Chicago: Open Court, 1908.

————. *Rules for the Direction of the Mind*. Indianapolis: Bobbs-Merrill Company, Inc., 1961.

Dewey, John. "Appearing and Appearance." In his *Philosophy and Civilization*. New York: Minton, Balch and Company, 1931. Pp. 56–76.

————. *Art as Experience*. New York: Minton, Balch and Company, 1934.

————. "The Development of American Pragmatism." In his *Philosophy and Civilization*. New York: Minton, Balch and Company, 1931. Pp. 13–35.

————. "Discussion. Experience and Existence: A Comment." *Philosophy and Phenomenological Research*, IX (1949), 712–13.

————. "An Empirical Account of Appearance." *The Journal of Philosophy*, XXIV (1927), 449–63.

————. *Essays in Experimental Logic*. Chicago: University of Chicago Press, 1916.

————. *Experience and Nature*. London: George Allen and Unwin, Ltd., 1929.

————. *The Influence of Darwin on Philosophy*. New York: Henry Holt and Co., 1910.

————. *Problems of Men*. New York: Philosophical Library, 1946.

————. "Qualitative Thought." In his *Philosophy and Civilization*. New York: Minton, Balch and Company, 1931. Pp. 93–116.

————. "Reality as Experience." *The Journal of Philosophy, Psychology, and Scientific Methods*, III (1906), 253–57.

———. *Reconstruction in Philosophy.* New York: Henry Holt and Co., 1919.

———. "The Subject Matter of Metaphysical Inquiry." *The Journal of Philosophy,* XII (1915), 337–45.

———. "Time and Individuality." *Time and Its Mysteries,* Series II, pp. 85–109. New York: New York University Press, 1940. (Reprinted in his *On Experience, Nature and Freedom.* Indianapolis: Liberal Arts Press, 1960. Pp. 224–43.)

———, and A. F. Bentley. *Knowing and the Known.* Boston: Beacon Press, 1949.

———, and James H. Tufts. *Ethics.* New York: Henry Holt and Company, 1908.

Drake, Durant, et al. *Essays in Critical Realism.* New York: Peter Smith, 1941.

Fuller, B. A. G. *A History of Philosophy.* New York: Henry Holt and Company, 1945.

Gibson, Walker. "Gotham." *Harper's Magazine,* CLXXXVI (1943), 531.

Hampshire, Stuart. "Are Philosophical Questions Questions of Language?" *Aristotelian Society Supplementary Volume,* XXII (1948), 31–48.

———. "Changing Methods in Philosophy." *Philosophy,* XXVI (1951), 142–45.

Hare, R. M. *The Language of Morals.* Oxford: Clarendon Press, 1952.

Harvard University. Committee on the Objectives of a General Education in a Free Society. *General Education in a Free Society.* Cambridge, Mass.: Harvard University Press, 1945.

Held, Richard. "Plasticity in Sensory-Motor Systems." *Scientific American,* CCXIII (November, 1965), 84–94.

Herskovits, Melville J. *The Influence of Culture on Visual Perception.* Indianapolis: Bobbs-Merrill Company, Inc., 1966.

Hospers, John. "What Is Explanation?" *Essays in Conceptual Analysis.* Edited by A. G. N. Flew. New York: St. Martin's Press, 1956.

Hume, David. *A Treatise of Human Nature*. Oxford: Clarendon Press, 1897.

James, William. *The Meaning of Truth*. New York: Longmans, Green and Co., 1914.

————. "The Moral Philosopher and the Moral Life." In his *The Will to Believe and Other Essays in Popular Philosophy*. New York: Longmans, Green and Co., 1897.

————. *A Pluralistic Universe*. New York: Longmans, Green and Co., 1920.

————. *Pragmatism*. New York: Longmans, Green and Co., 1922.

————. *The Principles of Psychology*. New York: Henry Holt and Co., 1890.

Jones, W. T. *A History of Western Philosophy*. New York: Harcourt, Brace and Company, 1952.

Kant, Immanuel. *Prolegomena to Any Future Metaphysics*. LaSalle, Ind.: Open Court, 1902.

Keller, Helen. *The World I Live In*. New York: Century Co., 1908.

Khatchadourian, Haig. "On Professor Lafferty's 'The Metaphysical Status of Qualities'." *The Journal of Philosophy*, LV (1958), 397–412.

Kilpatrick, F. P. "Statement of Theory." *Human Behavior from the Transactional Point of View*. Hanover, N.J.: Institute for Associated Research, 1952.

Lafferty, Theodore T. "Empiricism and Objective Relativism in Value Theory." *The Journal of Philosophy*, XLVI (1949), 141–55.

————. "The Metaphysical Status of Qualities." *The Journal of Philosophy*, L (1953), 313–28.

————. "Some Metaphysical Implications of the Pragmatic Theory of Knowledge." *The Journal of Philosophy*, XXIX (1932), 197–207.

————. "Valuation as Cognition." *The Journal of Philosophy*, XLV (1948), 181–88.

Lewis, H. D. *Clarity Is Not Enough*. New York: Humanities Press, 1963.

Locke, John. *An Essay concerning Human Understanding.* Ed. A. C. Fraser. Oxford: Clarendon Press, 1894.

Lovejoy, Arthur O. *The Revolt against Dualism.* Chicago: Open Court, 1930.

Macdonald, Margaret. "Natural Rights." *Proceedings of the Aristotelian Society,* XLVII (1946–47), 225–50.

Mead, George Herbert. "The Genesis of the Self and Social Control." *International Journal of Ethics,* XXXV (1925), 251–77. (Reprinted in his *The Philosophy of the Present* as Supplementary Essay V.)

————. *Mind, Self and Society.* Chicago: University of Chicago Press, 1934.

————. *Movements of Thought in the Nineteenth Century.* Chicago: University of Chicago Press, 1936.

————. "The Objective Reality of Perspectives." *Proceedings of the Sixth International Congress of Philosophy.* New York: Longmans, Green and Co., 1927. Pp. 75–85. (Reprinted in his *The Philosophy of the Present.*)

————. *The Philosophy of the Present.* Chicago: Open Court, 1932.

————. "A Pragmatic Theory of Truth." *University of California Publications in Philosophy,* XI (1929), 65–88.

Meyerson, Emile. *Identity and Reality.* New York: Macmillan, 1930.

Mill, John Stuart. *Utilitarianism.* Indianapolis: Bobbs-Merrill Company, Inc., 1957.

Millikan, Robert Andrews. *The Electron.* Chicago: University of Chicago Press, 1917.

Montague, William P. "The Story of American Realism." *Philosophy,* XII (1937), 1–22.

Moore, A. W. "Subsistence and Existence in Neo-Realism." *Proceedings of the Sixth International Congress of Philosophy.* New York: Longmans, Green and Co., 1927. Pp. 278–84.

Moore, G. E. *Principia Ethica.* Cambridge, Eng.: The University Press, 1922.

Parker, DeWitt H. *Human Values.* New York: Harper and Brothers, 1931.

Plato. *Theaetetus. The Dialogues of Plato.* Translated by B. Jowett. Vol. II. New York: Random House, 1937.

Randall, John Herman, Jr., and Justus Buchler. *Philosophy: An Introduction.* New York: Barnes and Noble, 1942.

Rollins, C. D., ed. *Knowledge and Experience.* Pittsburgh: University of Pittsburgh Press [1964].

Royce, Josiah. *The Spirit of Modern Philosophy.* Boston: Houghton Mifflin Company, 1892.

Russell, Bertrand. "The Cult of Common Usage." *The British Journal for the Philosophy of Science,* III (1952–53), 303–7.

———. *A History of Western Philosophy.* New York: Simon and Schuster, 1945.

———. *Human Knowledge.* New York: Simon and Schuster, 1948.

———. *Human Society in Ethics and Politics.* New York: Simon and Schuster, 1955.

———. *An Inquiry into Meaning and Truth.* New York: Norton, 1940.

———. *Mysticism and Logic.* New York: Norton, 1929.

———. *Our Knowledge of the External World.* New York: Norton, 1929.

———. *The Problems of Philosophy.* New York: Henry Holt and Co., 1912.

———. *Religion and Science.* London: T. Butterworth, Ltd., 1935.

———. "Reply to Criticisms." *The Philosophy of Bertrand Russell.* Ed. Paul Arthur Schilpp. Evanston, Ill.: Library of Living Philosophers, 1946.

———. *Wisdom of the West.* Garden City, N.Y.: Doubleday, 1959.

Ryle, Gilbert. *Dilemmas.* Cambridge, Eng.: The University Press, 1960.

Santayana, George. *Scepticism and Animal Faith.* New York: Charles Scribner's Sons, 1923.

———. *The Sense of Beauty.* New York: Charles Scribner's Sons, 1896.

Schlick, Moritz. *Philosophy of Nature.* New York: Philosophical Library, 1949.

Schneider, Herbert W. Review of Paul E. Pfuetze's *The Social Self.* In *The Journal of Philosophy,* LV (1958), 699–703.

Searle, John R. "Meaning and Speech Acts." In *Knowledge and Experience.* Ed. C. D. Rollins. Pittsburgh: University of Pittsburgh Press [1964].

The State (Columbia, S. C.), July 19, 1965.

Titus, H. H. *Living Issues in Philosophy.* New York: American Book Company, 1946.

Toulmin, Stephen Edelston. *An Examination of the Place of Reason in Ethics.* Cambridge, Eng.: The University Press, 1953.

Toulmin, S[tephen] E[delston], and K[urt] Baier. "On Describing." *Mind,* LXI (1952), 13–38.

Urmson, J. O. *Philosophical Analysis.* Oxford: Clarendon Press, 1956.

Whitehead, Alfred North. *Modes of Thought.* New York: Macmillan, 1938.

———. *The Principles of Natural Knowledge.* Cambridge, Eng.: The University Press, 1925.

———. *Science and the Modern World.* New York: Macmillan, 1947.

Wittgenstein, Ludwig. *Philosophical Investigations.* New York: Macmillan, 1953.

Wright, William Kelley. *A History of Modern Philosophy.* New York: Macmillan, 1941.

INDEX

Absolute: object, 111–12, 143, 193,
195, 197–99; values, 258–59
Absolute, the, 172
Absolutism, 195–97, 263
Abstraction, 78–79, 168–69. *See
also* Selection, abstraction as;
Universals
Analysis, chap. I passim, 82. *See
also* Logical positivism; Russell,
Bertrand
Analyst, 3–4, 5–6, 11–12, 14, 18,
21–22, 27, 32, 91–92
Appearance, 77–78, 160–62, 199,
217–18, 295 n. 34; subjectivity
of, 215. *See also* Perception; Phenomena; Sense-data; Transactions
Aristotle, 96, 97, 103, 105–6, 195–
96, 197–98
Attitudes, 54; terminal, 53–54. *See
also* Ends
Ayer, A. J., 4, 9–10, 13–14, 22–25,
80, 145. *See also* Logical positivism

Baier, Kurt, 11, 79
Barnes, Winston H. F., 212–14
Bentham, Jeremy, 253
Bentley, A. F., 95
Bergson, Henri, 59
Berkeley, George, 77–78, 99, 100–
101, 111, 124–25, 150–51, 161,
273
Bohr's equation, 10, 37
Bridgman, P. W., 72
Broad, C. D., 245

Causal explanation, 128
Causal laws, 8, 143
Causal theory of perception, 71,
153, 177–78. *See also* Causation;
Perception
Causation, 45, 98, 124–25, 142,

151–53, 228. *See also* Causal ex-
planation; Causal laws; Hume,
David
Cognition, 12. *See also* Epistemol-
ogy; Knowledge; Propositions,
cognitive
Common world, the, 66–67, 73
Communication, 56–58, 271–72.
See also Language
Concrete, 79, 127–28. *See also*
Empirical
Consciousness, 48–50, 52; states of,
244
Consummatory, 42–43, 62, 69–70,
106, 169–70. *See also* Ends;
Means-end relation; Values
Correspondence, 4, 127–28, 182.
See also Truth; Verification

Democritus, 98, 103–4, 110, 111,
136, 197
Descartes, René, 43, 45, 112, 121,
141, 210, 215, 235
Dewey, John, 6–7, 12, 19–21, 31,
32, 47, 79, 95, 133, 193, 205,
219, 235–36, 256, 272, 274,
277–79, 283–87 n. 74
Dualism, 46–47, 78, 81–82, 144–
46, 150, 154–55, 157, 183, 256–
57; epistemological, 181–82, 185;
metaphysical, 47–48, 151, 177,
181, 185, 219, 256, 291–92 n. 6;
psychophysical, 186. *See also*
Russell, Bertrand
Duhem, Pierre, 207

Empirical, 7–8, 180
Ends, 227–28, 232, 235, 238–39,
246–50, 253, 274–75. *See also*
Means-end relation; Values
Energy, 45, 97–98, 110, 126–27,
137. *See also* Forces; Self-

Nature and Values was manually composed on the Linotype and was printed letterpress by Heritage Printers, Charlotte, North Carolina. The book was sewn and bound by Delmar Companies, Inc., also of Charlotte.

The book was designed by Robert L. Nance and Larry Hirst. Electra type was used as text, with Deepdene as display type. The paper on which the book is printed was supplied by the S. D. Warren Company and is watermarked with the University of South Carolina Press colophon. This paper was developed for an effective life of at least three hundred years.

UNIVERSITY OF SOUTH CAROLINA PRESS
COLUMBIA